W9-AYA-065

BEGINNING
FLASH®, FLEX®, AND AIR® DEVELOPMENT
FOR MOBILE DEVICES

BEGINNING

Flash®, Flex®, and AIR® Development for Mobile Devices

BEGINNING

Flash®, Flex®, and AIR® Development for Mobile Devices

Jermaine G. Anderson

John Wiley & Sons, Inc.

Beginning Flash®, Flex®, and AIR® Development for Mobile Devices

Published by
John Wiley & Sons, Inc.
10475 Crosspoint Boulevard
Indianapolis, IN 46256
www.wiley.com

Published simultaneously in Canada

ISBN: 978-0-470-94815-6
ISBN: 978-1-118-19334-1 (ebk)
ISBN: 978-1-118-19335-8 (ebk)
ISBN: 978-1-118-19336-5 (ebk)

Manufactured in the United States of America

10 9 8 7 6 5 4 3 2 1

For general information on our other products and services please contact our Customer Care Department within the United States at (877) 762-2974, outside the United States at (317) 572-3993 or fax (317) 572-4002.

Wiley also publishes its books in a variety of electronic formats and by print-on-demand. Not all content that is available in standard print versions of this book may appear or be packaged in all book formats. If you have purchased a version of this book that did not include media that is referenced by or accompanies a standard print version, you may request this media by visiting http://booksupport.wiley.com. For more information about Wiley products, visit us at www.wiley.com.

Library of Congress Control Number: 2011905204

This book is dedicated to my wife, Joanna, and to the "little one," our beautiful darling daughter, Olivia.

Love you both to bits!

Xx

ABOUT THE AUTHOR

 **JERMAINE G. ANDERSON** works within the Software Engineering department of British Sky Broadcasting in London, UK, currently as Scrum Master, where he manages the technical delivery for an Agile team responsible for the short-form online video platform.

In recent years, Jermaine's work has predominantly centered on video streaming, where he has been instrumental in creating cutting-edge and innovative products, specializing in Flash, the Flex framework, and, more recently, AIR.

Jermaine grew up in the town of Wincobank, Sheffield, where he developed his passion for science, technology, art, design, and computing. From an early age he started coding on the family computer, using BASIC on an Amstrad CPC 6128. When Jermaine was eight years old, his father set him the task of designing a level for the critically acclaimed U.S. Gold computer game Gauntlet, which he completed, only to discover that there was a submission date for the level entry, and that date had passed, to Jermaine's disappointment. He cites this as one of the early lessons he learned, to always do something for the enjoyment, and rewards come in various guises. Ultimately, problem solving and working with technology are his main drivers working in online media, driven by the Internet.

Having earned a BSc (Hons) degree in Chemistry at The University of Birmingham, and a MSc in Computer Studies from Sheffield Hallam University, Jermaine devoted much of his professional career to working with Flash and online media over the last 11 years, taking a keen interest in mobile application development from early 2004.

In 2005, Jermaine was awarded the "Best Productivity" category for his Mobile TV application, a concept that he designed and developed for the Macromedia Flash Lite Contest.

Jermaine's first book, *Professional Flash Lite Mobile Application Development* (Wrox, 2010), focuses on structuring several mobile application concepts using the PureMVC framework targeting the Flash Lite player. His second book, *Beginning Flash, Flex, and AIR Development for Mobile Devices*, focuses on the Flex framework for mobile development, targeting Android, BlackBerry, and iOS devices.

Jermaine tweets at www.twitter.com/jganderson and writes his personal blog at www.jgorganic.co.uk/blog.

ABOUT THE TECHNICAL EDITOR

 **DARREN OSADCHUK** has been creating games and applications in Flash for approximately 10 years. In 2005, he started Ludicrous Software and began developing games for Flash Lite-enabled mobile devices. Since then, Ludicrous Software's games have been available on a variety of platforms, including Apple's App Store, the Android Market, Amazon's Appstore, BlackBerry App World, and Nokia's Ovi Store. In addition to games published under the banner of Ludicrous Software, Darren has developed mobile and web games and applications for clients around the world. He has a Bachelor of Arts in Political Science from the University of Manitoba and a Master of Arts in Contemporary Social and Political Thought from the University of Victoria, British Columbia.

CREDITS

ACKNOWLEDGMENTS

FIRST, I WANT TO THANK JOANNA for being an incredibly supportive wife, whom I have known for 12 years, and is still the most intelligent person I know. Jo is a real-life "firefighter" and has helped me to accomplish this book, every step of the way. Thank you for your patience and understanding as I worked to finish the book at all kinds of crazy hours. And thank you for taking care of all the things that would have been a distraction to me. And no, I don't mean LO. I love you.

Olivia, mummy and daddy love you lots. You have been a true inspiration over the 18 months since you came into our world. Thank you for being an angel.

I want to thank everyone at Wrox and Wiley for all their support. Thank you for sticking with the changes, especially when the volume of updates brought in for iOS seemed mega!

Thank you to the former Wiley acquisition editor Scott Meyers, for bringing the book to the attention of executive editor Robert Elliot. Bob, many thanks for your support and overall steer.

I would also like to say a big thank you to project editors William Bridges and John Sleeva, copy editor Kim Cofer, production editor Becca Anderson, editorial manager Mary Beth Wakefield, and technical editor Darren Osadchuk, for all your contributions and for helping the book become ship-shape.

Finally, many thanks to my family and friends, for the love and support they gave me while I was writing this book.

—JERMAINE G. ANDERSON

CONTENTS

INTRODUCTION

THERE'S A GREAT DEMAND TODAY for mobile content and applications. Many of the leading device manufacturers and platforms are supporting Adobe Flash Player, and since many of them are also integrating Adobe AIR directly into the mobile device's OS, there has never been a better time for getting to know how to author content designed for the small screen.

With the fast-moving pace of the mobile industry it's really important to keep abreast of the latest developments in the Adobe Flash Platform, and so *Beginning Flash, Flex, and AIR Development for Mobile Devices* includes all the key developments of "Flash on mobile" since my first book, *Professional Flash Lite Mobile Development* (Wrox, 2010).

Over the course of the book, you learn how to utilize industry-leading software for authoring mobile content. You'll become familiar with the Adobe Flex framework and the MXML components optimized for mobile devices. You'll also learn how to utilize the Flash Player 10.3 and AIR ActionScript 3.0 APIs.

The material set out in this book is really targeted for developers at all levels. At a base level it will help you start creating Flash-enabled mobile applications. This book also contains extensive code examples that are explained in detail and essentially cover how you create mobile applications from the ground up, targeted at Flash Player 10.1 and AIR 2.5, using ActionScript 3.0. The book is for anyone wanting to showcase mobile content across a range of mobile platforms.

WHOM THIS BOOK IS FOR

This book is aimed at mobile developers looking to create and distribute new mobile applications.

Programmers and developers of all experiences will be able to use the book as a reference on how to author content for mobiles and devices using Adobe Flash, Flex, and AIR.

The book is designed to help both experienced mobile developers and newcomers gain a comprehensive introduction to Flash, Flex, and AIR. As such, Chapters 1 and 2 are primarily aimed at newcomers to the Adobe Flash Platform; the background to Flash, Flex, and AIR is discussed, along with the tools used in the creation of mobile applications — namely, Flash Builder and Device Central CS5.5.

WHAT THIS BOOK COVERS

Beginning Flash, Flex, and AIR Development for Mobile Devices introduces the reader to a number of topics covering the key authoring aspects of developing for the current iteration of the Adobe Flash Platform, guiding the reader through the following chapters:

➤ **Chapter 1 — An Introduction to Flash, Flex, and AIR:** This chapter provides an overview of the Adobe Flash Platform covering the Flash Player, the Flex framework, and the Adobe

Integrated Runtime. It also takes the reader through the basics of programming with AS3 and a light introduction to MXML.

➤ **Chapter 2 — Getting Started:** This chapter focuses on getting started with the tools to carry out mobile development, taking a look at three essential tools used in developing and testing Flash content: Adobe Flash Builder, Adobe Flash Professional CS5, and Adobe Device Central CS5.

➤ **Chapter 3 — Building AIR Applications for Android, BlackBerry, and iOS:** This chapter takes you through building AIR 2.5 applications for the Google Android mobile platform, with a heavy portion of the chapter focusing on the Adobe AIR Application Descriptor settings. Here you also learn how you update AIR applications for the Google Android platform.

➤ **Chapter 4 — Touch, Multitouch, and Gestures:** This chapter covers the user input features introduced in Flash Player 10.1 and provides extensive code listings for you to follow, using Adobe Flash Builder 4.5 and Adobe Device Central CS5 to create and test the examples.

➤ **Chapter 5 — Developing for Multiple Screen Sizes:** This chapter guides you through the best practices for creating content for multiple devices with different screen sizes.

➤ **Chapter 6 — Debugging Applications:** This chapter shows you how to utilize the Flash Debug Perspective in Adobe Flash Builder. It also covers Error Handling and in particular Global Error Handling, a feature introduced in Flash Player 10.1.

➤ **Chapter 7 — Working with the Filesystem:** This chapter details how to use the AIR File System API, and walks you through creating a Files Explorer mobile application using MXML and the Flex framework in Adobe Flash Builder.

➤ **Chapter 8 — Working with Data:** This chapter introduces some of the ways you can utilize data within mobile applications. It also focuses on SQLite and guides you through the creation of a Teams database application.

➤ **Chapter 9 — Working with Audio and Video:** This chapter highlights multiple ways in which you can include sound and video in your mobile applications, and introduces you to the Open Source Media Framework (OSMF) framework.

➤ **Chapter 10 — Utilizing Device Features:** This chapter draws your attention to the APIs introduced in AIR 2.7 that particularly rely on device support, including utilizing the device's camera, microphone, web browser, and geolocation features.

HOW THIS BOOK IS STRUCTURED

The book is written in such a way that it allows the reader to pick up and start from any chapter.

By design, Chapters 1 through 3 contain relatively little code when compared to later chapters; from Chapter 4 onwards, you'll notice a substantial increase in the number of examples to follow and tasks to carry out.

Each chapter in the book will start with a list of chapter objectives and an introduction, and then end with a chapter summary, exercises, and a table of the key concepts learned in the chapter.

Chapter 10 will feature more tasks that rely on the reader using a mobile device to test content.

WHAT YOU NEED TO USE THIS BOOK

You will need to have one of the following Operating Systems:

➤ Mac OS

➤ Windows

➤ Linux

To use the code samples and run the example applications in this book you will need the following:

➤ Adobe Flash Builder 4.5

➤ Adobe Device Central CS5.5

➤ Adobe AIR 2.7 SDK

While you do not explicitly need a Flash- or AIR-enabled mobile device, to complete all the tasks, a Google Android device running Gingerbread 2.3.4 is recommended. Many of the examples covered in this book, in addition to Google Android, will run on Apple iOS devices with version 4.x and above, including the iPad, iPhone, and iPod Touch devices. Each of the examples will also work on the BlackBerry PlayBook device, running the BlackBerry Tablet OS.

CONVENTIONS

To help you get the most from the text and keep track of what's happening, we've used a number of conventions throughout the book. Among these are the Try It Out activity and the accompanying How It Works. A sample of the format follows:

TRY IT OUT **The *Try It Out* is an exercise you should work through, following the text in the book.**

1. The exercise usually consists of a set of steps.

2. Each step has a number.

3. Follow the steps through with your copy of the database.

WARNING *Boxes with a warning icon like this one hold important, not-to-be-forgotten information that is directly relevant to the surrounding text.*

 NOTE *The pencil icon indicates notes, tips, hints, tricks, and asides to the current discussion.*

As for styles in the text:

➤ We *highlight* new terms and important words when we introduce them.

➤ We show filenames, URLs, and code within the text like so: `object.method()`.

We present code in a few different ways:

```
We use this monofont type with no highlighting for some of the code examples.
```

```
We use bold to emphasize code that is particularly important in the present
context.
```

Also, the Source view in Flash Builder provides a rich color scheme to indicate various parts of code syntax. This is a great tool to help you learn language features in the editor and to help prevent mistakes as you code. To reinforce the colors used in Flash Builder, the code listings in this book are colorized using colors similar to what you would see on screen in Flash Builder working with the book's code. In order to optimize print clarity, some colors have a slightly different hue in print than what you see on screen. But all the colors for the code in this book should be close enough to the default Flash Builder colors to give you an accurate representation of the colors.

The following example taken from Chapter 4 shows how code could be colored and highlighted:

```
package
{
    import flash.display.Sprite;
    import flash.text.TextField;
    import flash.text.TextFieldAutoSize;
    import flash.ui.Multitouch;

    public class MultitouchAndGestures extends Sprite
    {
        private var multitouch:TextField;

        public function MultitouchAndGestures()
```

SOURCE CODE

As you work through the examples in this book, you may choose either to type in all the code manually, or to use the source code files that accompany the book. All the source code used in this book is available for download at www.wrox.com. When at the site, simply locate the book's title (use the Search box or one of the title lists) and click the Download Code link on the book's detail page to obtain all the source code for the book. Code that is included on the website is highlighted by the following icon:

Available for download on Wrox.com

Listings include the filename in the title and also are identified by a Listing number. If the downloaded item is just a code snippet, you'll find the filename in a code note such as this in the text:

Code snippet filename

NOTE *Because many books have similar titles, you may find it easiest to search by ISBN; this book's ISBN is 978-0-470-94815-6.*

Once you download the code, just decompress it with your favorite compression tool. Alternately, you can go to the main Wrox code download page at www.wrox.com/dynamic/books/download .aspx to see the code available for this book and all other Wrox books.

ERRATA

We make every effort to ensure that there are no errors in the text or in the code. However, no one is perfect, and mistakes do occur. If you find an error in one of our books, like a spelling mistake or faulty piece of code, we would be very grateful for your feedback. By sending in errata, you may save another reader hours of frustration, and at the same time, you will be helping us provide even higher quality information.

To find the errata page for this book, go to www.wrox.com and locate the title using the Search box or one of the title lists. Then, on the book details page, click the Book Errata link. On this page, you can view all errata that has been submitted for this book and posted by Wrox editors. A complete book list, including links to each book's errata, is also available at `www.wrox.com/misc-pages/booklist.shtml`.

If you don't spot "your" error on the Book Errata page, go to `www.wrox.com/contact/techsupport.shtml` and complete the form there to send us the error you have found. We'll check the information and, if appropriate, post a message to the book's errata page and fix the problem in subsequent editions of the book.

P2P.WROX.COM

For author and peer discussion, join the P2P forums at `p2p.wrox.com`. The forums are a web-based system for you to post messages relating to Wrox books and related technologies and interact with other readers and technology users. The forums offer a subscription feature to e-mail you topics of interest of your choosing when new posts are made to the forums. Wrox authors, editors, other industry experts, and your fellow readers are present on these forums.

At `p2p.wrox.com`, you will find a number of different forums that will help you, not only as you read this book, but also as you develop your own applications. To join the forums, just follow these steps:

1. Go to `p2p.wrox.com` and click the Register link.

2. Read the terms of use and click Agree.

3. Complete the required information to join, as well as any optional information you wish to provide, and click Submit.

4. You will receive an e-mail with information describing how to verify your account and complete the joining process.

 NOTE *You can read messages in the forums without joining P2P, but in order to post your own messages, you must join.*

Once you join, you can post new messages and respond to messages other users post. You can read messages at any time on the Web. If you would like to have new messages from a particular forum e-mailed to you, click the Subscribe to this Forum icon by the forum name in the forum listing.

For more information about how to use the Wrox P2P, be sure to read the P2P FAQs for answers to questions about how the forum software works, as well as many common questions specific to P2P and Wrox books. To read the FAQs, click the FAQ link on any P2P page.

An Introduction to Flash, Flex, and AIR

WHAT YOU WILL LEARN IN THIS CHAPTER:

➤ An overview of the Adobe Flash platform

➤ Outlining the key concepts of the ActionScript 3.0 language

➤ Exploring the Flex framework and MXML components

➤ A brief introduction to Adobe AIR

In this chapter you'll take a look at each of the core elements of the book: Flash, Flex, and AIR.

First you'll cover a number of the core aspects of Flash and the programming language ActionScript 3.0, which this book uses.

You'll then explore the key features of the Flex framework and MXML components, looking at examples through code snippets.

Lastly, you'll be introduced to features of AIR, the Adobe Integrated Runtime.

ADOBE FLASH

Adobe's Flash platform consists of several Flash-based runtime clients: Flash Player, Flash Lite, and Adobe AIR. Each run time has its own set of functions and APIs that are specific for that run time.

The Flash platform also encompasses a component framework, Flex. All these elements, the runtime clients and component frameworks, support and utilize the SWF format.

Flash is predominantly used for the web deployment of rich content and applications. It is installed as a web browser plug-in, and can also run content in standalone mode. The Adobe Flash logo is shown in Figure 1-1.

Flash on Mobile Devices

There are currently two ways in which Flash has dedicated support on mobile devices. These involve using Flash Lite and Flash Player, respectively.

Flash Lite 4.0

FIGURE 1-1: The Adobe Flash logo

Flash Lite runs Flash content and applications intended to run on performance-limited mobile devices. Flash Lite offers a different set of capabilities compared with Flash Player. Until recently Flash Lite supported only the ActionScript 2.0 (AS2). Currently Flash Lite is in version 4.0 and the run time now supports ActionScript 3.0 (AS3).

To learn more about Flash Lite and how you can create mobile applications using the technology, check out the book *Professional Flash Lite Mobile Application Development*, by Jermaine Anderson (Wrox, 2010).

Flash Player 10.x

Flash Player 10.1 was the first release of Flash Player aimed at supporting the development of content and SWF format deployment to both traditional web browser and mobile devices.

At the time of writing, a beta for Adobe Flash Player 11 was underway, allowing developers to preview new and enhanced features targeting the next release of the run time. With the potential for new APIs to be dropped, none of the features could be covered in this book, but look for an update. For more information, visit the Adobe Labs website (`labs.adobe.com/technologies/`) and search for Adobe Flash Player 11.

This book centers on the development of Flash content targeting the latest release, Adobe Flash Player 10.3 using AS3.

Flash is fully supported on Google Android and the BlackBerry Tablet OS mobile platforms. Unless you've been hiding under a rock for the past few years, you'll know Flash isn't supported on the Apple iOS platform. However, using AS3 and AIR, you can target your applications to run on the platform via standalone applications.

ACTIONSCRIPT 3.0

AS3 is an object-oriented language for creating media content for playback in the Flash runtime clients' Flash Player, Flash Lite, and Adobe AIR.

ECMAScript

The core of the AS3 language is based on the ECMAScript 4th Edition language specification, which you can view on the ECMA International website at `www.ecmascript.org/`. You can view the AS3 specification at `http://livedocs.adobe.com/specs/actionscript/3`.

AS3 has a syntax that is very similar to Java; it is also similar to the widely used JavaScript, the popular language used in web browsers. If you are from either of these programming disciplines, then AS3 will be very familiar.

ECMAScript 4 defines a number of rules for how code is written in AS3, including grammar and syntax. These dictate that code be written in a particular way, which should mean that code written by one developer will be recognizable to another.

A number of core programming concepts, such as variables, functions, classes, objects, expressions, and statements, form part of ECMAScript 4 and are inherited by AS3.

ECMAScript 4 also defines several built-in data types for AS3, allowing developers to utilize frequent data types such as an array, Boolean, number, and string.

Key Concepts

You need to grasp a number of important key concepts when programming with AS3; these will stand you in good stead for the rest of this book. Here you'll take a look at some of these concepts.

Classes, Objects, and Instances

A *class* is what gives an object its properties and the features by which an object accomplishes particular tasks through its methods and functions. A class is essentially a blueprint for an object.

AS3 classes are text-based files identified by the .as file extension. A class is defined by the class keyword, followed by the name of the class, which should start with a capital letter. It is this class name that must match the filename the class is created in. The following snippet shows you an example of a class called Mobile that's being defined:

```
class Mobile {}
```

An *object* represents part of a program that describes a particular thing. That thing could be a shape that has three sides and is colored blue; a film that has a PG rating; or a mobile device that allows you to store contacts. An object can be anything you can think of.

Objects have properties that give them their character and also have methods that allow them to carry out particular tasks.

In AS3, objects are created from classes by instantiating them, calling the new keyword before the class name and parentheses (). The following snippet shows you an example of the Mobile class being instantiated:

```
new Mobile();
```

Packages

A *package* defines the path to a class, which should be uniquely identified in respect to other classes that may have the same class name. Packages also reflect the folder structure.

Ultimately, packages are used to avoid conflicts between classes.

It is best practice to give packages meaningful names. Grouping similar classes together in a package is common practice and makes it easier to search and utilize different classes when programming.

The `Mobile` class could well be placed in a package called `devices`, sitting alongside another class called `Tablet`, if that class were to be created.

```
package devices
{
        class Mobile {}
}
```

While this example shows a fully qualified package, the naming convention is usually more granular, and with the package name defined for a class set as a dot-delimited, reverse-DNS-style string. For example, the `devices` package declaration could quite easily have been referenced as part of the Wrox.com domain, with the Chapter 1 name `com.wrox.ch1.devices`, as shown in the following snippet:

```
package com.wrox.ch1.devices
{
        class Mobile {}
}
```

Packages are also used when importing classes into AS documents, denoted by the `import` keyword, as shown in the following code snippet where the package `com.wrox.ch1.devices` example is used again:

```
import com.wrox.ch1.devices.Mobile;
```

A class has to be referenced by its full package reference before it can be used.

> **NOTE** In AS3 you need to specify the package declaration, ensuring that the class declaration is made inside the package curly brackets. The package name can be left blank, but this should be avoided. In AS2 the package declaration was absent in class creation.

Functions, Methods, and Scope

A *function* is what allows an object to do a particular task and perform a set of reusable instructions. Functions are defined using the function keyword followed by the name of the task.

Class Scope Modifiers

Four keywords give scope to the properties and functions of an object: `public`, `private`, `protected`, and `internal`.

The `public` scope modifier means that a variable property or function can be accessed anywhere. The `protected` scope modifier means that only the current class and subclasses can use the variable or function. The `private` scope modifier restricts access to within the class only, and the `internal` scope modifier restricts the scope to the package it is contained in.

The Class Constructor

The *constructor* of a class is what initializes an object and creates it. The constructor is basically a class method, which must be declared public. The following snippet shows the `constructor` for the `Mobile` class, which is simply `Mobile()`:

```
package devices
{
    public class Mobile
    {
        public function Mobile()
        {
            // Code to initialize Mobile
        }
    }
}
```

Return Types

Depending on the set of instructions found in the function, the return type gives an indication of the value that can be generated by the function call. In the following snippet, a public function called `launchApp()` is defined, with the return type specified as `void`:

```
package devices
{
    public class Mobile
    {
        public function Mobile()
        {
            // Code to initialize Mobile
        }

        public function launchApp():void
        {
            // Code to launch an app on the mobile.
        }
    }
}
```

The `void` keyword indicates that a value isn't expected to be returned by the function. Also note that class constructors don't specify a return type.

Variables

A *variable* is a unique identifier associated with an object that can hold a reference to a value. In AS3, data types are given to variables so that they can be checked at compile time. Variables are defined by the `var` keyword and then followed by the variable name.

In a class, variables that are added outside of functions can be referenced within the scope of the class; these are known as *instance variables*. These describe an object's characteristics and are what give an object its properties.

The following code snippet shows two private variables being declared: `contacts`, an `Array` data type, and `phoneNumber`, a `Number` data type:

```
package devices
{
    public class Mobile
    {
        private var contacts:Array;
        private var phoneNumber:Number;

        public function Mobile()
        {
            // Code to initialize Mobile
        }

        public function launchApp():void
        {
            // Code to launch an app on the mobile.
        }
    }
}
```

The following code demonstrates creating a `Mobile` object and assigning it to the variable `mobileObj`:

```
var mobileObj:Mobile = new Mobile();
```

Notice here that the data type assigned to the object is `Mobile`. Whenever you instantiate an object in this way, you need to define the data type on the variable; otherwise, you'll get a "variable has no type declaration" warning.

Within a method or function, instance variables can be used to set or reference data values. In the following code snippet the `phoneNumber` variable is assigned a value within the constructor method of `Mobile`, using the `this` keyword:

```
package devices
{
    public class Mobile
    {
        private var contacts:Array;
        private var phoneNumber:Number;

        public function Mobile()
        {
            this.phoneNumber = 011003637;
        }

        public function launchApp():void
        {
            // Code to launch an app on the mobile.
        }
    }
}
```

Static Variables and Methods

A *static* reference relates to class methods and variables that can be referenced without instantiating the class and creating an object.

In the following code snippet, the Mobile class is given the static variable deviceType which is defined as a string and is given the value Smartphone. A static function called switchOn() is also defined.

```
package devices
{
    public class Mobile
    {
        public static var deviceType:String = "Smartphone";

        private var contacts:Array;
        private var phoneNumber:Number;

        public function Mobile()
        {
            this.phoneNumber = 011003637;
        }

        public function launchApp():void
        {
            // Code to launch an app on the mobile.
        }

        public static function switchOn():void
        {
            // Code to switch on the device.
        }
    }
}
```

The following code demonstrates how you would call the switchOn() function:

```
Mobile.switchOn();
```

Parameters and Arguments

A *parameter* is a local variable that is defined and given a data type in the parentheses of a function declaration.

Instance methods allow you to define functions that exhibit an object's features and the things it can do. Parameters can be defined on instance methods to allow values to be passed to an object.

The following snippet shows a new instance method for the Mobile class defined, called addContact(). The method has a public scope and has two parameters: cName, a String data type representing a contact's name, and cNumber, a Number data type representing the contact's mobile number.

```
package devices
{
    public class Mobile
    {
```

```
public static var deviceType:String = "Smartphone";

private var contacts:Array;
private var phoneNumber:Number;

public function Mobile()
{
      this.phoneNumber = 011003637;
}

public function addContact(cName:String, cNumber:Number):void
{
      // Code to add a new contact
}

public function launchApp():void
{
      // Code to launch an app on the mobile.
}

public static function switchOn():void
{
      // Code to switch on the device.
}
        }
    }
```

Note that local variables are only temporary.

To invoke or call the addContact() method, you need to use an instance of the Mobile class and supply what are called the *arguments* for the method. In this case there are two arguments, as shown in the following snippet:

```
var mobileObj:Mobile = new Mobile();
mobileObj.addContact("Olivia", 736300110);
```

Here the values Olivia and 736300110 are both arguments. Each argument needs to match the data types of the parameters specified for the method.

Conditional and Loop statements

A *conditional* statement is code that executes when a specific condition has been met.

In the following code snippet another static function called switchOff() has been added to the Mobile class. Here you will see a conditional if statement that checks the variable isOn, a Boolean value which is initially set to false in the class. In switchOn(), there is an if statement to check to see if the isOn value is false; this is indicated by the exclamation (!) preceding the Boolean value (that is, !isOn). The switchOff() function demonstrates another way of writing the same by asking whether the isOn variable is equal to false, and then executing the code within the else block of the if statement by setting isOn to false.

```
package devices
{
```

```
public class Mobile
{
      public static var deviceType:String = "Smartphone";

      private var contacts:Array;
      private var phoneNumber:Number;
      private var isOn:Boolean = false;

      public function Mobile()
      {
            this.phoneNumber = 011003637;
      }

      public function addContact(cName:String, cNumber:Number):void
      {
            // Code to add a new contact
      }

      public function launchApp():void
      {
            // Code to launch an app on the mobile.
      }

      public static function switchOn():void
      {
            if(!isOn)
            {
                  isOn = true;

                  // Now add code to switch on the device.

            } else {

                  // Do nothing, device is already on.

            }
      }

      public static function switchOff():void
      {
            if(isOn == false)
            {

                  // Do nothing, device is already off.

            } else {

                  isOn = false;

                  // Now add code to switch off the device.

            }
      }
   }
}
```

A *loop* is a statement in which code is executed for as long as a particular condition is met.

The following code snippet shows how the switchOn() function could be updated to include a while loop statement, which executes the code within the block as long as the seconds variable is more than 0. The value held by seconds reduces by 1 each time the loop runs.

```
public static function switchOn():void
{
        if(!isOn)
        {
                isOn = true;

                var seconds:Number = 10;

                while(seconds > 0)
                {
                        seconds = seconds - 1;
                }

                // Now add code to switch on the device.

        } else {

                // Do nothing, device is already on.

        }
}
```

Another loop frequently used in AS development is the for loop statement. In the following code snippet you'll see how the switchOn() function could be updated to include a for loop statement, which executes the code within the block as long as the seconds variable is more than 10. This time the value held by seconds increases by 1 each time the loop executes.

```
public static function switchOn():void
{
        if(!isOn)
        {
                isOn = true;

                for(var seconds:Number = 0; seconds < 10; seconds++)
                {
                        // Now add code to switch on the device.
                }

        } else {

                // Do nothing, device is already on.

        }
}
```

Inheritance

Inheritance describes the relationship between two or more classes where one class inherits the properties and method definitions of another class.

In the following example you'll see how the class `GoogleNexusS` is created from the `Mobile` class:

```
package devices
{

    import devices.Mobile;

    public class GoogleNexusS extends Mobile
    {
        public function GoogleNexusS()
        {
            super();
        }
    }
}
```

Note here that the `extend` keyword is used to reference the class that is being extended. And the `super()` function called in the `GoogleNexusS` class constructor method indicates that, when an instance is created from instantiating `GoogleNexusS`, it will call the `Mobile` class constructor function also. In this context the `GoogleNexusS` class is referred to as a *subclass* of `Mobile`, and `Mobile` is the *parent* class of `GoogleNexusS`.

Over the course of this book you'll go through many more examples of using AS3 in mobile application development.

THE FLEX FRAMEWORK

Flex is a framework that leverages an underlying library of AS3 classes to provide UI components that allow developers to build rich media applications and compile to the SWF format. Adobe Flex builds on top of the core runtime APIs provided by Flash Player and Adobe AIR.

Flex is available through the Flash Builder IDE, a tool that you will take a look at in the next chapter. Flex is also available through a software development kit (SDK) allowing SWF format content to be created through command line tools. The Adobe Flex logo is shown in Figure 1-2.

FIGURE 1-2: The Adobe Flex logo

Flex 4.5.1

This release introduces support for developing mobile applications using the Flex framework. This book uses the components that are available in the Flex 4.5.1 SDK and the Flash Builder 4.5.1 update release of the latest Flash Builder tool. There will be more on Flash Builder in Chapter 2.

Mobile applications for touch screen devices undoubtedly should differ from desktop and web applications for a number of reasons. While mobile devices are becoming more capable, there are important considerations you need to be aware of when developing applications. These include:

> **UI design:** Mobile devices have small screens and high pixel densities, and so applications have to be designed to account for sizeable components on screens that are easy to interact with.

> **Screen resolution:** Mobile devices can have different screen resolutions, and the pixel densities across most mobile device screens are higher than those of desktop monitors. So applications have to adapt well to those displays.

> **Touch screen input:** Mobile devices that provide support for touch interaction must allow for touch input via the application.

> **Memory availability and processor performance:** Mobile devices in most cases have limited memory availability, as well as lower CPU and GPU performances, and so applications have to be processor-friendly.

Depending on your development experience or background, these points may or may not seem quite so obvious. But what is important here is for you to understand some of the features that the Flex framework helps to address in mobile application development.

The Flex framework introduces the MXML language.

MXML

MXML is an XML tag-based markup language, used in the layout and design of components and data assets for Flex-based user interfaces. As an XML format, MXML is also structured, so there are several rules you have to follow when you write it, and the contents must be well formed and valid XML to preserve the integrity of the document.

Every MXML file is a class, but instead of having a .as file extension, it has a .mxml file extension. And instead of simply having AS3 code and syntax, it can contain both the MXML markup and AS3.

XML Namespaces

In MXML documents, an XML namespace refers to a valid Uniform Resource Identifier (URI). There is a World Wide Web Consortium (W3C) URI clarification at www.w3.org/TR/uri-clarification/. The URI allows for declarative tags, attributes, and sets of components, to be uniquely identified within the scope of the MXML document.

Three default namespaces are used in this book:

> fx: This namespace references special language declarative tags, as defined by the *MXML 2009 – Functional and Design Specification* (Adobe Open Source Wiki, http://opensource.adobe.com/wiki/display/flexsdk/MXML+2009).

> s: This namespace references the Spark Components Library, introduced into the Flex 4 framework.

> mx: This namespace references the MXML Components Library that was introduced in the Flex 3 framework but also supported in the Flex 4 framework.

The following code snippet shows how the `fx`, `s`, and `mx` namespaces are defined with associated URIs, in the root of the opening `<s:Application>` tag:

```
<?xml version="1.0" encoding="utf-8"?>
<s:Application xmlns:fx="http://ns.adobe.com/mxml/2009"
               xmlns:s="library://ns.adobe.com/flex/spark"
               xmlns:mx="library://ns.adobe.com/flex/mx">

</s:Application>
```

The `<s:Application>` tag is a container that enables you to start adding visual and interactive components to your mobile application using the Flex framework, without the need to define other containers.

Notice that the namespace for `Application` is given the s prefix. This is because the `Application` component is derived from the Spark Component Library.

The Spark component features are specifically targeted for mobile development, to conserve memory.

Namespaces can also be referenced for local custom components.

Essentially, namespaces are used to do the following:

1. Specify the language version of the document
2. Map XML and CSS tag names to an AS class name

Both these allow the Flex compiler to resolve the implementation for both default and custom language and component tags.

In general, mobile applications should utilize the `fx` and `s` XML namespaces, the majority of which have been optimized for mobile devices.

 NOTE *If it makes it easier, think of the namespaces as individual import statements that allow you to use only certain AS3 classes that have been imported into that document. For each namespace a number of classes can be used, once that namespace has been declared in the document.*

The `<fx:Script>` tag declaration permits AS3 code to be added to the document and to be referenced by other elements in the MXML document, as you'll see shortly.

As with AS3, MXML follows particular rules for coding. One such MXML rule is that an element must have an opening and closing tag if it contains other values or nests other tags.

With MXML specifying components like the button requires a lot less code. This is mainly because the Flex framework contains a lot of the logic and hides it from the developer in design time. Tags that don't need to contain nested values in your application may simply be written with an enclosing forward slash (/), as shown in the following snippet, which highlights the `<fx:Declarations>` tag being empty:

```
<fx:Declarations/>
```

Usually, you will see the `<fx:Declarations>` tag with an MXML comment nested between the opening `<fx:Declarations>` tag and the closing `</fx:Declarations>` tag:

```
<fx:Declarations>
        <!-- Place non-visual elements (e.g., services, values objects) -->
</fx:Declarations>
```

As highlighted in the comment, the `<fx:Declarations>` tag enables you to define value objects for use within MXML and AS3.

The following code snippet shows how a string, `<fx:String>`, and an integer, `<fx:int>`, can be in `<fx:Declarations>` to specify two values, "Jermaine G. Anderson," and a random number "31," respectively:

```
<fx:Declarations>
        <fx:String id="myName">Jermaine G. Anderson</fx:String>
        <fx:int id="myAge">31</fx:int>
</fx:Declarations>
```

Notice the `id` attribute being used in each value object declaration.

The id Attribute

In MXML the `id` attribute is a special property used as a unique identifier for tags, setting the name property on the underlying AS3 class. This allows components to be referenced through AS3 defined in a `<fx:Script>` tag.

The following code snippet shows an instance of the `<s:Label>` component being referenced within the `<fx:Script>` declaration. The `id` property on `<s:Label>` has been set to `myLabel`, allowing the `text` property on the component to be set via AS3 within the function called `setLabelText()`, when it is called.

```
<fx:Script>
        <![CDATA[
                private function setLabelText():void
                {
                        myLabel.text = "Hello World";
                }
        ]]>
</fx:Script>

<s:Label id="myLabel"/>
```

In MXML, each property available for a particular tag component can be set or referenced in AS3 using the `id`.

Spark Library Components

Spark is the name of the component library, which is a key aspect of the Flex framework and Flash Builder.

These components and their skins have been optimized to run out of the box on mobile touch screen devices; in Flex 4.5.1, components have been added to address common application design problems specific to smartphones.

The Spark architecture encompasses a skinning model that provides a separation of a component's visual aspect from its working logic, allowing designers and developers more freedom, because the visual elements of a Flex component can be designed independently of the implementation of the logic behind the component.

While skinning isn't a key focus of this book, you'll get to know the Spark component library well, enabling you to build relatively robust mobile applications in a very short amount of time.

In Flex, components are declared in their own namespaces. The majority of the components and data elements defined by the <mx> namespace are not optimized for mobile, while the components derived from the <s> namespaces have been optimized for applications on mobile devices. This book predominantly uses the <s> set of components.

Once a namespace has been declared, the components can be referenced within the MXML document.

The following subsections detail some of the core mobile components that are used throughout this book.

The Label Component

The <s:Label> tag is a visual Spark component that renders a single line of text. The following code snippet shows how the <s:Label> component renders the text "Hello World":

```
<s:Label text="Hello World"/>
```

The Text Input and Text Area Components

Both the <s:TextInput> and <s:TextArea> tags are visual Spark components that allow users to enter text using a device's native keyboard. The following code snippet shows how the <s:TextInput> component displays the text "Type a name..." via a prompt property:

```
<s:TextInput prompt="Type a name..."/>
```

The text set by the prompt property will disappear when the user starts typing or when the component gains focus, and regain the prompt text if the component loses focus or the user deletes all the text.

Text for the components can be set and retrieved via the text property, as shown in the following code snippet, which shows how the <s:TextArea> component displays the text "Once upon a time..."

```
<s:TextArea text="Once upon a time..."/>
```

The <s:TextInput> component allows you to define whether the user input should be hidden by asterisks via the displayAsPassword property. The <s:TextArea> component allows for multiple lines of text to be written, whereas the <s:TextInput> does not.

The `<s:TextInput>` component is shown in Figure 1-3.

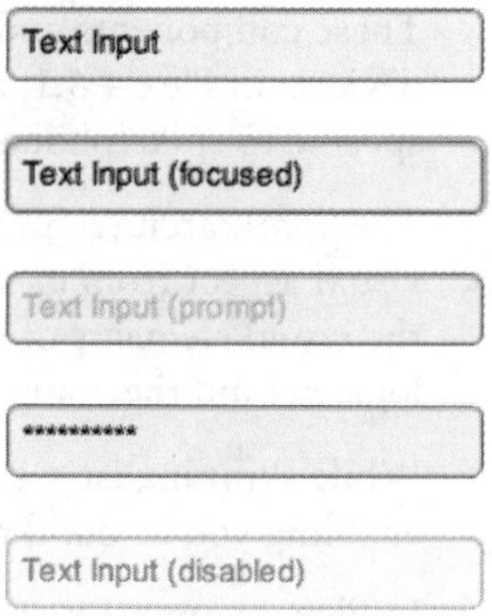

The Button Component

To add a Button component in an application, specify the `<s:Button>` tag. In the following code snippet the `<s:Button>` tag defines the `id` property as `myButton`, a `label` property with the text `Hit Me!`, and a `click` property set to a function named `onClick()`:

```
<s:Button id="myButton"
        label="Hit Me!"
        click="onClick(event)"/>
```

The `onClick()` function assigned to the click event handler needs to be defined in the `<fx:Script>` tag.

The `<s:Button>` is shown in Figure 1-4.

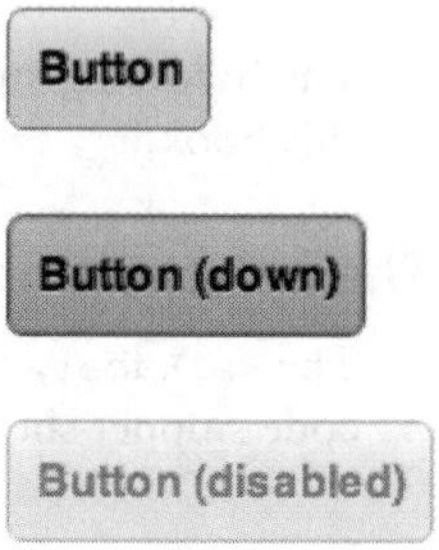

The Button Bar Component

The `<s:ButtonBar>` tag allows you to create a collection of buttons that are able to navigate between the views of the mobile application. Only one of the buttons in the bar may be selected at any one time.

In the following code snippet, the two buttons are defined in the `<s:ButtonBar>` component, Grid and Vertical List:

```
<s:ButtonBar>
    <s:dataProvider>
        <s:ArrayCollection>
            <s:NavigatorContent id="gridBtn"
                                label="Grid"/>

            <s:NavigatorContent id="listBtn"
                                label="Vertical List"/>
        </s:ArrayCollection>
    </s:dataProvider>
</s:ButtonBar>
```

The `<s:ButtonBar>` component is shown in Figure 1-5.

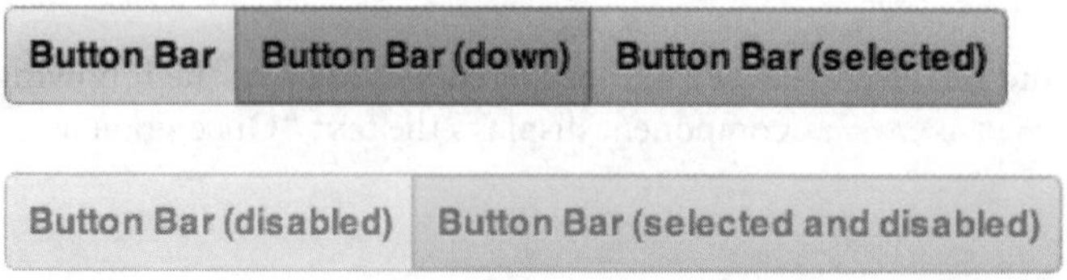

FIGURE 1-3: The Spark Text Input control, displaying the default, focused, prompt, password, and disabled states

FIGURE 1-4: The Spark Button control, displaying the default, down, and disabled states

FIGURE 1-5: The Spark Button Bar control, displaying the default, down, selected, and disabled states

The HTTP Service Component

Data can be accessed in a number of ways for applications, one of which is by using an HTTP Service.

To utilize data over HTTP using MXML, the `<s:HTTPService>` tag can be used. The following snippet shows how the `<s:HTTPService>` tag is defined:

```
<s:HTTPService id="httpService"
               url="http://localhost/HTTPService"
               fault="onFault(event)"
               result="onResult(event)"
               resultFormat="object"
               showBusyCursor="true"/>
```

The Web Service Component

To utilize data via a web service, the `<s:WebService>` tag can be used. The following snippet shows how the `<s:WebService>` tag is defined:

```
<s:WebService id="service"
              wsdl="wsdl"
              useProxy="false"
              showBusyCursor="true"
              result="onResult(event)"
              fault="onFault(event)"/>
```

The List Component

The following code snippet shows one of the ways in which nested tags can be used in MXML for a single component. In this example the `<s:dataProvider>` for the `<s:List>` component is an `<s:ArrayList>`:

```
<s:List id="myList">
    <s:dataProvider>
        <s:ArrayList id="arrList"
                     source="[One, Two, Three]"/>
    </s:dataProvider>
</s:List>
```

The `<s:List>` component is shown Figure 1-6.

FIGURE 1-6: The Spark List control, displaying the default, down, selected states for each List Item

Layout Declarations

A number of non-visual components can be used in MXML to specify the layout of an application and to group visual elements.

The `<s:layout>` component tag defines a layout, and this needs to nest an accompanying Layout component tag to give the layout its properties.

The following lists each of the tags that can be nested within the opening `<s:layout>` and closing `</s:layout>` tags:

➤ `<s:BasicLayout>`: Arranges components independently of each other, according to their individual settings. To position each component within a layout, each child element's position needs to be explicitly defined, using the x and y properties of the child, or constraints.

➤ `<s:ConstraintLayout>`: Gives you the ability to create sibling-relative layouts by constraining elements to the specified columns and rows.

➤ `<s:HorizontalLayout>`: To arrange the layout elements in a horizontal sequence, left to right, with optional gaps between the elements and optional padding around the elements.

➤ `<s:VerticalLayout>`: To arrange the layout elements in a vertical sequence, top to bottom, with optional gaps between the elements and optional padding around the sequence of elements.

➤ `<s:FormItemLayout>`: To provide a constraint-based layout to `FormItems`.

➤ `<s:TileLayout>`: To arrange equally sized cells of components in columns and rows, using a number of properties that control orientation, count, size, gap, and justification of the columns and the rows, in addition to an element's alignment within a cell.

In the following code you see how the horizontal layout tag `<s:HorizontalLayout>` is defined:

```
<s:layout>
      <s:HorizontalLayout/>
</s:layout>
```

Chapter 5 explores the use of the `<s:HorizontalLayout>` and the `<s:VerticalLayout>` declarations in more detail.

The Group, HGroup, and VGroup Containers

The `<s:Group>`, `<s:HGroup>`, and `<s:VGroup>` tags are non-visual containers that allow you to group components. Both the `<s:HGroup>` and `<s:VGroup>` containers are subclasses of the `<s:Group>` tag. The `<s:HGroup>` tag uses `<s:HorizontalLayout>`, and so components that are nested within the `<s:HGroup>` tag will be arranged horizontally from left to right. The `<s:VGroup>` tag uses `<s:VerticalLayout>`, and so components that are nested within the `<s:VGroup>` tag are arranged vertically from top to bottom.

In the following code snippet you see two buttons horizontally aligned using the `<s:HGroup>` tag, with their label properties set to Left and Right, respectively:

```
<s:HGroup id="buttonContainer"
          width="100%"
          height="100%">

    <s:Button id="button1" label="Left"/>
    <s:Button id="button2" label="Right"/>

</s:HGroup>
```

Contrast this with the following code snippet, where the two buttons are vertically aligned within the `<s:VGroup>` tag. This time the label properties are set to Top and Bottom, to indicate their arrangement.

```
<s:VGroup id="buttonContainer"
          width="100%"
          height="100%">

    <s:Button id="button1" label="Top"/>
    <s:Button id="button2" label="Bottom"/>

</s:VGroup>
```

Throughout the book you will see examples of using `<s:Group>`, `<s:HGroup>`, and `<s:VGroup>` tags.

The CheckBox and RadioButton Controls

The `<s:CheckBox>` and `<s:RadioButton>` components are controls that provide a way for users to make a selective choice.

To add a radio button, you need to specify the `<s:RadioButton>` tag. The following snippet shows two radio buttons with their `label` properties set to `Radio 1` and `Radio 2`, grouped by their `groupName` attributes, which are set to `myRadioGroup`. The `selected` property on the first radio button is set to `true`, which means this will be as follows:

```
<s:RadioButton label="Radio 1"
               groupName="myRadioGroup"
               selected="true"/>

<s:RadioButton label="Radio 2"
               groupName="myRadioGroup"/>
```

The `groupName` property is used so that only one button in a group of radio buttons is selected at a time.

The `<s:CheckBox>` and `<s:RadioButton>` components are shown in Figure 1-7.

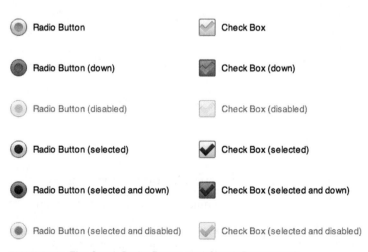

FIGURE 1-7: The Spark Radio Button and Check Box controls

The Image Component

Using the `<s:Image>` tag allows for image content to be included in an application via MXML. The following code shows how to render an image with both its `width` and `height` properties set to `100`:

```
<s:Image id="myImage"
         width="100"
         height="100"
         source="flash.png"/>
```

To reference a particular image you need to set the `source` property on the component to the image file path you want to load, relative to the .swf file generating the content. The component can also load image content via a URL over HTTP.

Throughout the book you will see examples of images being referenced using MXML like the one shown in the example.

Style Declarations

The `<fx:Style>` tag allows you to specify styles for components and views within an application.

In the following code snippet, you see the `backgroundColor` property of the spark `<s:Application>` container set to #CCCCCC, and the `fontSize` property of the `<s:Label>` component set to 24:

```
<?xml version="1.0" encoding="utf-8"?>
<s:Application xmlns:fx="http://ns.adobe.com/mxml/2009"
               xmlns:s="library://ns.adobe.com/flex/spark">

    <fx:Style>

        @namespace s "library://ns.adobe.com/flex/spark";

        s|Application
        {
            backgroundColor:#CCCCCC;
        }

        s|Label
        {
            fontSize:24;
        }

    </fx:Style>

</s:Application>
```

Note that hexadecimal code color values can be specified with either the # or the 0x prefix.

Defining styles in this way enables you to set the styles for components from within the main application file.

If you wanted a `<s:Label>` component to have a different font size from that set in the main application file, you would need to set the `fontSize` property on that specific `<s:Label>` instance, effectively overriding the main style.

You can also declare styles in a CSS file and by setting the `source` property on the `<fx:Style>` declaration. You can apply those as shown in the following snippet:

```
<?xml version="1.0" encoding="utf-8"?>
<s:Application xmlns:fx="http://ns.adobe.com/mxml/2009"
               xmlns:s="library://ns.adobe.com/flex/spark">

    <fx:Style source="mobileStyles.css"/>

</s:Application>
```

Data Binding

The Flex framework supports *data binding*, a mechanism in which data on one object can be tied to another object so that any updates or changes in one object are automatically reflected in the other.

The following code snippet demonstrates one of the ways in which data binding can be accomplished via the `<fx:Binding>` tag:

```
<?xml version="1.0" encoding="utf-8"?>
<s:Application xmlns:fx="http://ns.adobe.com/mxml/2009"
               xmlns:s="library://ns.adobe.com/flex/spark">

    <fx:Binding source="txtIn.text"
                destination="txtOut.text"/>

    <s:TextInput id="txtIn"/>

    <s:Label id="txtOut"/>

</s:Application>
```

Here, whenever text is written in the `<s:TextInput>` component, which has its `id` property value set to `txtIn`, the source data on the `text` property will be replicated to the `text` property on the `<s:Label>` component as the user types. To set the data binding, you need to specify the `source` and `destination` properties in the `<fx:Binding>` tag.

Another way data binding can be demonstrated is to use curly brackets (`{}`) and explicitly set a data object within those brackets to bind to. In the following code snippet, the `<fx:Binding>` tag is no longer used to assign the source and destination; instead, the `text` property on the `<s:Label>` references the `text` property on `<s:TextInput>` to assign its data:

```
<?xml version="1.0" encoding="utf-8"?>
<s:Application xmlns:fx="http://ns.adobe.com/mxml/2009"
               xmlns:s="library://ns.adobe.com/flex/spark">

    <s:TextInput id="txtIn"/>

    <s:Label id="txtOut"
             text="{txtIn.text}"/>

</s:Application>
```

Data binding can also be achieved by creating a bindable object variable. In the following snippet, you see that the textObj has been declared as a String object. The Bindable keyword is written above the variable within square brackets ([]), designating the variable as bindable:

```
<?xml version="1.0" encoding="utf-8"?>
<s:Application xmlns:fx="http://ns.adobe.com/mxml/2009"
               xmlns:s="library://ns.adobe.com/flex/spark">

    <fx:Script>
        <![CDATA[

            [Bindable]
            public var textObj:String = "String object";

            public function onClick():void
            {
                textObj = "String object has changed!";
            }

        ]]>
    </fx:Script>

    <s:TextInput text="{textObj}"/>

    <s:Button click="onClick()"/>

</s:Application>
```

When the button is clicked, the value of textObj changes, and those changes are reflected visually in the <s:TextInput> component, which has its text property assigned to the bindable textObj.

Flex Mobile Application Structure

The mobile application structure employed by the Flex framework consists of a view navigation pattern, where a user is able to navigate between views by selecting data items or other controls on screen.

By design, there are a number of components that are core to the mobile application structure supported by Flex 4.5. These include:

➤ View

➤ View menu

➤ View navigator

➤ Tabbed view navigator

➤ Action bar

The main application class recommended for building your Flex mobile applications is ViewNavigatorApplication, and this utilizes each of the core features.

The View Navigator Application

In MXML, the `<s:ViewNavigatorApplication>` tag is the entry point for your Flex-based mobile applications. The following code snippet shows how you would define the MXML, specifying the first view to render on the application on the `firstView` property:

```
<?xml version="1.0" encoding="utf-8"?>
<s:ViewNavigatorApplication xmlns:fx="http://ns.adobe.com/mxml/2009"
                            xmlns:s="library://ns.adobe.com/flex/spark"
                            firstView="views.FirstView">

</s:ViewNavigatorApplication>
```

Unlike the `<s:Application>` container, `<s:ViewNavigatorApplication>` is optimized for mobile but requires that a view be specified that displays content.

The View Component

The view component, as defined by the `<s:View>` tag and the `sparks.components.View` class, represents a single user interface screen in your mobile application. This is where you will be able to place each of the visual mobile components you want to appear within the application.

The following code snippet shows the MXML and `<fx:Script>` defined for a view. The `click` property on the `<s:Button>` component in the MXML is assigned to the `onClick()` method defined in the ActionScript within the `<fx:Script>` tag:

```
<?xml version="1.0" encoding="utf-8"?>
<s:View xmlns:fx="http://ns.adobe.com/mxml/2009"
        xmlns:s="library://ns.adobe.com/flex/spark"
        title="View Example">

    <fx:Script>
        <![CDATA[

            private function onClick(e:Event):void
            {
                myButton.label = "Ouch!";
            }

        ]]>
    </fx:Script>

    <s:Button id="myButton"
            label="Hit Me!"
            click="onClick(event)"/>

</s:View>
```

FIGURE 1-8: The view example

Note here that the `title` property on the view is simply set to View Example. The `title` property of a view will be displayed in the action bar area, at the top of the mobile application (Figure 1-8).

The View Menu Component

You can include a number of menu buttons that can control elements of your application by implementing the `<s:viewMenuItems>` tag.

The view menu in an application can be revealed when a user invokes the menu button on the device.

This is done by defining a set of `<s:ViewMenuItem>` components within a `<s:viewMenuItems>` declaration, as shown in the following code snippet:

```
<s:viewMenuItems>

    <s:ViewMenuItem label="Add"/>
    <s:ViewMenuItem label="Update"/>
    <s:ViewMenuItem label="Delete"/>

</s:viewMenuItems>
```

The menu appears at the bottom of the screen when the device's native menu button is pressed. When an item has been selected, the view menu will disappear from view.

The menu can also be invoked when you set the `viewMenuOpen` property on the `mx.core` `.FlexGlobals.topLevelApplication` object to `true`:

```
mx.core.FlexGlobals.topLevelApplication.viewMenuOpen = true;
```

The following code snippet shows how the `click` property on a `<s:Button>` component reveals the view menu:

```
<?xml version="1.0" encoding="utf-8"?>
<s:View xmlns:fx="http://ns.adobe.com/mxml/2009"
        xmlns:s="library://ns.adobe.com/flex/spark"
        title="View Menu Example">

    <fx:Script>
        <![CDATA[

            import mx.core.FlexGlobals;

            private function onClick(e:Event):void
            {
                FlexGlobals.topLevelApplication.viewMenuOpen = true;
            }

            private function onSelected(e:Event):void
            {
                myLabel.text = e.currentTarget.label + " selected";
            }

        ]]>
    </fx:Script>

    <s:Label id="myLabel"/>

    <s:Button id="myButton"
```

```
                label="Open Menu!"
                click="onClick(event)"/>

        <s:viewMenuItems>

            <s:ViewMenuItem label="Add"
                            click="onSelected(event)"/>
            <s:ViewMenuItem label="Update"
                            click="onSelected(event)"/>
            <s:ViewMenuItem label="Delete"
                            click="onSelected(event)"/>

        </s:viewMenuItems>

    </s:View>
```

This example is shown in Figure 1-9.

The View Navigator

The `ViewNavigator` class is what manages each of the view
containers in a mobile application. Using a stack-based history
mechanism, the main role of a view navigator is to conserve
memory used by the application, by ensuring that only one view is
in memory at a given time.

FIGURE 1-9: A view menu
example

When the mobile application starts, a view navigator will show the view specified by its `firstView`
property, which, as shown, can be defined on the `<s:ViewNavigatorApplication>` tag. Each view
created in an application has a reference to a view navigator via its `navigator` object.

In the following snippet, you see how to navigate to a new view in an application

```
navigator.pushView(views.HelloWorldAppHome, dObj);
```

As shown, the `pushView()` method on the `navigator` object is called, where the full name of
the view `views.HelloWorldAppHome` is supplied as the first argument, and a data object `dObj` is
supplied as the second argument. This method will normally be invoked by user input, like a button
call. The data object supplied can be retrieved on the `data` property of the next view. Thus, using
`pushView()`, data can also be passed between views as the user navigates around the application.

When new views are added to an application, they are stacked, like an endless deck of cards. The
`popView()` and `popToFirstView()` methods allow the user to navigate back through a series of
screens.

The `popView()` method can be called to return to the previous view:

```
navigator.popView();
```

If `navigator.popToFirstView()` is called, the user will be returned to the first view in a view stack:

```
navigator.popToFirstView();
```

The Tabbed View Navigator Application

The *tabbed* view navigator application allows you to build more complex mobile applications that are capable of switching between different view stacks. When the mobile application starts, the user is able to toggle between a defined number of tabs at the bottom of the screen. Each tab effectively represents a unique view navigator.

To include this feature in your mobile application, you define the `<s:TabbedViewNavigatorApplication>` tag in your main application file. This class utilizes the `TabbedViewNavigator` object, which manages a collection of view navigators.

When you define a `<s:ViewNavigator>` for the `<s:TabbedViewNavigatorApplication>`, you need to ensure the value for the `firstView` property is set to the class path of the view, and that the `width` and `height` properties are set to `100%`.

The following code snippet shows how to define three tabs with labels `Tab 1`, `Tab 2`, and `Tab 3`, respectively, for a tabbed view navigator application:

```xml
<?xml version="1.0" encoding="utf-8"?>
<s:TabbedViewNavigatorApplication xmlns:fx="http://ns.adobe.com/mxml/2009"
                                   xmlns:s="library://ns.adobe.com/flex/spark">

        <s:ViewNavigator label="Tab 1"
                         width="100%"
                         height="100%"
                         firstView="views.FirstTabView"/>

        <s:ViewNavigator label="Tab 2"
                         width="100%"
                         height="100%"
                         firstView="views.SecondTabView"/>

        <s:ViewNavigator label="Tab 3"
                         width="100%"
                         height="100%"
                         firstView="views.ThirdTabView"/>

</s:TabbedViewNavigatorApplication>
```

Figure 1-10 shows the tabs in a Flex mobile application.

The initial screen to appear in this example will be the `FirstTabView`, which is defined on the first `<s:ViewNavigator>` specified in the application.

You can also assign a `.png` file to the `icon` property on `<s:ViewNavigator>`. This will display an image on the tab (Figure 1-11).

FIGURE 1-10: Tabs being displayed in the tabbed view navigator application example

FIGURE 1-11: Icons displayed on the tabs of a tabbed view navigator application

The following code snippet shows that an image named search.png is assigned to the first tab, while an image named settings.png is assigned to the second tab:

```xml
<?xml version="1.0" encoding="utf-8"?>
<s:TabbedViewNavigatorApplication xmlns:fx="http://ns.adobe.com/mxml/2009"
                                  xmlns:s="library://ns.adobe.com/flex/spark">

        <s:ViewNavigator icon="search.png"
                         width="100%"
                         height="100%"
                         firstView="views.FirstTabView"/>

        <s:ViewNavigator icon="settings.png"
                         width="100%"
                         height="100%"
                         firstView="views.SecondTabView"/>

</s:TabbedViewNavigatorApplication>
```

The data for a view navigator can be set using the firstViewData property, as shown in the following snippet:

```xml
<?xml version="1.0" encoding="utf-8"?>
<s:TabbedViewNavigatorApplication xmlns:fx="http://ns.adobe.com/mxml/2009"
                                  xmlns:s="library://ns.adobe.com/flex/spark">

        <fx:Script>
```

```
        <![CDATA[

            private var dObj:Object = {name:"Jermaine G. Anderson"};

        ]]>
    </fx:Script>


    <s:ViewNavigator icon="search.png"
                     width="100%"
                     height="100%"
                     firstView="views.FirstTabView"/>

    <s:ViewNavigator icon="settings.png"
                     width="100%"
                     height="100%"
                     firstView="views.SecondTabView"
                     firstViewData="{dObj}"/>

</s:TabbedViewNavigatorApplication>
```

The Action Bar Component

The action bar is the visual header that appears by default at the top of a view in a Flex mobile application.

This header has space for three distinct content areas, including a central area designated for a view title. To the left of the title content is an area designated for navigational content, represented in MXML by the <s:navigationContent> tag, and to the right is an area designated for actionable content, represented by the <s:actionContent> tag.

Button components can be assigned to the action bar, when necessary, to allow the user to control navigation and perform actions in the application.

In the following code snippet, you see an example of the navigation and action content areas specified in a <s:ViewNavigatorApplication> declaration:

```
<?xml version="1.0" encoding="utf-8"?>
<s:ViewNavigatorApplication xmlns:fx="http://ns.adobe.com/mxml/2009"
                            xmlns:s="library://ns.adobe.com/flex/spark">

    <s:navigationContent>

        <s:Button label="Home"
                  click="navigator.popToFirstView()"/>

    </s:navigationContent>

    <s:actionContent>

        <s:Button label="Search"
                  click="onSearch()"/>

    </s:actionContent>

</s:ViewNavigatorApplication>
```

Action bar content is not limited to button controls within the navigation or action content areas. You can pretty much add any of the visual spark components to be placed in the action bar. In the following snippet, you also see an example of the title content area being defined via the `<s:titleContent>` tag to include a text input field:

```
<s:titleContent>

    <s:TextInput id="searchTxt"
                 width="100%"
                 prompt="Search field..."/>

</s:titleContent>
```

Figure 1-12 demonstrates the `<s:titleContent>` being set.

In this example, you see that icons are also specified on the navigation and action content areas of the action bar.

The action bar can be customized for each individual view of the application or have controls designated that persist across all the views of an application when defined in the main application file.

FIGURE 1-12: Action bar content defined within a view navigator application

View Transitions

When users navigate between views, they will see the current view transition out of the screen, while the next view transitions onto the screen via a set of defined animations.

There are two properties of the `ViewNavigator` object that can be defined to describe the type of view transition for the view:

➤ `defaultPushTransition`: The animation that occurs when a new view is added to the view stack — e.g., via `pushView()`

➤ `defaultPopTransition`: The animation that occurs when a view is removed from the view stack — e.g., via `popView()`

There are four view transition classes found in the `spark.transitions` package that can be customized and assigned to both the default transition objects:

➤ `CrossFadeViewTransition`: To fade out the existing view as the new view is revealed

➤ `FlipViewTransition`: To flip out the existing view as the new view is revealed

➤ `SlideViewTransition`: To slide out the existing view while the new view slides in

➤ `ZoomViewTransition`: To zoom out of the existing view as the new view is revealed, or to zoom in to the new view over the existing view

Each view transition has a number of properties that can be defined for animations, including `direction`, `duration`, and `mode`.

The following code snippet shows a zoom transition operating on the `pushView()` method to reveal a view called `FirstViewTab`. The mode is set to *zoom in* using the `ZoomViewTransitionMode.IN` constant, and the transition duration is set to *250 milliseconds*:

```
<fx:Script>
    <![CDATA[

        import spark.transitions.ZoomViewTransition;
        import spark.transitions.ZoomViewTransitionMode;

        private function zoomView():void
        {
            var zoom:ZoomViewTransition = new ZoomViewTransition();
            zoom.mode = ZoomViewTransitionMode.IN;
            zoom.duration = 250;

            navigator.pushView(views.FirstTabView, null, null, zoom);
        }
    ]]>
</fx:Script>
```

The `ZoomTransition` object is supplied as the fourth argument to the `pushView()` method on the `navigator` property of the view.

The following code snippet shows a slide transition, in which the slide mode is set to *push* using the `SlideViewTransitionMode.PUSH` constant, and the transition direction is set to *down*, using the `ViewTransitionDirection.DOWN` constant. The duration is set also to *250 milliseconds*:

```
<fx:Script>
    <![CDATA[

        import spark.transitions.ViewTransitionDirection;
        import spark.transitions.SlideViewTransition;
        import spark.transitions.SlideViewTransitionMode;

        private function slideView():void
        {
            var slide:SlideViewTransition = new SlideViewTransition();
            slide.direction = ViewTransitionDirection.DOWN
            slide.mode = SlideViewTransitionMode.PUSH;
            slide.duration = 250;

            navigator.pushView(views.FirstTabView, null, null, slide);
        }

    ]]>
</fx:Script>
```

Either of the transitions in the previous examples could also be assigned to the `navigator`
`.defaultPushTransition` or the `navigator.defaultPopTransition` on the view:

```
navigator.defaultPushTransition = slide;
navigator.defaultPopTransition = zoom;
```

By default, Flex uses the `SlideViewTransition` for view transitions.

Over the course of the book, you'll implement many of the key components of a Flex Mobile Application, including those that are core to the `<s:ViewNavigationApplication>` class.

Considerations for Mobile Development

Mobile applications for touch screen devices undoubtedly should differ from desktop and web applications for a number of reasons. Although mobile devices are becoming more capable, there are important considerations you need to be aware of when developing applications. These include:

➤   **UI design:** Mobile devices have small screens and high pixel densities, so applications have to be designed to account for sizeable components on screens that are easy to interact with.

➤   **Screen resolution:** Mobile devices can have different screen resolutions, and the pixel densities across most mobile device screens are higher than those of desktop monitors. Thus, applications have to adapt well to those displays.

➤   **Touch screen input:** Mobile devices that provide support for touch interaction must allow for touch input via the application.

➤   **Memory availability and processor performance:** In most cases, mobile devices have limited memory availability, as well as lower CPU and GPU performances. Thus, applications have to be processor-friendly.

Depending on your development experience or background, these points may or may not seem quite so obvious. What is important here is for you to understand some of the features that the Flex framework helps to address in mobile application development.

ADOBE AIR

The Adobe Integrated Runtime (AIR, www.adobe.com/products/air) is a cross-platform run time that allows developers to create and deploy applications for a variety of operating systems outside of Internet browsers.

AIR for smartphone and tablet devices allows developers to create applications that can be deployed in the same way as native applications across each mobile platform. And as previously mentioned, the Flex framework can be used to create mobile applications that are installed as standalone applications using the Adobe AIR run time. On Google Android devices supporting AIR, if AIR is not yet installed, the user will be prompted to download and install the run time on first launch of an AIR application. On RIM's BlackBerry PlayBook, AIR is integral to the operating system, so you need only be concerned with the version of AIR that has been installed on the device. On Apple iOS devices, such as the iPad and iPhone, AIR cannot be installed as a separate run time; an AIR application is installed as a self-contained package.

FIGURE 1-13: The Adobe AIR logo

The Adobe AIR logo is shown in Figure 1-13.

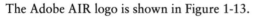

When Adobe AIR was first released, it was aimed at the creation of rich media content and enterprise applications that could run outside the traditional web browser, essentially targeting the desktop across multiple platforms.

In addition to the SWF format, Adobe AIR can render content produced with both HTML and JavaScript. Adobe AIR now runs Flash platform applications across a wide range of devices and operating systems, covering Desktop, TV, and Mobile Devices.

Adobe AIR 2.7 is the most recent release of the client. The first release, AIR 2.5, introduced support for the mobile device profile; this book uses references to AIR 2.7.

On each of the platforms AIR supports, the client must be installed directly on the end user's device at an OS level.

This book covers many of the APIs introduced in AIR 2.7 for mobile devices supported on Google Android, BlackBerry Tablet OS, and Apple iOS.

At the time of writing, a beta for Adobe AIR 3 was underway, allowing developers to preview new and enhanced features for desktop and mobile applications targeting the next release of the run time. With the potential for new APIs to be dropped, none of the features could be covered in this book, but look for an update. For more information, visit the Adobe Labs website (`labs.adobe.com/technologies/`) and search for Adobe AIR 3 in the Products section.

SUMMARY

This introduction to Flash, Flex, and AIR is just the beginning, and many of the topics touched on here, and more, will be explored in detail over the course of this book.

In this chapter, you learned about the Flash Player run time for mobile and covered many of the key concepts of AS3.

You then explored some of the core elements of the Flex framework and MXML components, and then were introduced to Adobe AIR.

In Chapters 2 and 3, you begin building mobile applications for Google Android, Apple iOS, and BlackBerry Tablet OS devices using AIR 2.7. Then from Chapter 4 onwards, there will be extensive coverage of AS3 and MXML. You expand on this in Chapters 7, 8, and 10, where you cover many of the runtime APIs available only via the Adobe AIR installed on mobile devices.

In the next chapter, you get started with mobile application development, creating the Hello World App example.

At the end of each chapter, you'll encounter exercises containing additional tasks that will help you build your knowledge about key aspects of that particular chapter. In the following section, you can either tackle the exercises now or wait until later; they don't have to be completed to follow on.

EXERCISES

1. Define a new AS3 class called `Tablet` that is contained in the devices package. Set a few properties for screen resolution and orientation to indicate whether the device is in portrait or landscape mode. Then add a public method to toggle between the device orientations.

2. Define how to create a tile arrangement of five images using MXML.

3. Define a view navigator application that has four views. Add a label and button to each view. For the button, implement a click that navigates the user to the next view using a unique view transition. Add a back button so that you can view.

4. Define a tabbed view navigator application that has three tab views. For the first view, specify a list of three items. For the second view, add a 100x100 image of the world that moves randomly around the screen. Then for the third view, add a label that displays a countdown timer in seconds. Every time the third view is selected, the countdown starts from 5 and stops at 0. When the countdown reaches 0, the background color for the view should change.

▶ **WHAT YOU LEARNED IN THIS CHAPTER**

TOPIC	KEY CONCEPT
Flash	Flash Lite 4.0 and Flash Player 10.3 are currently the run times that support SWF format mobile content out of the box.
Flex framework	Flex 4.5.1 is the latest version of the Flex framework.
	The Flex framework contains a library of components, styles, and skins optimized for developing mobile applications.
	MXML is the markup language used for developing Flex-based applications.
Adobe AIR	Adobe AIR 2.7 contains the mobile device profile, which allows for AIR applications to be deployed on devices across multiple platforms, including Google Android, Apple iOS, and BlackBerry Tablet OS.

Getting Started

WHAT YOU WILL LEARN IN THIS CHAPTER:

➤ Using Flash Builder 4.5.1

➤ Creating a Flex mobile project

➤ Defining run configurations for both desktop and devices

Adobe's portfolio includes numerous software products that enable you to author Flash-based mobile applications. These include Flash Builder, an Integrated Development Environment (IDE) that fully supports the build of Flex Framework and AS3-based mobile projects, Flash Professional for Flash-authored projects, Device Central for emulating content, and the AIR SDK for targeting multiple platforms.

In this chapter you take a close look at Flash Builder, learning how to create a Flex mobile project and how to run that project on the desktop, and also take a look at how to configure the project to run on Apple iOS, BlackBerry Tablet OS, and Google Android.

USING FLASH BUILDER 4.5.1

Flash Builder is the ideal tool of choice for creating mobile applications using the Flex framework. Built on top of Eclipse, an IDE widely used by many Java developers, Flash Builder is a robust development environment.

This book mainly focuses on building applications with the latest version of Flash Builder — at the time of writing, version 4.5.1.

> **NOTE** *If you are using Flash Builder 4.5.0, you will need to install the Flash Builder 4.5.1 updater, which you can find on the Adobe website (*www.adobe.com/support/flex/downloads_updaters.html*).*

Toward the end of this chapter, you are guided through setting up a Flex mobile project using the IDE.

Flash Builder has numerous features that simplify the task of building mobile applications, making it easier and fun.

Cool features in the latest version include wizards to target new devices that support Adobe AIR, such as the BlackBerry Playbook and Google Nexus One. You can run content on supported devices connected to your development environment, so you can install, test, and run an application instantly.

Within the IDE are tabs to switch between a mobile application's source code and the Design view. Within the Design view you can drag and drop components from panels within the IDE. The Source code view supports color schemes that can be applied to AS3 syntax and MXML script, making it easier to code documents. There is also an integrated debugger facilitating testing and advanced code hinting, and autocomplete commands that insert full class paths. Flash Builder is nothing short of a developer's dream.

The official requirements for Flash Builder are listed at the Adobe website (`www.adobe.com/products/ flash-builder/tech-specs.html`).

The following sections take a look at the following Flash Builder features:

- ➤ Workspaces
- ➤ Flash perspective
- ➤ Flash Debug perspective
- ➤ Source view
- ➤ Design view

Working with Workspaces

Flash Builder enables you to create different workspaces. A workspace contains each of the projects that you create in Flash Builder, and, by default, the workspace is the Flash Builder installation path, but this can be changed. You can also add multiple workspaces to keep collections of projects separate. I recommend for the examples used in this book that you create a workspace and keep the projects separate.

In this section you take a look within the workspace and a closer look at the tools within the IDE used to build Flex and ActionScript-based mobile applications.

Flash Builder includes a number of view panels that provide various features and configurable options for developing and testing applications.

Perspectives are a specific arrangement of view panels displayed together, aimed at providing suitable tools for a particular task.

By default, Flash Builder has two perspectives: the *Flash perspective*, which contains an arrangement of view panels for authoring your applications, and the *Flash Debug perspective*, which contains an arrangement of view panels for debugging applications.

Flash Builder will ask you to switch to a different perspective if you are debugging an application.

Using the Flash Perspective

The following lists some of the view panels available in the Flash Perspective by default:

➤ **Editor Area:** This is where you can edit files that contain your source code, including .mxml, .as, .xml, and .txt files. MXML source has two subpanels, which are available under the tabs labeled Source and Design. The Source view panel is where the MXML source is written, and the Design view panel is where the appearance of the application can be viewed or edited. When you add visual elements like a button component to the layout in Design view, the changes are automatically reflected in the Source view. The same happens when you add visual elements in the Source view; changes are reflected in the Design view. Using the Design view allows you to drag and drop components to the screen, instead of typing code, allowing you also to visually customize the appearance of the application and individual elements.

➤ **Package Explorer:** This is where you can see each of the files within the projects of a workspace. Here you not only see the contents of the project, but if you open an .as or .mxml file you see a detailed list of all class functions, methods, and variables, whether they are public, private, or protected.

➤ **Outline:** This is where you can see all the ingredients of an .mxml file or .as file. The outline contains a list of all the import, variable, and method declarations in the file. After opening or selecting an .as file, in the Editor Area you can see a list of imports, functions, methods, and properties utilized by a class in the Outline panel. The Outline panel has controls that enable you to hide non-public members, to hide static functions and variables, and to sort the list alphabetically, making it easier to find an item. Outlines are available only for an .as or .mxml file.

➤ **Problems:** This is where you see any particular issues relating to open projects in the workspace. Here you will be given warnings and compiler errors detailing the problem. This details the type of problem along with a description, the resource, the package path, and the line location on which the error has occurred.

➤ **Data/Services:** This is where you can create and integrate data services into your applications. In the Data/Services view panel you can specify and connect to a number of different data sources including BlazeDS, ColdFusion, HTTP, LiveCycle Data Services, PHP, WSDL Web Services, and XML. This view panel enables you to connect to remote and local data services while authoring your applications, giving you the option to specify input values for services and returns types, and ultimately generating code snippets to create a service call within the Flex-based project. The Data/Services panel also launches a Test Operation panel, which enables you to select one of the services you've created for your application and specify variables to run and test the service.

➤ **Network Monitor:** For Flex-based projects this is where you can monitor and record request times and response times for the particular service request calls an application makes.

Figure 2-1 shows the Flash Perspective with the view panels displayed at the bottom of the IDE and the button highlighted on the top right.

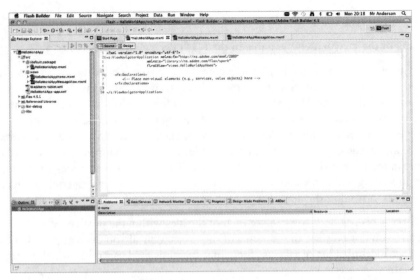

FIGURE 2-1: The Flash Perspective shown from the Hello World App project

Using the Flash Debug Perspective

The Flash Debug perspective contains view panels that enable you to rigorously test your application using a variety of features in a debugging session, including the ability to step through your code while the application is running.

The aim of the perspective is to help you to examine the source code and values assigned to variables, ultimately helping you to find problems in your application. The Flash Debug perspective launches when you select to run a debug session.

When you first run Flash Builder the option to show the Flash Debug perspective is unavailable. You need to have opened it at least once before within the workspace. Navigate to Window ➪ Perspective ➪ Flash Debug. You can also open the perspective by clicking the Open Perspective button and then selecting Flash Debug.

The following lists some of the view panels that are displayed when the Flash Debug perspective is open:

➤ **Breakpoints:** This is where you can manage the breakpoints that have been added in your application.

➤ **Console:** This is where you can see several outputs from your application while it is running, including runtime errors and trace statements.

➤ **Debug:** This panel contains all the controls you need to step through your source code in the debugging session while the application is running.

➤ **Expressions:** This is where you can manage expressions on the variables you have set to watch in your application.

➤ **Variables:** This panel is where you can find all of the variables in the current thread of the application.

Each of these panels can be seen in Figure 2-2.

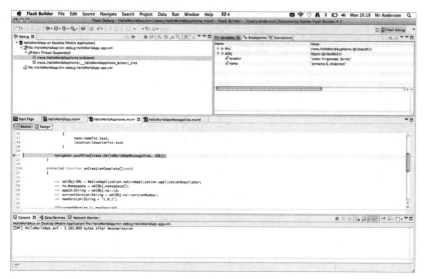

FIGURE 2-2: The Flash Debug Perspective for the Hello World project

Using the Source and Design Views

The Source view is simply the code editor where for the majority of this book you will be spending time following many of the example listings covered (Figure 2-3). Next take a look at the Design view contained within the Editor Area view panel (Figure 2-4). The Design view gives you a preview of your application.

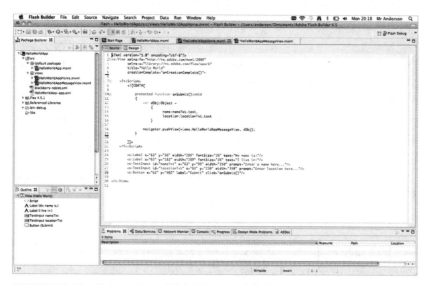

FIGURE 2-3: The Source view of HelloWorldAppHome.mxml

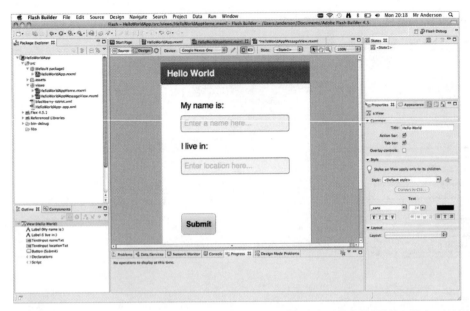

FIGURE 2-4: The corresponding Design view for the Source view of HelloWorldAppHome.mxml

In the Design view are several panels you can use to help facilitate the design of an application:

➤ **Components:** This is where you can see each of the Flex user interface components that are available to drag onto the view of the application.

➤ **States:** This is where you can manage each of the states available in a view of an application. States represent variations in the user interface, which are usually associated with a task a user has performed, such as changing the orientation of a device.

➤ **Properties:** This is where you can set the default properties for each of the components selected in the view.

➤ **Appearance:** This is where you can apply a project theme and edit the styles for the project. For mobile applications using Flex, this includes defining the text properties, the color properties, and the content background.

By default, the Components panel appears in the same pane as the Outline view panel on the left of the screen, and the States and Properties view panels appear on the right. The Design view is fully interactive, so you can drag and drop components directly onto the Stage area of the design.

Flash Builder also has controls to select the orientation of the mobile device, so you can choose to preview content in landscape or portrait mode.

 NOTE *You can only switch to the Design mode when the source is MXML and error free. You cannot switch to Design mode when editing an* .as *file.*

The Properties view located to the bottom right of the Flash Builder has multiple sections for editing:

➤ **Common:** This is where you edit the component properties.

➤ **Style:** This is where you define the style properties for a component. Depending on the component these properties may include the chrome color, padding, text, and content background.

➤ **Size and Position:** This is where you can provide the width and height of the component.

➤ **Layout:** This is where you can set the layout properties for a container component. You can select from one of the default Spark layouts to base the component's layout on, including the `HorizontalLayout` and the `VerticalLayout` classes.

When you make updates to the style properties the changes are reflected in the Design view, and depending on which component you select in the Design view, the sublist of properties that appear in the Properties view panel may change.

CREATING A MOBILE PROJECT USING FLASH BUILDER

A number of different features were covered in the previous section on Flash Builder. In this section, you take a look at using the IDE for yourself.

Creating a Hello World App Example

Over the course of this chapter you'll follow the creation of the Hello World App project. This mobile application simply enables you to enter your name onscreen and present it back with the text "Hello World, my name is . . ." — a simple example, but enough to get you started using Flash Builder.

Defining the Flex Mobile Project Settings

The first few steps take you through defining the Flex Mobile Project settings, which are usually the first things you encounter when you start a new project.

1. In Flash Builder select File ➪ New ➪ Flex Mobile Project to open the New Flex Mobile Project panel.

2. In the Project Location tab, set the Project Name field to **HelloWorldApp**. Use the default location for the project files, and then for the Flex SDK selection, use the default version (Figure 2-5). The minimum version used should be version 4.5. Once the project location details have been set, click Next.

FIGURE 2-5: Setting the Project Location for the Hello World App in the New Flex Mobile Project dialog

Targeting Mobile Devices on Different Platforms

Within the Flex Mobile Project panel, you also target your development for the mobile platforms supported by Flash Builder.

After defining the Project Settings, the next few steps take you through targeting the three mobile platforms: Apple iOS, Google Android, and BlackBerry Tablet OS.

1. For the Mobile Settings tab, ensure Apple iOS, Google Android, and BlackBerry Tablet OS are selected in the Target Platforms section. In the Application Template section select View-based Application, ensuring the Initial View Title is set to Hello World. Then at the bottom of the panel, in the Application Settings section, leave the Automatically Reorient checkbox selected (Figure 2-6).

2. Return to the section under Target Platforms and select Permission. Select Apple iOS as the platform from the drop-down, which should be the default selection. Notice in the description that you do not need to set permissions for the Apple iOS platform (Figure 2-7).

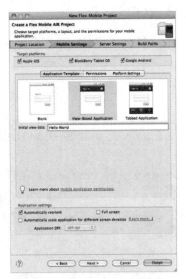

FIGURE 2-6: Setting the Mobile Settings for the Hello World App in the New Flex Mobile Project dialog

FIGURE 2-7: Setting the permissions for Apple iOS Platform for the Hello World App in the New Flex Mobile Project dialog

3. Select BlackBerry Tablet OS as the platform selection from the drop-down. You will see a number of permissions that can be set for your application should it require a particular feature (Figure 2-8).

4. Select Google Android as the platform selection from the drop-down. You will see a different set of permissions that can be set, very similar to BlackBerry Tablet OS (Figure 2-9).

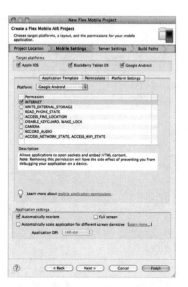

FIGURE 2-8: Setting the permissions for BlackBerry Tablet OS for the Hello World App in the New Flex Mobile Project dialog

FIGURE 2-9: Setting the permissions for Google Android for the Hello World App in the New Flex Mobile Project dialog

5. Take a look at the Platform Settings tab, with Apple iOS selected as the platform. Here you can set the target devices for the platform. Select from either iPad, both the iPhone and iPod Touch, or all the devices. Leave the default setting in place (Figure 2-10).

6. In the Server Settings tab, under the Server Technology section, leave the default setting for application server type selected as None/Other, and in the Compiled Flex Application Location section leave the default setting for Output Folder set to bin-debug. Then click Next (Figure 2-11).

7. In the Build Paths tab, check that the Main Source Folder is set to src, the Main Application File is set to `HelloWorldApp.mxml`, and the Application ID is set to `com.wrox.ch2.HelloWorldApp`, before clicking Finish (Figure 2-12).

FIGURE 2-10: Configuring the target devices for the Apple iOS platform for the Hello World App in the New Flex Mobile Project dialog

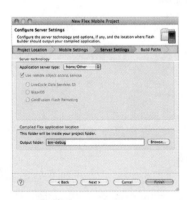

FIGURE 2-11: Configuring the Server Settings for the Hello World App in the New Flex Mobile Project dialog

FIGURE 2-12: Setting the Build Paths for the Hello World App in the New Flex Mobile Project dialog

NOTE *At this point you should familiarize yourself with the steps under "Defining the Flex Mobile Project Settings" and "Targeting Mobile Devices on Different Platforms" because these will be mentioned only briefly when you start other example projects in later chapters.*

In the Flash Builder Package Explorer panel, you should see that the Hello World project has now been created, and several files have been automatically generated for the project.

In the `src` directory, you will see the default package folder, with the main application file `HelloWorldApp.mxml`.

In the views package folder, you will see a file called `HelloWorldAppHelloWorldView.mxml`. The name of the file is built from a combination of the project name and the initial view title defined. The file represents the first view class that the application will see when launched.

Rename the class via Flash Builder to `HelloWorldAppHome.mxml`. Do this by highlighting the file and selecting File ➪ Rename from the Flash Builder menu. In the Rename Class panel that opens, ensure the Update references box is checked, enter **HelloWorldAppHome** as the name for the file, and then click OK to confirm.

The third file generated is `HelloWorldApp-app.xml`; this is the AIR application descriptor file template. AIR application descriptor files are explored in more detail in Chapter 3.

Last, the fourth file generated is the `blackberry-tablet.xml` file, which is generated when you target your projects to run on the BlackBerry Tablet OS. BlackBerry Tablet OS files are explored in more detail in Chapter 3.

Building the Hello World Project

In Listing 2-1 you see the main application file `HelloWorldApp.mxml`, with the `fx` and `s` namespaces defined. Notice here that the `firstView` property on the application has been set to `views` `.HelloWorldAppHome` to reflect the updated filename.

LISTING 2-1: The HelloWorldApp.mxml application file for the Hello World project

```
<?xml version="1.0" encoding="utf-8"?>
<s:ViewNavigatorApplication xmlns:fx="http://ns.adobe.com/mxml/2009"
                            xmlns:s="library://ns.adobe.com/flex/spark"
                            firstView="views.HelloWorldAppHome">

</s:ViewNavigatorApplication>
```

In Listing 2-2 you see the `<s:View>` container defined in the `HelloWorldAppHome.mxml` file. This has been modified slightly from the generated file, with the `title` property set to display `Hello World`.

LISTING 2-2: The HelloWorldAppHome.mxml view for the Hello World project

```
<?xml version="1.0" encoding="utf-8"?>
<s:View xmlns:fx="http://ns.adobe.com/mxml/2009"
        xmlns:s="library://ns.adobe.com/flex/spark"
        title="Hello World">

</s:View>
```

Ensure these two files have been modified as shown in the first two listings, and then follow these steps to build on the example:

1. In `HelloWorldAppHome.mxml` add two `<s:Label>` components. For the first label set the value of the `y` position to `56` and the value of the `text` property to `My name is:`. Then for the second label set the value of the `y` position to `182` and the value of the `text` property to `I live in:`. Then on both components set the value of the `x` position to `63`, the value of the `width` property to `289`, and the value for the `fontSize` property to `26` (Listing 2-3).

LISTING 2-3: Adding two <s:Label> components to the view in HelloWorldAppHome.mxml

```
<?xml version="1.0" encoding="utf-8"?>
<s:View xmlns:fx="http://ns.adobe.com/mxml/2009"
        xmlns:s="library://ns.adobe.com/flex/spark"
        title="Hello World">

    <s:Label x="63"
             y="56"
             width="289"
             fontSize="26"
```

continues

LISTING 2-3 *(continued)*

```
                    text="My name is:"/>

    <s:Label x="63"
             y="182"
             width="289"
             fontSize="26"
             text="I live in:"/>

</s:View>
```

2. Add two `<s:TextInput>` components to the view. On the first, set the value of the `prompt` property to `Enter a name here...`, the value of the `id` property to `nameTxt`, and the value of the `y` position to `98`. On the second component, set the `prompt` to `Enter location here...`, the value of the `id` property to `locationTxt`, and the `y` position to `230`. Then, on both components, set the value of the `x` position to `63` and the value of the `width` property to `350` (Listing 2-4).

LISTING 2-4: Adding two `<s:TextInput>` components to the view in HelloWorldAppHome.mxml

```
<?xml version="1.0" encoding="utf-8"?>
<s:View xmlns:fx="http://ns.adobe.com/mxml/2009"
        xmlns:s="library://ns.adobe.com/flex/spark"
        title="Hello World">

    <s:Label x="63"
             y="56"
             width="289"
             fontSize="26"
             text="My name is:"/>

    <s:Label x="63"
             y="182"
             width="289"
             fontSize="26"
             text="I live in:"/>

    <s:TextInput id="nameTxt"
             x="63"
             y="98"
             width="350"
             prompt="Enter a name here..."/>

    <s:TextInput id="locationTxt"
             x="63"
             y="230"
             width="350"
             prompt="Enter location here..."/>

</s:View>
```

3. Add a `<s:Button>` control to the view. Set the value of the `label` property to `Submit`, and the values of the `x` and `y` properties to `63` and `402`, respectively (Listing 2-5).

LISTING 2-5: Adding a <s:Button> component to the view in HelloWorldAppHome.mxml

```xml
<?xml version="1.0" encoding="utf-8"?>
<s:View xmlns:fx="http://ns.adobe.com/mxml/2009"
        xmlns:s="library://ns.adobe.com/flex/spark"
        title="Hello World">

    <s:Label x="63"
             y="56"
             width="289"
             fontSize="26"
             text="My name is:"/>

    <s:Label x="63"
             y="182"
             width="289"
             fontSize="26"
             text="I live in:"/>

    <s:TextInput id="nameTxt"
             x="63"
             y="98"
             width="350"
             prompt="Enter a name here..."/>

    <s:TextInput id="locationTxt"
             x="63"
             y="230"
             width="350"
             prompt="Enter location here..."/>

    <s:Button x="63"
              y="402"
              label="Submit"/>

</s:View>
```

4. Save the project, and then open the Design view, where you will see the components you've just added.

5. Next add another view to the application to display the message when the user clicks Submit. From the Flash Builder menu select File ➪ New ➪ MXML Component. Then in the window that opens enter the details for the new view. Enter **views** in the Package field, and **HelloWorldAppMessageView** for the Name. Leave the default values for the Layout and Based On fields (Figure 2-13).

FIGURE 2-13: Creating a new view via the New MXML Component panel for the Hello World App

After clicking OK the file will be generated in the Project Explorer.

6. Open the `HelloWorldAppMessageView.mxml` file, updating the value of the `title` property to `Your message....` Then add a single `<s:Label>` component to the view, setting the value of the `id` property to `messageTxt`, the values of the `width` and `height` properties to `100%`, the values for the `paddingLeft`, `paddingRight`, and `paddingTop` properties to `20`, the value of the `color` property to `#868686`, and the `fontSize` property to `32` (Listing 2-6).

Available for
download on
Wrox.com

LISTING 2-6: Adding a <s:Label> to the view in HelloWorldAppMessageView.mxml

```
<?xml version="1.0" encoding="utf-8"?>
<s:View xmlns:fx="http://ns.adobe.com/mxml/2009"
        xmlns:s="library://ns.adobe.com/flex/spark"
        title="Your message...">


    <s:Label id="messageTxt"
             color="#868686"
             paddingLeft="20"
             paddingRight="20"
             paddingTop="20"
             width="100%"
             height="100%"
             fontSize="32"/>

</s:View>
```

7. Return to the `HelloWorldAppHome.mxml` view, and add a new `<fx:Script>` declaration containing a protected function called `onSubmit()` (Listing 2-7).

Available for
download on
Wrox.com

LISTING 2-7: Adding a new function called onSubmit() to the <fx:Script> declaration in HelloWorldAppHome.mxml

```
<?xml version="1.0" encoding="utf-8"?>
<s:View xmlns:fx="http://ns.adobe.com/mxml/2009"
        xmlns:s="library://ns.adobe.com/flex/spark"
        title="Hello World">

    <fx:Script>

        <![CDATA[

            protected function onSubmit():void {}

        ]]>

    </fx:Script>

    <s:Label x="63"
             y="56"
```

```
            width="289"
            fontSize="26"
            text="My name is:"/>

<s:Label x="63"
         y="182"
         width="289"
         fontSize="26"
         text="I live in:"/>

<s:TextInput id=""
             x="63"
             y="98"
             width="350"
             prompt="Enter a name here..."/>

<s:TextInput id=""
             x="63"
             y="230"
             width="350"
             prompt="Enter location here..."/>

<s:Button x="63"
          y="402"
          label="Submit"/>

</s:View>
```

8. In onSubmit() create an object called dObj, which will hold two values, a property called name set by the first <s:TextInput> component nameTxt, and a property called location, set by the second <s:TextInput> component locationTxt (Listing 2-8).

Available for download on Wrox.com

LISTING 2-8: Defining name and location properties on a data object dObj via onSubmit() in HelloWorldAppHome.mxml

```
<fx:Script>

    <![CDATA[

        protected function onSubmit():void
        {
            var dObj:Object =
            {
                name:nameTxt.text,
                location:locationTxt.text
            }
        }

    ]]>

</fx:Script>
```

9. Invoke the `pushView()` method on the `navigator` object for the view, supplying `views`
`.HelloWorldAppMessageView` and `dObj` as the arguments for `onSubmit()` (Listing 2-9).

LISTING 2-9: Calling the pushView() method via the onSubmit() method in
HelloWorldAppHome.mxml

```
protected function onSubmit():void
{
    var dObj:Object =
    {
        name:nameTxt.text,
        location:locationTxt.text
    }

    navigator.pushView(views.HelloWorldAppMessageView, dObj);
}
```

10. Assign the `onSubmit()` method to the `click` property on the `<s:Button>` component
(Listing 2-10).

LISTING 2-10: Assigning the onSubmit() method to the click property on the <s:Button>
component in HelloWorldAppHome.mxml

```
<s:Button x="63"
          y="402"
          label="Submit"
          click="onSubmit()"/>
```

In `onSubmit()`, you've created a function that will use the data set via the text input fields,
pushing the data object `dObj` and the `name` and `location` properties set on that object
through to the `HelloWorldAppMessageView`. To utilize the data object, you will need to
update the `HelloWorldAppMessageView`.

You can use one of the following event properties to handle what happens when the
`<s:View>` component renders to the screen:

➤ `creationComplete`: When a component has completed its construction, property
processing, measuring, layout, and drawing

➤ `viewActivate`: When the current view has been activated

Similar to the `click` event property used for the `<s:Button>` component, you assign a
method to handle the `creationComplete` and `viewActivate` properties.

11. Return to the `HelloWorldAppMessageView.mxml` view, and add a new `<fx:Script>`
declaration containing a protected function called `onCreationComplete()`. Assign the
method to the `creationComplete` event property on the view (Listing 2-11).

LISTING 2-11: Assigning the onCreationComplete() method to the creationComplete property in HelloWorldAppMessageView.mxml

```xml
<?xml version="1.0" encoding="utf-8"?>
<s:View xmlns:fx="http://ns.adobe.com/mxml/2009"
        xmlns:s="library://ns.adobe.com/flex/spark"
        title="Your message... "
        creationComplete="onCreationComplete()">

    <fx:Script>

        <![CDATA[

            protected function onCreationComplete():void {}

        ]]>

    </fx:Script>

</s:View>
```

12. In onCreationComplete() update the value of the text property on the <s:Label> to utilize the name and location properties defined on the view's data object, and incorporate the values into a message saying Hello World, My name is with and I live in phrases (Listing 2-12).

LISTING 2-12: Assigning the name and location properties to the <s:Label> component in HelloWorldAppMessageView.mxml

```
protected function onCreationComplete():void
{
    messageTxt.text = "Hello World, \n\n"
                    + "My name is " + data.name
                    + ", and I live in " + data.location + "...";
}
```

Here you see that the data object for HelloWorldAppMessageView is utilized, and the name and location properties that were set in HelloWorldAppHome are referenced and assigned to the text property on messageTxt. Now, whenever the pushView() method is invoked via the onSubmit() method in HelloWorldAppHome, the onCreationCompete() method will display the text entered by the user.

The Hello World App is now ready for testing. Next you take a look at running your project by setting up run configurations.

DEFINING RUN CONFIGURATIONS

Run configurations are a key feature of Flash Builder that enable you to *create* and *manage* how you run and debug your mobile projects. You can elect to run your mobile application on the desktop, or directly on a connected device.

When you run your project on the desktop you can select from a number of devices, enabling you to run your applications using different screen sizes and pixel densities.

The next few sections take you through defining run configurations for desktop and devices.

Running Mobile Applications on the Desktop

First, to set up a project that runs on the desktop, follow these steps:

1. In Flash Builder, select Run ⇨ Run Configurations (Figure 2-14).

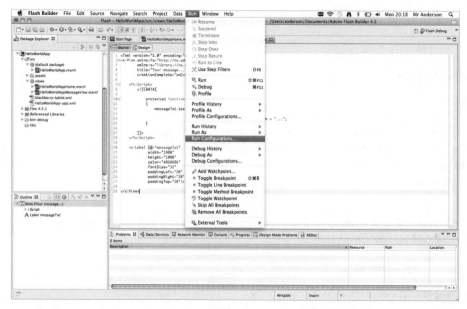

FIGURE 2-14: Navigating to the Run Configurations in Flash Builder

2. In the Run Configurations window that opens, select Mobile Application ⇨ New, to create a mobile configuration type. Then in the Name field for the configuration replace `HelloWorldApp` with `HelloWorldApp on Desktop`. Leave the Application File set as `src/HelloWorldApp`. Then for the Target Platform select Google Android. For the Launch Method, first select On Desktop. Then from the list of devices to run the application on, choose the Google Nexus One. Finally, click Apply. This should update the Mobile Application options in the left-hand panel (Figure 2-15).

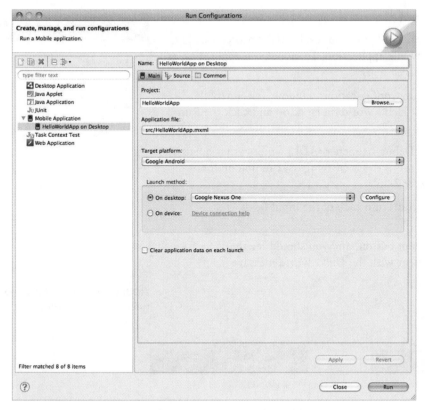

FIGURE 2-15: Creating a run configuration for the Hello World App running on the desktop

At this stage you could also elect to choose BlackBerry Tablet OS or Apple iOS and select a device that runs on those target platforms. For the majority of the book the example projects will be emulated using the Google Android platform and the Google Nexus One device profile.

> **WARNING** *Be aware that selections for the Target Platform in the Run Configuration window will appear only if you have enabled your application to be targeted on that platform. So, if you have targeted your application to run only on Google Android Platform, neither Apple iOS nor BlackBerry Tablet OS devices will be selectable here.*

Launching the Project

Once your project's run configuration has been defined you will be able to launch your mobile application. To launch the application as it is currently follow these steps:

1. Within the Run Configurations window, select Mobile Application ➪ Hello World on Desktop and click the Run button.

2. In the Adobe Debug Launcher (ADL) window that opens you'll see the project as it currently is, running on the desktop (Figure 2-16).

3. Enter some details into each of the input fields (Figure 2-17).

4. Click the Submit button, and you should see the new view appear with the *Hello World* message (Figure 2-18).

FIGURE 2-16: Hello World App running on the desktop

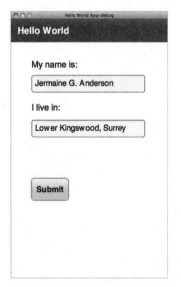

FIGURE 2-17: Hello World App with the name and location fields completed

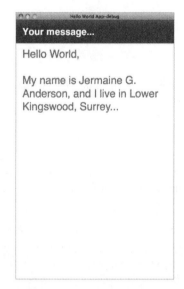

FIGURE 2-18: Hello World App displaying the *Hello World* message view

In the next section you take a look at the steps to create run configurations on Apple iOS, BlackBerry Tablet iOS, and Google Android devices.

Running Mobile Applications on the Device

Once you've set up a run configuration for the Hello World application on the desktop, return to the Run Configurations window to set up run configurations for an actual mobile device on each of the target mobile platforms supported, starting with Google Android.

Creating Run Configurations for Google Android

Follow the next steps to create a run configuration for devices running the Google Android OS platform:

1. Within the Run Configurations window, click the New Launch configuration, and update the name of the configuration to `HelloWorldApp on Google Android`.

2. Leave the Application File set to `src/HelloWorldApp.mxml`, and then for the Launch Method select On Device.

3. Click Apply; the device run configuration will appear in the Mobile Application drop-down (Figure 2-19).

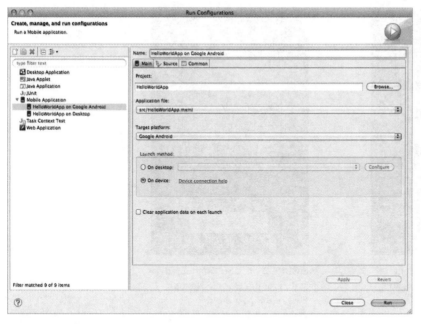

FIGURE 2-19: Run configuration for the Hello World App on Google Android now ready to launch on a USB-connected device

These are the only steps you need to take to create a run configuration for Google Android devices in Flash Builder. You will also need to make sure your device is connected and has USB debugging enabled.

Enabling USB debugging

For Google Android devices running Android version 2.3.4, you need to ensure USB debugging is enabled.

1. On the Google Nexus One running Android 2.3.4, navigate to the Development settings. From the Applications menu, select Settings ➪ Applications ➪ Development.

2. In the Development settings, ensure the USB debugging option is enabled, and when asked whether to enable USB debugging, select OK. Also ensure the Stay Awake option is enabled, to prevent your Android device screen from sleeping while you are testing the application (Figure 2-20).

3. Once you connect your device via USB you will be able to run mobile applications directly from your Android run configuration. This is indicated by the debugging and USB connection, in the top left of the status bar (Figure 2-21).

FIGURE 2-20: Development settings for the Google Nexus One device running Android version 2.3.4

FIGURE 2-21: USB Connected status for the Google Nexus One running Android version 2.3.4

If you have a BlackBerry Tablet OS device like the BlackBerry PlayBook, the next section covers the creating run configurations for BlackBerry Tablet OS.

Creating Run Configurations for BlackBerry Tablet OS

Next take a look at defining a run configuration for devices running the BlackBerry Tablet OS.

1. Within the Run Configurations window, click the New Launch configuration, and update the name of the configuration to `HelloWorldApp on BlackBerry Tablet OS`.

2. Leave the Application File set to `src/HelloWorldApp.mxml`, and then select On Device for the Launch Method.

    Unlike the Google Android platform, you will need to configure a BlackBerry Tablet OS device in order for the run configuration to be completed (Figure 2-22).

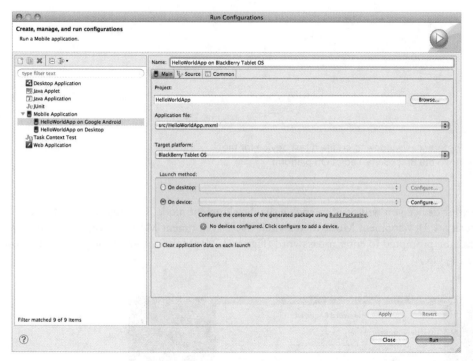

FIGURE 2-22: Creating a run configuration for the Hello World App on a BlackBerry Tablet OS device

3. Click the Configure button next to the On Device drop-down. This brings up a Preferences window where you can add test devices to the BlackBerry Tablet OS (Figure 2-23).

    The next few steps in Flash Builder require that you use some properties from your BlackBerry Tablet OS device. Here you use the BlackBerry PlayBook, where you will need to obtain an IP address and a password to run you applications on the device.

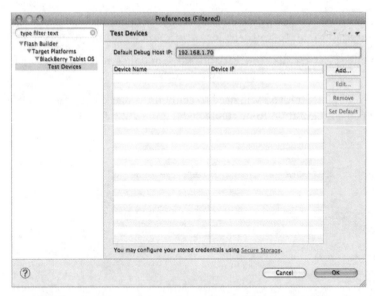

FIGURE 2-23: Preferences window to create a test device for the
Hello World App on the BlackBerry Tablet OS platform

4. On your device you will need to enable the development mode. For this go to Settings ➪
    Security ➪ Development Mode then switch Use Development Mode to On, where you
    should be prompted to enter a password (Figure 2-24). Make a note of the password before
    clicking OK.

FIGURE 2-24: Enabling the use of the development mode for the Hello World App
on a BlackBerry PlayBook

5. Next connect your device via USB to your PC or Mac. In the home screen on the device make a note of the IP address from the Development settings on the main bar (Figure 2-25).

 NOTE *In Figure 2-25 you will actually see that the PlayBook is connected via USB and Wi-Fi; thus, there are two IP addresses. The first IP address shown, 169.254.168.221, corresponds to the USB connection, whereas the second IP address, 10.0.1.2, is the Wi-Fi network connection. Either can be used for the Device IP, which is set in step 5. However, in this example, follow the USB route. Also, note that the IP address will change whenever you connect your device.*

FIGURE 2-25: IP Address displayed when the Development mode is enabled and BlackBerry PlayBook is connected

6. Returning to Flash Builder, within the Preferences window, click the Add button, and then in the window that opens enter the details of the BlackBerry Tablet OS device. First set the Device Name to PlayBook. Then for the Device IP and Password fields, use the values you used in steps 4 and 5. Also ensure that the Debug Host IP and Debug Token checkboxes are selected before clicking OK (Figure 2-26).

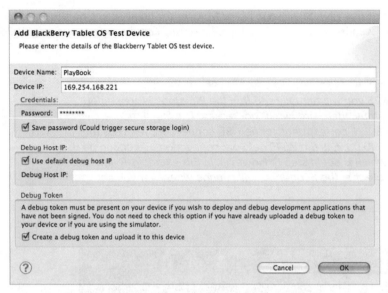

FIGURE 2-26: Details window when adding a test device for the
BlackBerry Tablet OS platform

Before you complete your test device you will need to ensure the device has a
debug token installed. This will enable you to run applications on your device that are
not digitally signed. For this you will need
to register with RIM, who will be able
to send you RDK and PBDT versions of
a CSJ file, both required to create your
debug tokens.

The window in Figure 2-27 shows an
example of the completed details you will
need to provide when creating a debug
token and uploading it straight to the
device.

FIGURE 2-27: Details window when creating a
debug token for the BlackBerry Tablet OS platform

NOTE *For more information on debug tokens, I recommend reading the*
Running unsigned applications using a debug token *article on the BlackBerry*
Developers website (`http://docs.blackberry.com/en/developers`*).*

7. Once you have completed your test device, the device name and device IP address appear in
the Preferences window (Figure 2-28).

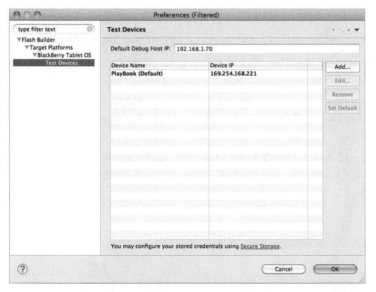

FIGURE 2-28: Preferences window with PlayBook test device created for the Hello World App on the BlackBerry Tablet OS platform

8. Click OK and return to the Run Configurations window where you will see you are now able use your BlackBerry Tablet OS configuration. Click Apply to save the configuration (Figure 2-29).

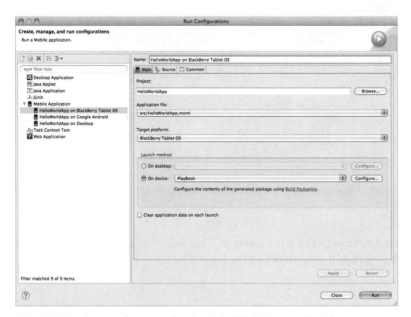

FIGURE 2-29: Run configuration for the Hello World App on BlackBerry Tablet iOS ready for launch to a USB connected device

Creating Run Configurations for Apple iOS

Next take a look at defining a run configuration for devices running on the Apple iOS platform.

1. Within the Run Configurations window, click the New Launch configuration, and update the name of the configuration to `HelloWorldApp on Apple iOS`.

2. Leave the Application File set to `src/HelloWorldApp.mxml`, and then for the Launch Method select On Device. For the Packaging Method select the Fast Packaging option.

Unlike the Google Android and the BlackBerry Tablet OS platforms, for Apple iOS you will have to define the package settings before the run configuration is complete. Note the error message in Figure 2-30.

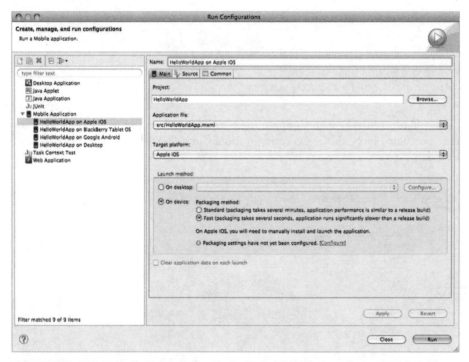

FIGURE 2-30: Creating a run configuration for the Hello World App on the Apple iOS platform

3. Click the Configure link next to the error message. This will open the Packaging Properties for the project, where you will need to define the Digital Signature settings.

This requires you to obtain an Apple iOS Developer Certificate and Mobile Provisioning profile, which you will need to install on your device prior to deploying your mobile application. Before you can do this, you need to become a member of the iOS Dev Center.

The window in Figure 2-31 shows an example of the completed Digital Signature details.

FIGURE 2-31: Properties window for the Hello World App on the Apple iOS platform, displaying paths to a developer certificate and iOS provisioning file

 NOTE *For more information on generating certificates and installing mobile provisioning profiles on your iOS device, visit the* iOS Provisioning Portal *at the Apple iOS Developer website (*http://developer.apple.com/devcenter/ios*).*

4. Once you have completed your Digital Signature settings, you will be able to apply the run config settings for the Apple iOS device (Figure 2-32).

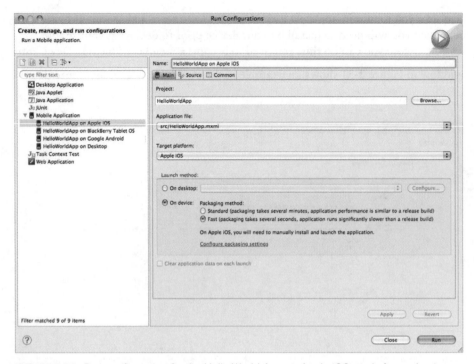

FIGURE 2-32: Run configuration for the Hello World App on Apple iOS ready for packaging

At this stage you have learned how to create configurations for running your mobile applications on a connected device. The next chapter covers building and packaging for the three mobile platforms in more detail.

SUMMARY

In this chapter you created a Flex-based mobile application using Flash Builder. Along the way you also explored the Flash Builder IDE in depth, gaining an understanding of some of the key concepts.

Over the course of the book, the Flash Builder IDE will become more and more familiar as you build on and create further examples.

You learned how to create run configurations that targeted each of the different mobile platforms supported in Flash Builder, and may have noticed the differences in how running on a Google Android is definitely the easier of the three platforms, closely followed by BlackBerry Tablet OS, and then Apple iOS. The latter two both rely on you registering with the development communities of Apple and BlackBerry, before you can get started.

In the next chapter you take a closer look at the AIR application descriptor file and building for each of the mobile platforms in more detail.

EXERCISES

1. Create another desktop run configuration for the Hello World App, this time for the BlackBerry Tablet OS platform.

2. Add a new `<s:Button>` component next to the existing Submit button that clears the text in the two input fields when clicked.

3. Define a splash image for the application that displays for two seconds.

4. Specify a navigational button in the Action Bar that returns the user back to the first view when clicked. Then randomize the color of the *Hello World* message set on the label each time the message is generated.

▶ **WHAT YOU LEARNED IN THIS CHAPTER**

TOPIC	KEY CONCEPT
Run configurations for Apple iOS devices	Obtain a developer certificate and provisioning profile from Apple.
	Define the package settings.
Run configurations for BlackBerry Tablet OS devices	Register with RIM for debug token details.
	Create a test device profile.
	Enable development mode on the device.
	Set the IP address for the device.
	Connect the device via USB.
Run configurations for Google Android devices	Ensure USB debugging is enabled on the Google Android device.
	Connect the device via USB.

3

Building AIR Applications for Android, BlackBerry, and iOS Devices

WHAT YOU WILL LEARN IN THIS CHAPTER:

➤ Setting the properties of an application descriptor file manually

➤ Specifying image icons for an application

➤ Setting permissions for Android and BlackBerry applications

➤ Packaging AIR applications for Android, BlackBerry, and iOS

➤ Updating AIR applications

In this chapter you'll take a look at some of the elements involved in constructing AIR apps, outside the task of actually coding an application.

First, you'll explore the core components of the AIR application descriptor file, understanding how to specify settings for it, covering image icon assignment, and setting Android permissions and specifying iOS settings.

You'll close the chapter by packaging a mobile application using Flash Builder, and then look at how you can update AIR applications that aren't uploaded to a target platform's marketplace.

AIR APPLICATION DESCRIPTOR FILES

An Adobe AIR application descriptor file contains parameters that are used to identify, install, and launch an AIR application.

Each new project created in Flash Builder automatically generates an AIR application descriptor file template. The AIR application descriptor file name is usually generated by the name of the application set in the Flash Builder New Project wizard, as covered in Chapter 2, in which HelloWorldApp generates `HelloWorldApp-app.xml`.

This section takes a look at editing an application descriptor file focusing on each of the core elements.

Setting Properties in the AIR Application Descriptor File

The AIR application descriptor file is essentially an XML file consisting of many elements that you need to specify for your mobile applications to be built. When these are packaged and then deployed to the mobile device, the installation of AIR on that device can interpret the package correctly and ascertain where to install files, write directories, and set data. Some of the elements in the application descriptor file are required, and some are optional.

In Table 3-1 you see each of the core elements used in the AIR application descriptor file for mobile applications listed.

TABLE 3-1: AIR Application Descriptor File Elements

ELEMENT	USAGE
`<application>`	Sets the AIR namespace declaration. Required for building AIR apps.
`<id>`	A unique identity for the application.
`<filename>`	The name used for the Android Package file (APK, `.apk` file).
`<name>`	Sets the application name displayed on the device.
`<versionNumber>`	The version number of the application.
`<versionLabel>`	Used to display a label to users in the application's installation dialog.
`<initialWindow>`	Contains properties for the initial appearance of the application.
`<content>`	To set the path to the main content `.swf` file of the application.
`<visible>`	To set the visibility of the content.
`<fullScreen>`	Defines whether the application should use the entire screen of the device.
`<aspectRatio>`	To specify whether the application is in portrait or landscape mode.
`<autoOrients>`	To set whether the orientation of content in the application automatically reorients as the device changes orientation.
`<supportedProfiles>`	Defines the supported profile that best fits the type of AIR application.
`<icon>`	To specify the icon images used to launch the application.

Manually Editing the Application Descriptor File for the Hello World App

Next you edit the contents of `HelloWorldApp-app.xml`, the AIR application descriptor file that can be found in the src folder of the Hello World App project from Chapter 2. Here are the steps:

1. First, remove the automatically generated content in the `HelloWorldApp-app.xml` file, as if you were creating the file from the beginning. Then begin with the `<?xml>` declaration, setting the `version` attribute to `1.0`, `encoding` to `utf-8`, and `standalone` property to `no` (Listing 3-1).

LISTING 3-1: Setting the XML declaration in the Hello World App AIR application descriptor file

```
<?xml version="1.0" encoding="utf-8" standalone="no"?>
```

> **NOTE** When Flash Builder generates `HelloWorldApp-app.xml`, it will contain numerous comments for properties used for AIR desktop applications that we're not going to cover here. Nevertheless, those comments would be self-explanatory if you were to read them. Thus, clearing the contents of `HelloWorldApp-app.xml` will make it easier to convey some of the settings and their corresponding values.

2. Add the AIR 2.7 namespace declaration in the `<application>` element (Listing 3-2).

LISTING 3-2: Setting the AIR namespace declaration in the Hello World App AIR application descriptor file

```
<?xml version="1.0" encoding="utf-8" standalone="no"?>
<application xmlns="http://ns.adobe.com/air/application/2.7">
```

Setting an ID for the Application

The recommended form for the AIR application's ID is a dot-delimited, reverse-DNS-style string, as shown in the following snippet:

```
<id>com.wrox.ch3.AppName</id>
```

> **WARNING** Each new application you install on a device should have a unique ID associated with it. If it doesn't, chances are it will override an existing application with the same ID.

3. In the `HelloWorldApp-app.xml` file, set the `<id>` property for the application to `com.wrox` `.ch3.HelloWorldApp` (Listing 3-3).

LISTING 3-3: Setting the Application ID property in the Hello World App AIR application descriptor file

```
<?xml version="1.0" encoding="utf-8" standalone="no"?>
<application xmlns="http://ns.adobe.com/air/application/2.7">
      <id>com.wrox.ch3.HelloWorldApp</id>
```

Setting the Name and Filename Properties

The `<name>` property in the AIR application descriptor file is used for display purposes. It is the label the end user will see once the application has been installed on the user's mobile device. While the `<filename>` property is used for the actual file name and file path on the device, it is usually hidden from the end user's view. The value for the filename should be a string with no spaces.

4. In `HelloWorldApp-app.xml` set `<filename>` to `HelloWorldApp` and the `<name>` setting to `Hello World App` (Listing 3-4).

LISTING 3-4: Setting the Name and Filename properties in the Hello World App AIR application descriptor file

```
<?xml version="1.0" encoding="utf-8" standalone="no"?>
<application xmlns="http://ns.adobe.com/air/application/2.7">
      <id>com.wrox.ch3.HelloWorldApp</id>
      <filename>HelloWorldApp</filename>
      <name>Hello World App</name>
```

Setting the Application Version

The `<versionNumber>` property is required to identify an instance of the application installed on the device. The version number's representation should be a numerical value that incrementally changes each time an update or new release of the mobile application has been produced, since the version number can be used to distinguish between applications that have the same `<id>` values in their AIR application descriptor files.

Version numbers should contain three integers separated by periods, as shown in the following snippet:

```
<versionNumber>7.3.6</versionNumber>
```

The three integers represent the *major*, *minor*, and *revision* numbers assigned for the application's release. These usually refer to an automated build of the application. Each value should be between 0 and 999.

5. Returning to `HelloWorldApp-app.xml`, set the `<versionNumber>` to `0.9.0` (Listing 3-5).

LISTING 3-5: Setting the Version Number property in the Hello World App AIR application descriptor file

```xml
<?xml version="1.0" encoding="utf-8" standalone="no"?>
<application xmlns="http://ns.adobe.com/air/application/2.7">
    <id>com.wrox.ch3.HelloWorld</id>
    <filename>HelloWorldApp</filename>
    <name>Hello World App</name>
    <versionNumber>0.9.0</versionNumber>
```

You can also supply the version as a label via the `<versionLabel>` element, as shown in the following snippet:

```xml
<versionLabel>0.9.0 (BETA)</versionLabel>
```

The `<versionNumber>` is required and takes precedence over the `<versionLabel>`, and if `<versionLabel>` is not used, then the value set in `<versionNumber>` is displayed to users.

Setting the Supported Profile

Three values can be supplied to `<supportedProfiles>` for AIR applications:

➤ `desktop`: An AIR application for the desktop

➤ `extendedDesktop`: An AIR application with support for the native process API on the desktop

➤ `mobileDevice`: An AIR application for mobile devices

For AIR mobile applications, you need to set `<supportedPropfiles>` to the `mobileDevice` profile.

6. In `HelloWorldApp-app.xml`, under the `<versionNumber>` declaration, set the `<supportedProfiles>` property to `mobileDevice` (Listing 3-6).

LISTING 3-6: Setting the Supported Profiles property in the Hello World App AIR application descriptor file

```xml
<?xml version="1.0" encoding="utf-8" standalone="no"?>
<application xmlns="http://ns.adobe.com/air/application/2.7">
    <id>com.wrox.ch3.HelloWorldApp</id>
    <filename>HelloWorld</filename>
    <name>Hello World App</name>
    <versionNumber>0.9.0</versionNumber>
    <supportedProfiles>mobileDevice</supportedProfiles>
```

Setting the Initial Appearance

Several properties can define the initial appearance of the application when it starts up: the content path; whether the content is visible; whether it is showing full-screen; the initial screen orientation; and whether the application changes to a landscape or portrait orientation when the user rotates the device.

The `<initialWindow>` element of the AIR application descriptor file is what defines these properties. Here you can specify the `<content>`, `<visible>`, `<fullScreen>`, `<aspectRatio>`, and `<autoOrients>` elements to specify the properties for the initial appearance of the application.

In the following snippet, the `HelloWorldApp.swf` is specified at the `<content>` property, the `<visible>` property is set to true, `<fullScreen>` is set to true, `<aspectRatio>` is set to landscape, and the `<autoOrients>` property is set to `false`:

```
<initialWindow>
        <content>HelloWorldApp.swf</content>
        <visible>true</visible>
        <fullScreen>true</fullScreen>
        <aspectRatio>landscape</aspectRatio>
        <autoOrients>false</autoOrients>
</initialWindow>
```

The last two properties set by `<aspectRatio>` and `<autoOrients>` indicate that the application will always be in landscape mode, since the application is prevented from automatically changing its orientation. Device orientation is covered in greater detail in Chapter 5.

7. In `HelloWorldApp-app.xml`, under the `<supportedProfiles>` declaration, add the initial window declaration setting the `<content>` to `HelloWorldApp.swf`, the `<visible>` property to true, the `<initialOrientation>` property to portrait, and the `<autoOrients>` property to true (Listing 3-7).

LISTING 3-7: Setting the Initial Window properties in the Hello World App AIR application descriptor file

```
<?xml version="1.0" encoding="utf-8" standalone="no"?>
<application xmlns="http://ns.adobe.com/air/application/2.7">
        <id>com.wrox.ch3.HelloWorldApp</id>
        <filename>HelloWorldApp</filename>
        <name>Hello World App</name>
        <versionNumber>0.9.0</versionNumber>
        <supportedProfiles>mobileDevice</supportedProfiles>
        <initialWindow>
                <content>HelloWorldApp.swf</content>
                <visible>true</visible>
                <fullScreen>false</fullScreen>
                <aspectRatio>portrait</aspectRatio>
                <autoOrients>false</autoOrients>
        </initialWindow>
```

Specifying Paths to Image Icons

The *launch icon* for an application needs to be specified before packaging. Because devices across platforms tend to have different screen resolutions, you need to be very specific about the images you reference. Thus, icon or image size needs to be carefully considered. For the Google Android and Apple iOS platforms, you set paths to the application icons in the AIR application descriptor file.

For the BlackBerry Tablet OS platform, you specify the icon in the BlackBerry Tablet settings file, which will be covered in more detail later.

For the BlackBerry PlayBook, the application icon should be supplied as a single 86×86 pixel .png image file that is an image with an 86 pixel width and 86 pixel height.

On Android devices, the icon should be supplied as 36×36, 48×48, and 72×72 pixel .png file images. These icon sizes are used for low-, medium-, and high-density screens, respectively.

On the iPad, iPhone, and iPod Touch iOS devices, there are a number of different screens on the platform that require different sized icons to be packaged for an application. The following details the sizes that can be supplied and where they are used:

➤ **29×29**: Used for the Spotlight and Settings screens of iPhone and iPod Touch devices, and also the settings screen on an iPad.

➤ **57×57**: Used for the Home screens of iPhone and iPod Touch devices.

➤ **72×72**: Used for the Home screen of an iPad.

➤ **114×114**: Used for the Home screen of an iPhone with retina display (e.g., iPhone 4).

The following snippet shows the `<icon>` declaration in the AIR application descriptor file that specifies the path to each of the image files that can be used on Android and iOS devices:

```
<icon>
      <image29x29>assets/i29x29.png</image29x29>
      <image36x36>assets/i36x36.png</image36x36>
      <image48x48>assets/i48x48.png</image48x48>
      <image57x57>assets/i57x57.png</image57x57>
      <image72x72>assets/i72x72.png</image72x72>
      <image114x114>assets/i114x114.png</image114x114>
</icon>
```

The images are located in a folder called `assets`, in a folder relative to the content and main .swf file. Notice that for each image you need to use a different element in the AIR application descriptor file. For example, to specify a 72×72 pixel file image that can be used for the Home screen of an iPad and a Google Nexus One, the path to the image is specified in the `<image72x72>` tag.

If you do not supply an icon of a given size, the next largest size is used and scaled to fit the occupied space. For example, on a Google Android device, if the `<image36x36>` icon is not specified, the `<image48x48>` declaration is used, and if `<image48x48>` isn't set, the application will default to `<image72x72>`.

If you don't specify any of the image icons permitted, or if you incorrectly specify the path to an image, you will see a default application image icon for the application set by the OS.

 NOTE For the remaining chapters, the defining of properties in the AIR application descriptor file process is omitted, so you may notice when you install the examples on Android devices that the default system icon is used.

Figure 3-1 shows the default Google Android application icon you will see on the device in the three sizes.

Figure 3-2 shows the six application icons that will be used in the Hello World App project.

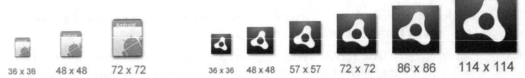

FIGURE 3-1: The default Android application icons, shown in three different sizes

FIGURE 3-2: The application icons used for the Hello World App project, shown in six different sizes

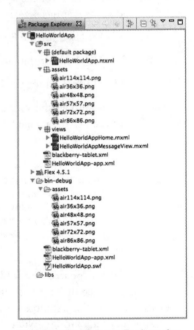

8. Ensure the six files, `air36x36.png`, `air48x48.png`, `air58x58.png`, `air72x72.png`, `air86x86.png`, and `air114x114.png`, are present in the `src/assets` folder of the project (Figure 3-3).

You should notice that once you've added the images and the `assets` folder, the `bin-debug` folder gets automatically replicated. Later you'll see a `bin-release` folder created and used for the final export of the AIR application.

9. Returning to the `HelloWorldApp-app.xml` file, under the `<initialWindow>` declaration, add the `<icon>` declaration, setting the paths to the five images, `air36x36.png` to `<image36x36>`, `air48x48.png` to `<image48x48>`, `air57x57.png` to `<image57x57>`, `air72x72.png` to `<image72x72>`, and `air114x114.png` to `<image114x114>` (Listing 3-8).

FIGURE 3-3: Package Explorer for the Hello World App project

LISTING 3-8: Setting the Icon properties in the Hello World App AIR application descriptor file

Available for download on Wrox.com

```
<initialWindow>
        <content>HelloWorldApp.swf</content>
        <visible>true</visible>
        <fullScreen>false</fullScreen>
        <initialOrientation>portrait</initialOrientation>
        <autoOrients>false</autoOrients>
</initialWindow>
<icon>
        <image36x36>assets/air36x36.png</image36x36>
        <image48x48>assets/air48x48.png</image48x48>
        <image57x57>assets/air57x57.png</image57x57>
```

```
        <image72x72>assets/air72x72.png</image72x72>
        <image114x114>assets/air114x114.png</image114x114>
    </icon>
```

Referencing the five images, as shown here, will allow application icons to be shown for both Google Android and Apple iOS.

Setting Android OS Permissions

For Android applications the security model for the OS requires that each application requests a particular permission in order to use a feature that has security or privacy implications. These permissions cannot be requested or changed at run time and so must be requested when the application is packaged in the AIR application descriptor file.

When a user installs an Android application, the operating system informs the user which permissions an application is requesting.

Android permissions are specified inside the `<android>` element of the AIR application descriptor file.

In the following snippet, you'll see that the `android:name` attribute inside the `<uses-permissions>` element is specified as the value `android.permission.NAME`, representing the full name of an Android permission.

```
<android>
    <manifestAdditions>
        <manifest>
            <data>
                <![CDATA[
                    <uses-permission android:name="android.permission.NAME"/>
                ]]>
            </data>
        </manifest>
    </manifestAdditions>
</android>
```

Each of the `uses-permission` statements in the AIR application descriptor file is added directly to an Android manifest document, when you target the Google Android platform in the New Flex Mobile Project wizard, as covered in Chapter 2.

The following lists some of the permissions that are required by AIR Android apps, in order for an application to use particular mobile device features:

➤ `android.permission.ACCESS_FINE_LOCATION`: Allows the application to access GPS data through the `Geolocation` class

➤ `android.permission.CAMERA`: Allows the application to gain access to the device's camera

➤ `android.permission.INTERNET`: Allows the application to make network requests

➤ `android.permission.READ_PHONE_STATE`: Allows the AIR run time to mute audio when an incoming call occurs

➤ `android.permission.RECORD_AUDIO`: Allows the application to access the microphone

➤ `android.permission.WAKE_LOCK`: Prevents the device from going to sleep while an application is running

➤ `android.permission.DISABLE_KEYGUARD`: Disables the key guard and stops the device from locking while an application is running

➤ `android.permission.WRITE_EXTERNAL_STORAGE`: Allows the application to write to the external memory card on the device

So, for example, to allow an application to use the camera you would use the `android.permission` `.CAMERA` Android permission, as shown in the following snippet:

```
<android>
    <manifestAdditions>
        <manifest>
            <data>
                <![CDATA[
                    <uses-permission android:name="android.permission.CAMERA"/>
                ]]>
            </data>
        </manifest>
    </manifestAdditions>
</android>
```

 NOTE *Throughout this book different AIR application descriptor files will be in use, and depending on the application covered, the file will contain a different value for each of the settings. For instance, in Chapter 10 you need to use the* `ACCESS_FINE_LOCATION`, `CAMERA`, `INTERNET`, *and* `RECORD_AUDIO` *Android permissions.*

10. In `HelloWorldApp-app.xml`, under the `<icon>` image settings, add an empty `<android>` declaration (Listing 3-9).

LISTING 3-9: Setting an empty Android permissions declaration in the HelloWorld AIR application descriptor file

```
<initialWindow>
        <content>HelloWorldApp.swf</content>
        <visible>true</visible>
        <fullScreen>false</fullScreen>
        <initialOrientation>portrait</initialOrientation>
        <autoOrients>false</autoOrients>
</initialWindow>
<icon>
        <image36x36>assets/air36x36.png</image36x36>
        <image48x48>assets/air48x48.png</image48x48>
        <image57x57>assets/air57x57.png</image57x57>
        <image72x72>assets/air72x72.png</image72x72>
        <image114x114>assets/air114x114.png</image114x114>
</icon>
<android>
        <manifestAdditions>
                <![CDATA[
                        <manifest/>
```

```
            ]]>
        </manifestAdditions>
    </android>
```

Defining iOS Capabilities

For iOS, you set application settings inside the `<iPhone>` element of the AIR application descriptor file.

Setting Info Additions

There are a numerous *key-value* pairs that define particular settings for your application running on iOS. These need to be set within the child element `<InfoAdditions>`. The following lists commonly used keys and some of their associated values:

➤ `UIApplicationExitOnSuspend`: A string that when set to `<true/>` will exit the application completely and not just suspend it.

➤ `UIDeviceFamily`: An array of strings defining the type of iOS device that the application should run on. A value of 1 specifies iPhone and iPod Touch devices, whereas a value of 2 specifies iPad.

➤ `UIPrerenderedIcon`: A string that when set to YES will remove the default gloss applied to the application's launch icon on iOS devices.

➤ `UIRequiredDeviceCapabilities`: An array of strings listing the device capabilities that are required in order for the application to be installed. Possible values include:

  ➤ `accelerometer`

  ➤ `auto-focus-camera`

  ➤ `camera-flash`

  ➤ `gps`

  ➤ `location-services`

  ➤ `microphone`

  ➤ `sms`

  ➤ `still-camera`

  ➤ `telophony`

  ➤ `video-camera`

  ➤ `wifi`

➤ `UIRequiresPersistentWifi`: A string that when set to YES requires the device to have a Wifi connection open for the length of duration the application is running; otherwise, it will close after 30 minutes.

➤ `UIStatusBarStyle`: A string determining how the status bar at the top of an iOS device will appear. A value of `UIStatusBarStyleBlackOpaque` means the status bar will not be clear; a value of `UIStatusBarStyleDefault` uses the iOS default grey status bar; and a value of `UIStatusBarStyleBlackTranslucent` sets the status bar to black with an alpha of 0.5.

Setting iOS Screen Resolution

Setting the `<requestedDisplayResolution>` to `high` allows you to specify that the application should utilize the full 940 x 640 retina display. This should be set when you want to target iPhone 4, as shown in the following snippet:

```
<requestedDisplayResolution>high</requestedDisplayResolution>
```

By default, this property is set to `standard`, which means the device screen will appear to your application as a standard resolution screen of 480 x 320. The application will try to adapt and upscale a single pixel in standard mode to four equivalent pixels on the high-resolution screen, giving a blurred appearance.

On non-high resolution iOS devices, if the `<requestedDisplayResolution>` property is set to `high`, the value is ignored and the application defaults to the `standard` setting.

11. Returning to the AIR application descriptor file, add the iOS capabilities for the application running on an iPhone 4 under the `<android>` manifest declaration (Listing 3-10).

LISTING 3-10: Setting iOS capabilities for the Hello World App in the AIR application descriptor file

```
<icon>
        <image36x36>assets/air36x36.png</image36x36>
        <image48x48>assets/air48x48.png</image48x48>
        <image57x57>assets/air57x57.png</image57x57>
        <image72x72>assets/air72x72.png</image72x72>
        <image114x114>assets/air114x114.png</image114x114>
</icon>
<android>
        <manifestAdditions>
                <![CDATA[
                        <manifest/>
                ]]>
        </manifestAdditions>
</android>
<iPhone>
        <InfoAdditions>
                <![CDATA[
                        <key>UIDeviceFamily</key>
                        <array>
                                <string>1</string>
                        </array>
                        <key>UIStatusBarStyle</key>
                        <string>UIStatusBarStyleBlackTranslucent</string>
                        <key>UIPrerenderedIcon</key>
                        <string>YES</string>
                ]]>
        </InfoAdditions>
        <requestedDisplayResolution>high</requestedDisplayResolution>
</iPhone>
```

12. Lastly, save the file as `HelloWorldApp-app.xml`.

You've now covered each of the settings required for a valid AIR application descriptor file to run on Google Android and Apple iOS devices. Later you'll you'll take a look at exporting a release package for the application, using this descriptor file via Flash Builder. In the final section on updating AIR applications you also reference several values saved to the file, in particular the `<versionNumber>` property. Next take a look at the configuration settings required for BlackBerry Tablet OS.

BlackBerry Tablet OS Configuration

The configuration settings for BlackBerry Tablet OS are found in the `blackberry-tablet.xml` file, which is generated when you choose to include the BlackBerry Tablet OS as a target platform during project setup. In this file you can specify a number of settings and permissions, which are used in addition to the AIR application descriptor file settings and permissions.

QNX is the platform on which the BlackBerry Tablet OS is based. By default, the XML file simply has an `<?xml>` declaration and an empty `<qnx/>` node:

```
<?xml version="1.0" encoding="UTF-8"?>
<qnx/>
```

The `<qnx>` element must have nested elements defined to set the appearance and behavior of the application on the device. The following code snippet shows an example of a configuration file:

```
<?xml version="1.0" encoding="UTF-8"?>
<qnx>
        <author>jganderson</author>
        <authorId>gYAAgFbt6rihu</authorId>
        <category>core.media</category>
        <buildId>1</buildId>
        <platformVersion>1.0.0.0</platformVersion>
        <icon>
                <image>i86x86.png</image>
        </icon>
        <splashscreen>s600x1024.jpg:s1024x600.jpg</splashscreen>
        <permission>access_internet</permission>
</qnx>
```

The following sections cover each of the core elements.

Setting the Author and Author Id

The `<author>` and `<authorId>` values need to match the values specified in the debug token generated for the device.

Setting the Build Id and Platform Version

The `<buildId>` is a value that represents an incremental build number for your application, which needs to be a whole number. It is combined with the `<versionNumber>` element of the AIR application descriptor file, which holds the *(Major).(Minor).(Revision)* values, and represents the *build* portion of a full version number reference in *(Major).(Minor).(Revision).(Build)*.

The `<platformVersion>` is the minimum version of the BlackBerry Tablet OS required to run the application. If this number exceeds the number on the device, it won't install.

The following snippet gives an example of how both these elements should be set:

```
<buildId>1</buildId>
<platformVersion>1.0.6.2390</platformVersion>
```

Note that the `1.0.6.2390` value specified for the `<platformVersion>` here is the version of the BlackBerry Tablet OS that had AIR version 2.7.0195 installed.

Setting the Category

On a BlackBerry PlayBook device, there are four categories in which you'll find applications: All, Favorites, Media, and Games.

Every applications installed on the PlayBook appears under the All category. Setting the `<category>` field in the settings file also allows you to add the application's launch icon to either the Media or Games categories. Specifying `core.games` adds the application to Games, while setting to `core.media` adds the application to the Media section, as shown in the following snippet:

```
<category>core.media</category>
```

This configuration setting is optional.

Setting the Application Icon

As previously mentioned, you need to define only one application icon in the configuration file for the BlackBerry PlayBook, which needs to be 86px width by 86px height. This is specified as shown in the following snippet:

```
<icon>
        <image>assets/i86x86.png</image>
</icon>
```

This configuration setting is also optional.

 WARNING *The list of icons specified in the AIR application descriptor file override the icon set in the BlackBerry Tablet Settings file. To use your 86×86 icon set in the BlackBerry Tablet settings file, you need to remove those specified in the AIR application descriptor.*

Setting the Permissions

The following lists some of the permissions that need to be added in the configuration settings, in order for an application to use particular device features on BlackBerry Tablet OS:

➤ `access_internet`: Allows the application to make network requests

➤ `access_shared`: Allows the application to access files and grants access to the file system on the device

➤ `play_audio`: Allows the application to access the device PIN and serial number

➤ `read_geolocation`: Allows the application to access GPS data through the `Geolocation` class

➤ `record_audio`: Allows the application to access the microphone

➤ `set_audio_volume`: Allows the application to control the device's native volume controls

➤ `use_camera`: Allows the application to gain access to the device's camera

Permissions are set through the either the `<permission>` or `<action>` element of the BlackBerry Tablet OS configuration file.

The following snippet shows how to allow an application to use network services and access GPS data:

```
<permission>access_internet</permission>
<permission>read_geolocation</permission>
```

Like with the Google Android platform, permissions can be automatically added to the configuration file when you target the BlackBerry Tablet OS in the New Flex Mobile Application wizard, as covered in Chapter 2.

These configuration settings are optional, but bear in mind if they are not set, you may run into issues not being able to use particular features in your applications.

Setting the Splash Image

While the application is loading you can display an image, known as the *splash screen* image.

The application can potentially run in both landscape and portrait orientation, so you are able to specify a value representing two images in the `<splashscreen>` element.

The screen size of the BlackBerry PlayBook is 1024 x 600. In the following snippet, you see the value for `<splashscreen>` is separated by a colon (`:`). The first image path, `s1024x600.jpg`, before the colon, represents the splash image to be shown when the application is in a landscape orientation. The second image path following the colon, `s600x1024.jpg`, represents the splash image to be shown when the image is in a portrait orientation.

```
<splashscreen>s1024x600.jpg:s600x1024.jpg</splashscreen>
```

If only a single image is specified, the device will default to that image, regardless of the size. Remember, though, setting the `<autoOrients>` and `<initialOrientation>` properties in the AIR application descriptor file will allow you to control the orientation of the application on launch; so, you could potentially get away with setting one splash image in a situation where your application will only use one orientation.

Also be aware that a splash screen image can also be specified for Flex mobile applications in the main application file. In the following code snippet you see a splash .png image is set to display for 5 seconds before the application launches:

```
<?xml version="1.0" encoding="utf-8"?>
<s:ViewNavigatorApplication xmlns:fx="http://ns.adobe.com/mxml/2009"
                             xmlns:s="library://ns.adobe.com/flex/spark"
                             firstView="views.HelloWorldAppHome"
                             splashScreenImage="@Embed('assets/splash.png')"
                             splashScreenMinimumDisplayTime="5000"
                             splashScreenScaleMode="none">

</s:ViewNavigatorApplication>
```

If this were to be set in addition to the <splashscreen> setting, you would have two splash images displayed, with the BlackBerry Tablet OS splash image showing first.

Before moving onto the next section, ensure the blackberry-tablet.xml file for the Hello World App project is updated with the configuration settings specified in Listing 3-11.

Available for download on Wrox.com

LISTING 3-11: Configuration settings for the Hello World BlackBerry Tablet OS Configuration File

```
<?xml version="1.0" encoding="UTF-8"?>
<qnx>
        <author>authorName</author>
        <authorId>authorId</authorId>
        <category>core.media</category>
        <buildId>1</buildId>
        <platformVersion>1.0.0.0</platformVersion>
        <icon>
                <image>assets/air86x86.png</image>
        </icon>
</qnx>
```

Note that in Listing 3-11 you will need to replace authorName and authorId with your own values for deploying to a device that has a debug token installed.

Packaging for Google Android

Using Flash Builder, you can package native AIR Android applications via the Export Release Build panel.

Packaging applications requires you to use self-signed digital certificates, which associate the application with an identity, with the aim of forging a trust between the application's creator and an end user. A few of the following steps will reference the creation of a self-signed digital certificate for use with packaging an AIR Android application.

The native application file package for Android is a `.apk` file. At the end of this section, you should be able to install the Hello World App onto an Android device.

1. In Flash Builder, returning to the `HelloWorldApp-app.xml` file, ensure that only the image paths required for displaying application icons on devices running the Google Android platform are set (Listing 3-12).

LISTING 3-12: Setting the Icon properties in the Hello World App AIR application descriptor file targeting the Google Android platform

```
<icon>
        <image36x36>assets/air36x36.png</image36x36>
        <image48x48>assets/air48x48.png</image48x48>
        <image72x72>assets/air72x72.png</image72x72>
</icon>
```

2. Ensure the Hello World App project is highlighted, and then select File ➪ Export to open the Export panel (Figure 3-4).

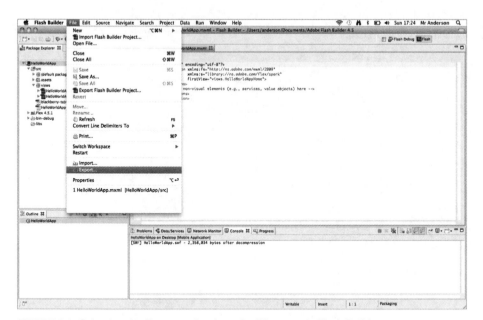

FIGURE 3-4: Selecting the Export option from the File menu in Flash Builder

3. In the Export panel that opens, select Flash Builder ⇨ Release Build (Figure 3-5).

4. Click Next. In the Export Build Release panel that opens, you should see that the Project, Application, and Base filename settings have been pre-populated with the HelloWorldApp, with the Application field automatically set to HelloWorldApp .mxml. For the Target platforms section, ensure that Google Android is selected and uncheck both Apple iOS and BlackBerry Tablet OS options. For the Export section, leave the Export to folder field blank, as the .apk file package will be created in the project folder. Leave the Base filename field as HelloWorldApp (Figure 3-6).

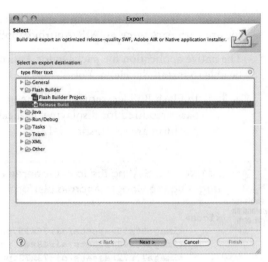

FIGURE 3-5: Selecting the Release Build option from the Export panel in the Hello World App project

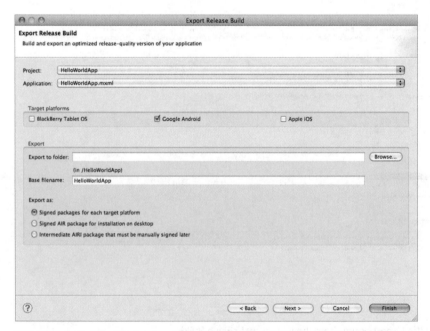

FIGURE 3-6: Setting the details of the Export Release Build for the Hello World App project targeting Google Android

5. Still within the Export Release Build panel, click Next. You should see the Exporting release progress status to the bottom of the panel, before being presented with the Packaging

Settings. Here you will see Google Android listed as one of the device platforms to the left in the Target platforms area. This panel also contains three tabs. The first is the Digital Signature tab where you can see the Target platforms and specify a Certificate and Password for the packaging. The second is the Package Contents tab, which allows you to see each of the files that will be packaged in the AIR application. The third is the Deployment tab, which allows you to specify whether the application should be installed on the device. Note that there is a No certificate selected error highlighted in the panel at this stage (Figure 3-7).

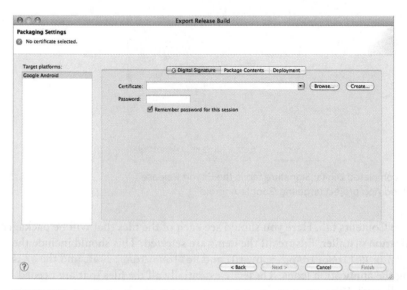

FIGURE 3-7: Displaying the Digital Signature tab for the Hello World App project targeting Google Android

6. In the Digital Signature section, create a certificate by clicking the Create button. Then in the Create Self-Signed Digital Certificate panel that opens, enter some details for the Publisher Name, Organizational Unit, and Organization Name. Select the Country, and then enter and confirm a password. Leave the Type selection as `1024-RSA`. Save the file as **helloWorldCert** (Figure 3-8).

7. Click the OK button. This will create the `helloWorldCert.p12` file. By default, the certificate will be located in the default project workspace for Adobe Flash Builder 4.5, although you can specify an alternative location. After the file is generated, you will be returned to the Digital Signature panel. Complete the section by entering the password that you set for the certificate (Figure 3-9).

FIGURE 3-8: Creating a Self-Signed digital certificate for the Hello World App project targeting Google Android

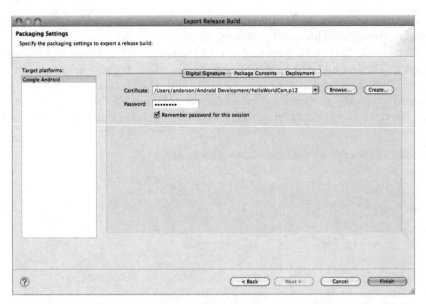

FIGURE 3-9: Displaying the completed Digital Signature tab in the Export Release Build panel for the Hello World App project targeting Google Android

8. Select the Package Contents tab. Here you should see each of the files that will be packaged in the AIR application installer. Ensure all the items are selected. This should include the application descriptor `HelloWorldApp-app.xml`, and `HelloWorldApp.swf`, and the `assets` folder containing the application icons. These are essentially all the files that are needed by the application (Figure 3-10).

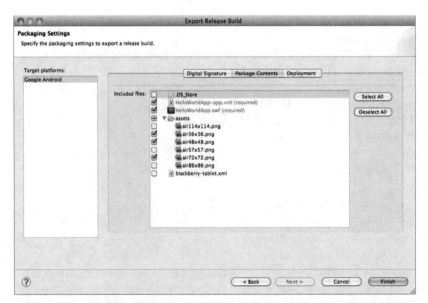

FIGURE 3-10: Displaying the package contents in the Export Release Build panel for the Hello World App project targeting Google Android

9. Select the Deployment package and ensure that the option for Install and launch application on any connected device is selected. Here you can also define the Application Store settings. So, if you plan on deploying an application to the Android Market or the Amazon Appstore, you can provide those users who download your application, who don't have the correct version of AIR installed, a URL to obtain the version from the relevant Application Store (Figure 3-11).

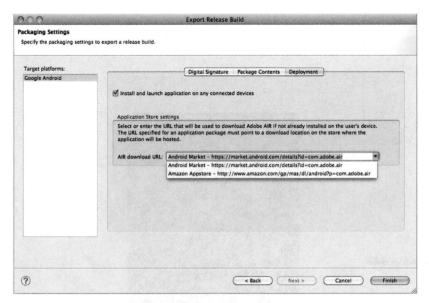

FIGURE 3-11: Displaying the Deployment settings in the Export Release Build panel for the Hello World App project targeting Google Android

10. Click the Finish button to finally create the `.apk` file. At this point, if you had selected the checkbox for automatic deployment, Flash Builder will attempt to automatically install the application onto the device, but only if it is connected via USB. When the publishing is complete, you'll get a message indicating that the application was successfully packaged, but no connected devices were found (Figure 3-12).

FIGURE 3-12: Confirmation of a successful export release build for the Hello World App targeting Google Android

As you will see in Figure 3-13, the newly generated `HelloWorldApp.apk` file will be located alongside the project's `src` folder. You may also see a new folder called `bin-release`, which contains all the files for the package.

If you have an Android device, try connecting it to Flash Builder via USB and then use the export release function to install the application onto the device. Figure 3-14 shows the app installed on the home screen.

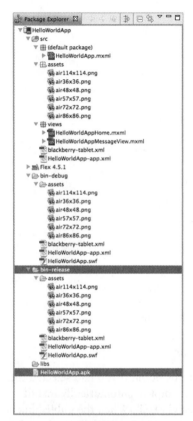

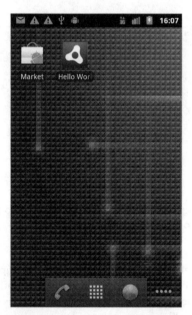

FIGURE 3-13: Package Explorer highlighting the HelloWorldApp .apk file generated for the Hello World App project targeting Google Android

FIGURE 3-14: Hello World App on the home screen of a Google Nexus One running Android 2.3.4

Packaging for Apple iOS

The native application file package for the Apple iOS platform is an `.ipa` file. At the end of this section, you should be able to install the Hello World App onto an iPhone 4.

Follow the next steps to create a release version of Hello World App using Flash Builder:

1. Returning to the `HelloWorldApp-app.xml` file, ensure that only the image paths required for displaying application icons on devices running the Apple iOS platform are set (Listing 3-13).

LISTING 3-13: Setting the Icon properties in the Hello World App AIR application descriptor file
targeting the Apple iOS platform

```
<icon>
        <image57x57>assets/air57x57.png</image57x57>
        <image72x72>assets/air72x72.png</image72x72>
        <image114x114>assets/air114x114.png</image114x114>
</icon>
```

2. Ensure the Hello World App project is highlighted. Select Project ➪ Export Release Build...,
to open the Export Release Build panel. Then select Apple iOS as the Target Platform, and
ensure the Signed packages for each target platform option is selected in the Export as
list (Figure 3-15). Click Next.

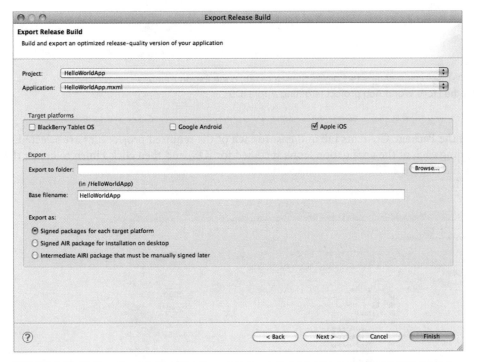

FIGURE 3-15: Setting the details of the Export Release Build for the Hello World App project
targeting Apple iOS

3. In the Digital Signature tab, ensure the Certificate, accompanying Password and
Provisioning file have been specified correctly. Then in the Package type field you have the
option of Ad hoc package for limited distribution, or Final Release Package for Apple App
store. Select Ad hoc (Figure 3-16).

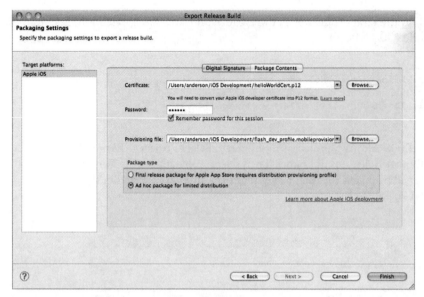

FIGURE 3-16: Displaying the completed Digital Signature tab in the Export Release Build panel for the Hello World App project targeting Apple iOS

4. Select the Package Contents tab and ensure each of the required project files are selected, including each of the application icons specified for iOS, and then click Finish to create the .ipa file (Figure 3-17).

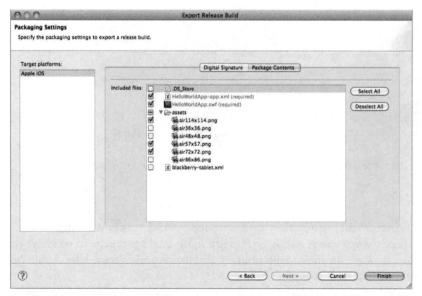

FIGURE 3-17: Displaying the package contents in the Export Release Build panel for the Hello World App project targeting Apple iOS

WARNING *The process of exporting a release build when targeting the Apple iOS platform may take several minutes.*

5. In the Package Explorer, you should see the .ipa file located in the root project folder. This should be named HelloWorldApp.ipa (Figure 3-18).

6. Double-click the newly created .ipa file. This should open iTunes and install the application into the local library (Figure 3-19).

FIGURE 3-18: Package Explorer highlighting the HelloWorldApp.ipa file generated for the Hello World App project targeting Apple iOS

FIGURE 3-19: iTunes displaying the Hello World App installed in the Library

 NOTE *At this stage, you will probably notice that the application icon for ITunes doesn't have an icon. In the AIR application descriptor file, you will need to specify an image that is 512x512 for the* <image512x512> *property.*

7. Before transferring the application to an iPhone 4, you will need to connect the device to the computer via USB. Then simply drag and drop the application from the Library to your iPhone (Figure 3-20). The iPhone will display a "sync in progress" status while the application is installing on the device, before revealing the Home screens.

FIGURE 3-20: Transferring the Hello World App to the iPhone

8. Navigate through your Home screen on the device to find the Hello World App is installed, with the correct application icon displayed, ready for launch (Figure 3-21).

    You can also navigate to the Spotlight screen and search for the Hello World App and find the application there, too (Figure 3-22).

FIGURE 3-21: Hello World App on the home screen of an iPhone 4 running iOS 4.3.3

FIGURE 3-22: Spotlight search screen listing the Hello World App on an iPhone 4 running iOS 4.3.3

At this point, realize that the settings defined in the AIR application descriptor file for iOS, while subtle, are significant. If you remember setting the `<UIPrerenderedIcon>` to `YES` earlier, then take notice of the gloss that was removed from the default setting, as shown in Figure 3-23.

Also, if you have already run the application on the iPhone 4 without making the changes in this chapter, you will see the difference from the previous chapter — that the `<requiredDisplayResolution>` setting has made in fully utilizing the screen resolution. Figures 3-24 through 3-26 show the Hello World App in action.

FIGURE 3-23: Default Hello World App icon with no gloss removed on an iPhone 4 running iOS 4.3.3

FIGURE 3-24: Hello World App on an iPhone 4 with iOS 4.3.3

FIGURE 3-25: Entering information using the native keyboard in the Hello World App, running on an iPhone 4 with iOS 4.3.3

FIGURE 3-26: Message screen in the Hello World App running on an iPhone 4 with iOS 4.3.3

For the remaining chapters, you will need to repeat the steps learned here to package applications for iOS devices.

Packaging for BlackBerry Tablet OS

The native application file package for BlackBerry Tablet OS is a `.bar` file. At the end of this section, you should be able to create a release package for the Hello World App onto a BlackBerry PlayBook.

Follow the next steps to create a release version of Hello World App for the BlackBerry PlayBook using Flash Builder:

1. In `HelloWorldApp-app.xml`, remove any image references for the application icon. This should be set in the `blackberry-tablet.xml` file (Listing 3-14).

LISTING 3-14: The Icon property setting in the Hello World App AIR application descriptor file targeting the BlackBerry Tablet OS platform

```
<icon/>
```

2. Ensure the Hello World App project is highlighted, then select Project ➪ Export Release Build…, to open the Export Release Build panel. Select BlackBerry Tablet OS as the Target Platform, and ensure the Export as a signed packages for each target platform option is selected. Click next (Figure 3-27).

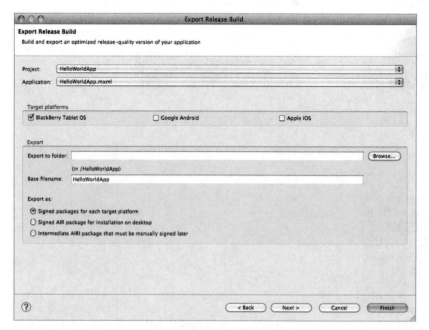

FIGURE 3-27: Setting the details of the Export Release Build for the Hello World App project targeting BlackBerry Tablet OS

3. In the Digital Signature tab, ensure the Enabling digital signing option has been selected. You will need to have created a debug token and a BlackBerry Tablet OS certificate, as highlighted in Chapter 2 (Figure 3-28).

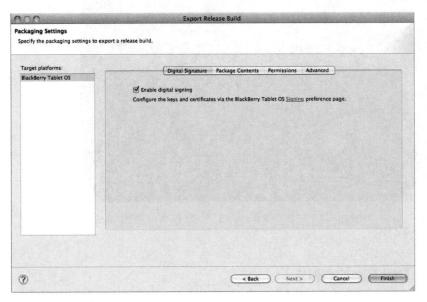

FIGURE 3-28: Enabling the digital signing for the Hello World App project targeting BlackBerry Tablet OS

4. In the Package Contents tab, ensure each of the required project files are selected. These should include the BlackBerry Tablet OS configuration file and the 86 x 86 application icon.

5. For the Permissions tab and the Advance tab, leave the default settings untouched. Here you would need to specify the permissions, as covered earlier. For the Hello World App, there are no permissions that need to be specified, so leave all the options unselected.

6. Click Finish to create the .bar file. In the Package Explorer, you should see the .bar file located in the root of the project folder, named HelloWorldApp .bar (Figure 3-29).

Figure 3-30 shows the Hello World App installed on the BlackBerry PlayBook under the Media category.

FIGURE 3-29: Package Explorer highlighting the HelloWorldApp.bar file generated for the Hello World App project targeting BlackBerry Tablet OS

FIGURE 3-30: Hello World App on the home screen of a BlackBerry PlayBook running BlackBerry Tablet OS 1.0.6.2390

UPDATING AIR APPLICATIONS

In this chapter, you've explored targeting each of the platforms supporting AIR mobile applications. For more information, I recommend visiting each platform's Mobile and Devices Developer Center page on Adobe's website:

➤ **Google Android:** www.adobe.com/devnet/devices/android.html

➤ **Apple iOS:** www.adobe.com/devnet/devices/ios.html

➤ **BlackBerry Tablet OS:** www.adobe.com/devnet/devices/blackberry.html

Updating your application involves your amending the <versionNumber> value in the application descriptor file, repackaging the application to the native platform, and uploading the new version of the application to the target marketplace. For Android, this is the Android Market or Amazon Appstore; for BlackBerry, it's AppWorld; and for Apple, it's App Store.

The process of updating an application installed on a device is simple enough for marketplaces and usually the process is automatic. However, when you download a mobile application from the Android marketplace, you can select whether or not to have automatic updates, where you will be notified when an updated version is available. The user could potentially decide to avoid using the marketplace to grab the update, choosing to manually check for new versions. In this scenario, there is a way you can notify users within an application that there is an upgrade available, when they haven't requested automatic updates.

Retrieving Details from the Application Descriptor File

Presenting a user with an update notification in the mobile app involves adding code to your application that uses namespaces to retrieve the descriptor file details and then compares those details with a reference to the new version.

The first step is to programmatically retrieve the version number from the application descriptor file. The following snippet shows how to use the NativeApplication class to retrieve an AIR application's descriptor file and assign the applicationDescriptor property to a variable called xmlObj of XML type:

```
var xmlObj:XML = NativeApplication.nativeApplication.applicationDescriptor;
```

Once the application descriptor's XML has been assigned to the variable, the Namespace class can be used to retrieve particular values in the XML file, as shown in the following snippet, where the application id and version number are retrieved and assigned to variables id and currentVersion respectively:

```
var xmlObj:XML = NativeApplication.nativeApplication.applicationDescriptor;
var ns:Namespace = xmlObj.namespace();
var appId:String = xmlObj.ns::id;
var currentVersion:String = xmlObj.ns::versionNumber;
```

As previously mentioned, to create an updated release version of your mobile application you will need to update the version number in the application descriptor file.

Using the Version Number

Using the preceding code snippet, the application can check the value of the version number and present the user with a message to indicate there is an update available.

In the following snippet the variable newVersion is assigned the value 1.0.1, a number that represents the new version number for an application. This should be different from the value retrieved from the one present in the application descriptor; you'll recall that earlier, the <versionNumber> property was set to 0.9.0:

```
var xmlObj:XML = NativeApplication.nativeApplication.applicationDescriptor;
var ns:Namespace = xmlObj.namespace();
var appId:String = xmlObj.ns::id;
var currentVersion:String = xmlObj.ns::versionNumber;
var newVersion:String = "1.0.1";

if(currentVersion != newVersion)
{
        // The version numbers are not the same...
        // Present the user with an update...

} else {

        // The version numbers are the same...
        // No need to present the user with an update...

}
```

Here the `if` statement uses the `currentVersion` value, retrieved from the descriptor file, and checks that number against the value held by the `newVersion` variable.

The code within the `if` statement is simply a comment which indicates what can be done.

Essentially the `newVersion` number should be retrieved from a file residing on a server which can be updated whenever a new release of the application is available.

For this you would have to use the `URLLoader` class to load in the data from a file on the server. Working with data is covered in detail in Chapter 8.

SUMMARY

This chapter took a detailed look at building applications that target the Google Android, BlackBerry Tablet OS, and Apple iOS platforms, noting the contents of the AIR application descriptor file, specifying the image icons, setting Android and BlackBerry permissions, and packaging applications.

In the next chapter, you will look at *touch*, *multitouch*, and *gestures*, some of the key features introduced in Flash Player 10.1.

Once you have completed some of the following chapters, you may want to return here to package some of the example applications using the steps listed in the walk-through.

EXERCISES

1. Package another AIR Android application using the Flash Builder, this time changing some of the initial viewing options. For example, instead of using portrait for the `<aspectRatio>` try using landscape to see the effect.

2. Create and package your own `.png` file icon for the Hello World App application.

3. Try packaging each of the examples found in the later chapters.

▶ **WHAT YOU LEARNED IN THIS CHAPTER**

TOPIC	KEY CONCEPT
AIR application descriptor files	Be aware of each of the required elements in the AIR application descriptor file.
Application IDs	Use reverse-DNS style strings to uniquely identify your application via the Application ID — for example, `com.wrox.ch3.HelloWorldApp`.
Application's initial appearance	To define the initial appearance of the application when it launches, define the `<initialWindow>` element. Use the `<content>`, `<visible>`, `<fullScreen>`, `<aspectRatio>`, `<initialOrientation>`, and `<autoOrients>` elements to set the initial appearance of the application.
Launch icons	To set an application's icons, define the `<icon>` element. Three image sizes are used on Android: 36x36, 48x48, and 72x72. Five image sizes are used across Apple iOS devices: 29x29, 57x57, 72x72, and 114x114, and 512x512. One image size is used on BlackBerry Tablet OS: 86x86.
Platform configurations	For the Google Android platform, define the configuration settings within the `<android>` element of the AIR application descriptor file. For the Apple iOS platform, define the configuration settings within the `<iphone>` element. For the BlackBerry Tablet OS platform, define the configuration settings within the `<qnx>` element of the `blackberry-tablet.xml` file.
Setting permissions	For Google Android, define the `<uses-permission>` element to manually define each permission that your application uses. For BlackBerry Tablet OS, define the `<permissions>` element in the `blackberry-tablet.xml` file to manually define each permission that your application uses. For Apple iOS, no permissions are defined.
Packaging applications	In Flash Builder, use the Export Release Build Panel to generate release packages. The Google Android platform uses an `.apk` file package. The Apple iOS platform uses an `.ipa` file package. The BlackBerry Tablet OS uses a `.bar` file package.
Updating AIR mobile applications	Use the `NativeApplication` class to retrieve details from the AIR application descriptor file. Use the `<versionNumber>` property as an indicator to decipher whether the user needs to be informed of an upgrade.

4

Touch, Multitouch, and Gestures

WHAT YOU WILL LEARN IN THIS CHAPTER:

➤ Determining mobile device support for touch points and gesture input

➤ Setting the input mode in an application to detect touch points or gestures

➤ Understanding touch and gesture event object types

➤ Handling touch and gesture events

➤ Utilizing touch input to draw shapes

➤ Implementing gestures to interact with shapes

➤ Using the Multitouch panel in Device Central

Many original equipment manufacturers (OEMs) now opt for user interfaces on their devices that are designed specifically for touch screens, which gives end users a visual display of information. In addition, these give users the whole area of the display to contact and navigate around various screens within the OS and applications. Usually this is with a finger, or an accompanying device accessory such as a stylus.

The alternative to the touch screen of course is the more traditional mobile device, which provides the visual display but without touch support. These mobile devices tend to receive end-user input through a combination of trackball, 4-way D-pad, soft keys, qwerty keyboard, and alphanumeric keypads.

Mobile devices with touch screen interfaces have been at their height of popularity since the introduction of the first iPhone, which had a capacitive touch screen implementation, meaning even the most sensitive of touches will be recognized by a user. The success of the iPhone, in part, can be attributed to the integration of multitouch and gesture support, which when implemented in the right way can provide a fun and satisfying end-user experience for mobile applications.

Flash Player 10.1 introduced native support for multitouch and gesture support, and in this chapter you'll take a look at these features and how you can implement them as part of your mobile applications.

Over the course of the chapter you'll construct an example that highlights some of the multitouch features, beginning with single touch point interactions.

MULTITOUCH INTERACTIONS

As the name indicates, in the context of mobile applications, *multitouch* is an interaction defining when a user uses two or more fingers to make contact and interact with a touch-enabled mobile device screen that is capable of receiving multiple points of input.

With the touch of a single finger being the absolute basic requirement for touch-enabled mobile devices, multitouch-enabled screens can potentially offer a more natural way for a user to interact with the device and its applications, by using two, three, four, or even more fingers simultaneously. And they provide an alternative to menu- or key-driven interactions on a device.

In this section you'll examine how you can apply multitouch within Flash mobile applications.

 NOTE *While the Flash Player from version 10.1 supports multitouch natively, not all devices can receive multiple points of touch input. You should therefore take into consideration non-multitouch user interactions.*

Determining Touch Input Support

Not every mobile device on the market will support multiple touch interactions, so when you are implementing multitouch features, or should you need to ensure that you are able to develop and target applications for devices that do not support multitouch, it is best practice to determine whether a device supports touch input in the first instance.

Next take a look at how to determine support for touch input. You can detect touch support with AS3 by retrieving the value returned by `Multitouch.supportsTouchEvents`.

In Listing 4-1 you will see the early stages of the `MultitouchAndGestures.as` file. You'll build on this example throughout the chapter. This class makes four initial imports: `flash.display.Sprite` for drawing shapes; `flash.text.TextField` for rendering text; `flash.text.TextFieldAutoSize` for setting the `autoSize` property on text fields; and the `flash.ui.Multitouch` class.

Above the class declaration four properties are defined for the creation of the swf application: the `backgroundColor` property, which is set to 0xFFFFFF (white); `frameRate`, which is set to 25 frames per second; `width`, which is set to 320; and `height`, which is set to 480.

In `MultitouchAndGestures` you see two `Textfield` objects declared. The first is called `coordinates`, which will be referenced later. The second is called `multitouch`, which is added to the stage after it has been populated with the result of `Multitouch.supportsTouchEvents` via a switch statement in the class constructor (Listing 4-1).

LISTING 4-1: Determining support for touch point events in MultitouchAndGestures.as

```
package
{
        import flash.display.Sprite;
        import flash.text.TextField;
        import flash.text.TextFieldAutoSize;
        import flash.ui.Multitouch;

        [ SWF(backgroundColor="0xFFFFFF",
                frameRate="25",
                width="320",
                height="480") ]

        public class MultitouchAndGestures extends Sprite
        {
                private var coordinates:TextField;
                private var multitouch:TextField;

                public function MultitouchAndGestures()
                {
                        multitouch = new TextField();
                        multitouch.autoSize = TextFieldAutoSize.LEFT;

                        switch(Multitouch.supportsTouchEvents)
                        {
                                case true:
                                {
                                        multitouch.text = "Touch Supported";
                                }
                                break;
                                case false:
                                {
                                        multitouch.text = "Not Supported";
                                }
                                break;
                        }

                        stage.addChild(multitouch);
                }
        }
}
```

The supportsTouchEvents property has a return type of Boolean, so will return true should the device be capable of receiving touch screen input, and false if it isn't.

Creating a Multitouch and Gestures App Example

You will need to set up a new ActionScript Project in Flash Builder, taking the following steps:

1. From the main menu select File ➪ New ➪ ActionScript Project. Set the Project name to MultitouchAndGestures, set the Project location to use the default location, set the Application type to Web, and then use the default SDK version (Figure 4-1). Click Next before moving to the next step.

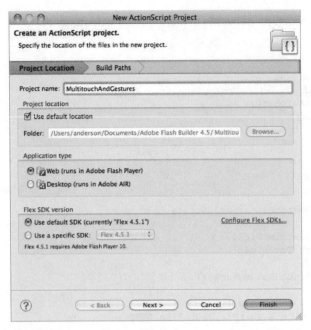

FIGURE 4-1 The New ActionScript Project panel in Flash Builder for the creation of the Multitouch and Gestures App project

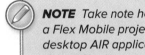

NOTE *Take note here that the example project is neither created from either a Flex Mobile project or an ActionScript Mobile project, nor does it use the desktop AIR application type. The approach used in this chapter is to create a* .swf *file that can be used in Device Central to simulate multitouch and gestures through the emulator. Unfortunately, there is no such emulator if you run the application via Flash Builder alone. The only other option is to run the example project first hand on a device, which you can do on each of the mobile platforms supporting AIR, including Apple iOS, Google Android, and BlackBerry Tablet OS.*

2.   Next confirm the build path for the project. Ensure the Main source folder is set to src, that the Main application file is set to `MultitouchAndGestures.as`, and the output folder is set to bin-debug (Figure 4-2).

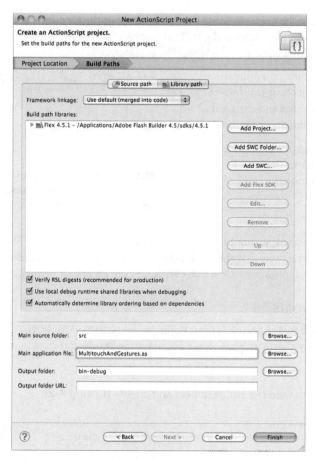

FIGURE 4-2 Defining the build path for the creation of the Multitouch and Gestures App project

3. Once you've clicked Finish, the project and its associated files should be generated. Now open the MultitouchAndGestures.as file from the src folder, adding the code from Listing 4-1.

4. Run the project using a Web application run configuration. Select Run ➪ Run as ➪ Web application. This should launch the application in a browser window, generating the .swf file for the project.

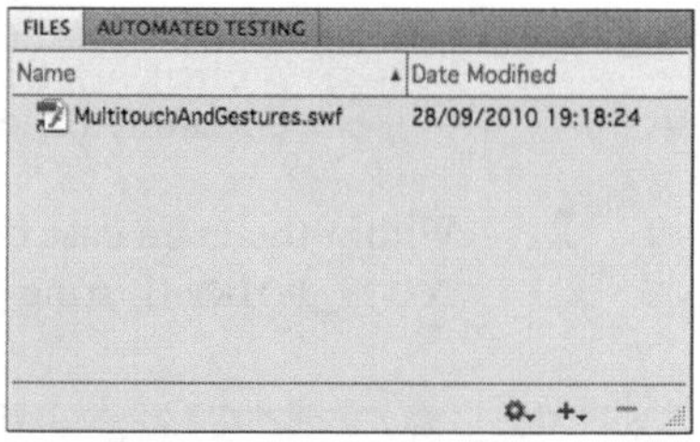

FIGURE 4-3 The Files tab in Device Central displaying the MultitouchAndGestures.swf file

5. In Device Central, add the MultitouchAndGestures.swf file generated to the Files tab. At the bottom of the tab select Add ➪ Add Files, then browse for the MultitouchAndGestures.swf file. Once selected it should appear in the Files tab (Figure 4-3).

6. While still in Device Central, select the Generic Multitouch device from the Devices panel and then run the first example by double-clicking the `MultitouchAndGestures.swf` file. Ensure that in the Info panel the Embedded in HTML option is selected.

In Device Central, attempting to interact with an application that isn't capable of dispatching touch events will result in the output window's displaying a warning message indicating no touch support for the emulated device, as shown in Figure 4-4.

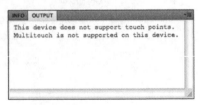

Try running the example in Listing 4-1 using other devices that support Flash Player from version 10.1 to determine whether multitouch input events can be handled.

FIGURE 4-4 The output window in Device Central displaying the warning message for no touch support

Touch Event Handling

Once support for touch input has been established, you need to set the *input mode* for multitouch. Touch point events are not exclusive multitouch interactions that the Flash player can detect; so you will need to decide whether the events dispatched in your applications are touch events, gesture events, or neither.

Setting the Input Mode for Touch Events

To handle touch events, you need to set the `Multitouch.inputMode` property to `TOUCH_POINT`. This is one of the three static values held by the `flash.ui.MultitouchInputMode` class.

Follow the next few steps to set the input mode:

1. Add the `MultitouchInputMode` class to the list of import statements (Listing 4-2).

LISTING 4-2: Importing the MultitouchInputMode class in MultitouchAndGestures.as

```
package
{
    import flash.display.Sprite;
    import flash.text.TextField;
    import flash.text.TextFieldAutoSize;
    import flash.ui.Multitouch;
    import flash.ui.MultitouchInputMode;
```

2. Within the `true` case of the switch statement in the class constructor, set the input mode to `TOUCH_POINT` (Listing 4-3).

LISTING 4-3: Setting the input mode for touch events via the class constructor method in MultitouchAndGestures.as

```
switch(Multitouch.supportsTouchEvents)
{
    case true:
    {
```

```
Multitouch.inputMode = MultitouchInputMode.TOUCH_POINT;

            multitouch.text = "Touch events - Supported";
    }
    break;
    case false:
    {
            multitouch.text = "Touch events - Not Supported";
    }
    break;
}
```

Touch Event Types and Properties

After determining the input mode for multitouch, the next step is to register the application's interest in a particular touch event. When selecting TOUCH_POINT as the input mode, the events returned will be of the event type flash.events.TouchEvent.

Eight event-type values are associated with the TouchEvent class, each essentially being treated as a different *phase* of a single touch event interaction:

➤ TouchEvent.TOUCH_BEGIN: A string with the value touchBegin, signaling when the touch event begins

➤ TouchEvent.TOUCH_END: A string with the value touchEnd, signaling when the touch event has ended

➤ TouchEvent.TOUCH_MOVE: A string with the value touchMove, signaling when the touch event has moved

➤ TouchEvent.TOUCH_OUT: A string with the value touchOut, signaling when the touch event is out

➤ TouchEvent.TOUCH_OVER: A string with the value touchOver, signaling when the touch event is over

➤ TouchEvent.TOUCH_ROLL_OUT: A string with the value touchRollOut, signaling when the touch event is a roll out

➤ TouchEvent.TOUCH_ROLL_OVER: A string with the value touchRollOver, signaling when the touch event is a roll over

➤ TouchEvent.TOUCH_TAP: A string with the value touchTap, signaling when the touch event is a tap

To register one of the touch events, you need to supply one of the event types as the first argument to the addEventListener() method; then for the second argument you supply a reference to an event handler, which you need to define.

Follow the next few steps to register touch events:

1. First add the TouchEvent class to the list of import statements (Listing 4-4).

LISTING 4-4: Importing the TouchEvent class in MultitouchAndGestures.as

```
package
{
        import flash.display.Sprite;
        import flash.events.TouchEvent;
        import flash.text.TextField;
        import flash.text.TextFieldAutoSize;
        import flash.ui.Multitouch;
        import flash.ui.MultitouchInputMode;
```

2. Under the constructor for the class, create an event handler function called onTouch().
This event handler should have one parameter defined, e, which should be of the type
TouchEvent (Listing 4-5).

LISTING 4-5: Creating the touch event handler in MultitouchAndGestures.as

```
private function onTouch(e:TouchEvent):void {}
```

3. In onTouch() add a switch statement that detects the three touch event types,
TOUCH_BEGIN, TOUCH_MOVE and TOUCH_END via the e.type property on the TouchEvent
object (Listing 4-6).

LISTING 4-6: Detecting the TOUCH_BEGIN, TOUCH_MOVE, and TOUCH_END event
types via the onTouch() method in MultitouchAndGestures.as

```
private function onTouch(e:TouchEvent):void
{
        switch(e.type)
        {
                case TouchEvent.TOUCH_BEGIN:
                {
                }
                break;
                case TouchEvent.TOUCH_MOVE:
                {
                }
                break;
                case TouchEvent.TOUCH_END:
                {
                }
                break;
        }
}
```

Here the value of the type property returned on the e touch event object is used to distinguish
between the three event types.

Each touch event type represents a unique value, so for every touch interaction you have an interest in responding to, you have to register it using addEventListener().

4. Returning to the constructor, register the three touch event types on the stage, referencing onTouch() as the event handler (Listing 4-7).

LISTING 4-7: Registering touch events with the stage via the class constructor method in MultitouchAndGestures.as

```
case true:
{
        Multitouch.inputMode = MultitouchInputMode.TOUCH_POINT;
        multitouch.text = "Touch events - Supported";

        stage.addEventListener(TouchEvent.TOUCH_BEGIN, onTouch);
        stage.addEventListener(TouchEvent.TOUCH_MOVE, onTouch);
        stage.addEventListener(TouchEvent.TOUCH_END, onTouch);
}
break;
case false:
{
        multitouch.text = "Touch events - Not Supported";
}
break;
```

Here the TOUCH_BEGIN, TOUCH_MOVE, and TOUCH_END events are all handled via the generically defined event handler called onTouch(). Registering the events with the stage means that the full stage will listen to any touch input.

The TouchEvent object returned by the event handler has the following core properties associated with it:

➤ type: A string value representing one of the eight touch event types

➤ touchPointID: An integer representing the touch point, which is unique for each touch point generated

➤ localX: A number representing the horizontal coordinate of the touch point, along an x-axis

➤ localY: A number representing the vertical coordinate of the touch point, along a y-axis

➤ sizeX: A number indicating the width of the touch point along the x-axis

➤ sizeY: A number indicating the height of the touch point along the y-axis

Next take a look at how some of the object properties returned by the three touch event types are used.

TRY IT OUT Tracking Multiple Touch Points in an Application

1. In onTouch(), assign properties of the e touch event object to three new variables. The value of the touchPointID property should be assigned to the variable id, stageX to the variable x, and stageY to y (Listing 4-8).

LISTING 4-8: Assigning properties of the touch point event via the onTouch() method in MultitouchAndGestures.as

```
private function onTouch(e:TouchEvent):void
{
        var id:Number = e.touchPointID;
        var x:Number = e.stageX;
        var y:Number = e.stageY;

        switch(e.type)
        {
                case TouchEvent.TOUCH_BEGIN:
                {
                }
                break;
                case TouchEvent.TOUCH_MOVE:
                {
                }
                break;
                case TouchEvent.TOUCH_END:
                {
                }
                break;
        }
}
```

2. After the onTouch() method, create four empty method stubs called drawLines(), moveLines(), removeLines(), and setCoordinates() (Listing 4-9).

LISTING 4-9: Creating stub functions to draw, move, remove, and set coordinates

```
private function onTouch(e:TouchEvent):void
{
        var id:Number = e.touchPointID;
        var x:Number = e.stageX;
        var y:Number = e.stageY;

        switch(e.type)
        {
                case TouchEvent.TOUCH_BEGIN:
                {
                }
                break;
                case TouchEvent.TOUCH_MOVE:
                {
                }
```

```
                break;
                case TouchEvent.TOUCH_END:
                {
                }
                break;
        }
    }

    private function drawLines(id:Number, x:Number, y:Number):void {}

    private function moveLines(id:Number, x:Number, y:Number):void {}

    private function removeLines(id:Number):void {}

    private function setCoordinates(x:Number, y:Number):void {}
```

3. Returning to onTouch(), call each of the newly created functions within the switch statement. For the TOUCH_BEGIN case call drawLines(), for TOUCH_MOVE call moveLines(), and for TOUCH_END call removeLines(). Each of the methods called should have the appropriate parameters supplied (Listing 4-10).

Available for download on Wrox.com

LISTING 4-10: Assigning the functions to each touch event type via the onTouch() method in MultitouchAndGestures.as

```
private function onTouch(e:TouchEvent):void
{
        var id:Number = e.touchPointID;
        var x:Number = e.localX;
        var y:Number = e.localY;

        switch(e.type)
        {
                case TouchEvent.TOUCH_BEGIN:
                {
                        drawLines(id, x, y);
                }
                break;
                case TouchEvent.TOUCH_MOVE:
                {
                        moveLines(id, x, y);
                }
                break;
                case TouchEvent.TOUCH_END:
                {
                        removeLines(id);
                }
                break;
        }
    }
```

4. Within setCoordinates(), set the x and y values on the coordinates.text property so they can be displayed. First check whether the TextField object, coordinates has been created;

if it hasn't been, instantiate a new `TextField` object and add it to the stage. Finally, position the text field along the x and y, reducing the position of the y by 15 pixels, while adding 2 pixels to x (Listing 4-11).

LISTING 4-11: Displaying the x and y coordinates of the touch point via the setCoordinates() method in MultitouchAndGestures.as

```
private function setCoordinates(x:Number, y:Number):void
{
        if(!coordinates)
        {
                coordinates = new TextField();
                stage.addChild(coordinates);
        }

        coordinates.text = "(" + x + ", " + y + ")";
        coordinates.x = x + 2;
        coordinates.y = y - 15;
}
```

5. In the private variable declarations add two new variables, `offsetX` and `offsetY` (Listing 4-12).

LISTING 4-12: Declaring new class variables in MultitouchAndGestures.as

```
public class MultitouchAndGestures extends Sprite
{
        private var coordinates:TextField;
        private var multitouch:TextField;
        private var offsetX:Number;
        private var offsetY:Number;
```

6. Within `drawLines()` add two lines to the stage. Use the x and y values to position them along with the `stage.stageWidth` and `stage.stageHeight` to define the length of each line. One line should be positioned vertically, the other horizontally, and both sprites should be named with reference to the `id` value. Then assign values to `offsetX` and `offsetY` before finally making a call to `setCoordinates()` (Listing 4-13).

LISTING 4-13: Drawing the vertical and horizontal lines via the drawLines() method in MultitouchAndGestures.as

```
private function drawLines(id:Number, x:Number, y:Number):void
{
        offsetX = x;
        offsetY = y;

        var vertical:Sprite = new Sprite();
        vertical.name = id + "v";
        vertical.graphics.lineStyle(2, 0x000000);
```

```
vertical.graphics.moveTo(x, 0);
vertical.graphics.lineTo(x, stage.stageHeight);
stage.addChild(vertical);

var horizontal:Sprite = new Sprite();
horizontal.name = id + "h";
horizontal.graphics.lineStyle(2, 0x000000);
horizontal.graphics.moveTo(0, y);
horizontal.graphics.lineTo(stage.stageWidth, y);
stage.addChild(horizontal);
setCoordinates(x, y);
}
```

7.   Within moveLines() reset the positions of the horizontal and vertical lines. Set the x property of
     the vertical line and the y property of the horizontal line, adjusting with offsetX and offsetY,
     respectively. Then call setCoordinates(), passing a reference to the x and y (Listing 4-14).

LISTING 4-14: Moving the vertical and horizontal lines, while displaying the x and y coordinates
of the touch point via the moveLines() method in MultitouchAndGestures.as

```
private function moveLines(id:Number, x:Number, y:Number):void
{
      var child1:Sprite = Sprite(stage.getChildByName((id + "v")));
      var child2:Sprite = Sprite(stage.getChildByName((id + "h")));

      var vertical:Sprite = child1;
      vertical.x = x - offsetX;

      var horizontal:Sprite = child2;
      horizontal.y = y - offsetY;

      setCoordinates(x, y);
}
```

8.   Within removeLines() remove both the vertical and horizontal lines from stage via
     removeChild(), using the id as a reference to retrieve the display object. The coordinates Text
     field should also be removed at this stage (Listing 4-15).

LISTING 4-15: Removing the vertical and horizontal lines via the removeLines() method in
MultitouchAndGestures.as

```
private function removeLines(id:Number):void
{
      stage.removeChild(Sprite(stage.getChildByName((id + "h"))));
      stage.removeChild(Sprite(stage.getChildByName((id + "v"))));
      stage.removeChild(coordinates);

      coordinates = null;
}
```

How It Works

The TOUCH_BEGIN event responds to a user's touch by initiating the drawing of horizontal and vertical lines, using the stageX and stageY of the touch event to define where those lines should be drawn. These values are supplied as parameters to a method called drawLines(), which creates two sprites representing each line. The touchPointID property is also passed onto the method. This is used to reference the sprite drawing of each in the lines array as seen in Listing 4-12.

For the TOUCH_MOVE event, the vertical and horizontal line sprites are retrieved using the getChildByName() function and then re-positioned along new x and y coordinates. Each time the TOUCH_MOVE event is dispatched, moveLines() is called, responding to the user's touch point movement. The key thing to note here is the id value, which should be the same number passed to the drawLines() method in order for the lines to move. The id is also required as the sole parameter for removeLines(), which is called when the TOUCH_END event has been dispatched. This time the line sprites are removed from the screen by a call to removeChild().

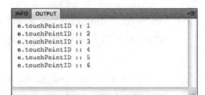

If you trace touchPointID in Device Central, you can see in the output window that every time a touch event has been created with one finger, a unique touchPointID value is generated (Figure 4-5).

FIGURE 4-5 The output window in Device Central, displaying the unique touchPointID values

At this point you should deduce that the touchPointID is a pretty significant property of the TouchEvent object.

While up to now you have created an example that handles one touch event at a time, next you'll take a look at how you can handle multiple touch events, taking full advantage of the touchPointID value.

Registering Touch Events on Interactive Objects

Multitouch is best served in an application when users can visually see the benefits of their input, like scrolling a list of contacts, increasing the size of an image, or moving on to the next picture in an image gallery. The lines and coordinates give a pretty accurate indication of a user's finger position on a device screen. Next let's examine using touch data to draw shapes to the screen:

1. First create a function called drawShape(). The function requires three parameters: id, x, and y. The function should create a Sprite object called shape, and then add it to the stage of the application, but only if the shape does not already exist (Listing 4-16).

Available for download on Wrox.com

LISTING 4-16: Creating a new shape sprite via the drawShape() method in MultitouchAndGestures.as

```
private function setCoordinates(x:Number, y:Number):void
{
    if(!coordinates)
```

```
        {
                coordinates = new TextField();
                stage.addChild(coordinates);
        }

        coordinates.text = "(" + x + ", " + y + ")";
        coordinates.x = x + 2;
        coordinates.y = y - 15;
    }

    private function drawShape(id:Number, x:Number, y:Number):void
    {
        var shape:Sprite;
        var shapeId:String = id.toString();

        if(!stage.getChildByName(shapeId))
        {
                shape = new Sprite();
                shape.name = shapeId;

                stage.addChild(shape);

        } else {

                shape = stage.getChildByName(shapeId) as Sprite;
        }

    }
```

In Listing 4-16, the id is used to define the name of each newly created shape object. Using stage.getChildByName(), you can retrieve any display object that has been added to the stage. Here this method is used to check that a shape with the same id, that is, finger touch, hasn't already been added to the stage. If getChildByName() returns a DisplayObject, a new shape doesn't have to be added to the stage. The object returned by the method can simply be cast as a Sprite. At present the shape doesn't have any properties, so if you run the example nothing will be visible on stage. You'll take a look at this shortly.

2. Next use the shape object to draw a rectangle. Calling the graphics.drawRect() method, the first two parameters should be offsetX and offsetY, representing the starting x and y position of the rectangle. The third and fourth parameters are the width and height of the rectangle, and are calculated by the x and y of the current touch point and the *offset values* defined when you first touch the screen (Listing 4-17).

Available for download on Wrox.com

LISTING 4-17: Defining the graphic properties of the shape sprite via the drawShape() method in MultitouchAndGestures.as

```
private function drawShape(id:Number, x:Number, y:Number):void
{
        var shape:Sprite;
        var shapeId:String = id.toString();
```

continues

LISTING 4-17 *(continued)*

```
if(!stage.getChildByName(shapeId))
{
        shape = new Sprite();
        shape.name = shapeId;

        stage.addChild(shape);

} else {

        shape = stage.getChildByName(shapeId) as Sprite;
}

var width:Number = x-offsetX;
var height:Number = y-offsetY;

shape.graphics.clear();
shape.graphics.lineStyle(2, 0x000000, 1.0);
shape.graphics.beginFill(0x000000, 0.0);
shape.graphics.drawRect(offsetX, offsetY, width, height);
shape.graphics.endFill();

}
```

3. Finally, within the TOUCH_BEGIN and TOUCH_MOVE events of onTouch(), call the drawShape() method (Listing 4-18).

LISTING 4-18: Drawing a shape when a finger touches the screen and when it moves via the onTouch() method in MultitouchAndGestures.as

```
private function onTouch(e:TouchEvent):void
{
        var id:Number = e.touchPointID;
        var x:Number = e.stageX;
        var y:Number = e.stageY;

        switch(e.type)
        {
                case TouchEvent.TOUCH_BEGIN:
                {
                        drawLines(id, x, y);
                        drawShape(id, x, y);
                }
                break;
                case TouchEvent.TOUCH_MOVE:
                {
                        moveLines(id, x, y);
                        drawShape(id, x, y);
                }
                break;
                case TouchEvent.TOUCH_END:
```

```
        {
                removeLines(id);
        }
        break;
    }
}
```

Determining the Supported Touch Points

Once you have set the input mode to TOUCH_POINT, you can also determine the number of touch points for an application by referencing Multitouch.maxTouchPoints.

This is another property of the Multitouch class that should give you the total number of touch points that can be handled by the device running your application. For instance, if maxTouchPoints returns 3, then only three fingers would be detectable on the device; if maxTouchPoints returns 1, then only one touch point, one finger, would be detectable.

The exact number of touch points recognized by a particular device may not always be the same as on another. The maxTouchPoints property is potentially useful for cross-device multitouch support. The Google Nexus One running Android 2.3.4 supports two touch points, whereas the Apple iPhone 4, running iOS 4, supports no fewer than five.

 WARNING *At the time of writing, the value returned by* Multitouch.maxTouchPoints *has not always been reported accurately and, in some instances, has returned inaccurate readings, depending on the device the application was running on. So, be careful if you decide you want to use the property for key logic in your applications.*

Now let's take a look at gestures.

GESTURE INTERACTIONS

Gestures are an extension of multitouch input, characterized more explicitly by specific movement and direction of the touch point interactions. Their definitive natures are encapsulated in a given term, like "zoom," "pan," or "swipe."

Determining Which Gestures Are Supported on a Device

Support for various gesture input types should be determined within an application before they are utilized, similarly to touch points.

You need to use Multitouch.supportsGestureEvents to detect gesture support. In addition, you can retrieve exactly which types of gestures are supported by calling the Multitouch.supportedGestures property, as in the following snippet:

```
if(Multitouch.supportsGestureEvents)
{
```

```
        var gestures:Vector.<String> = Multitouch.supportedGestures;

        for(var i:int=0; i < gestures.length; i++)
        {
               trace(gestures[i]);
        }
}
```

In the preceding snippet the `Multitouch.supportedGestures` property returns a `Vector` of strings.

A vector is simply an array with a specified data type to signify that all the elements in the array are of that same data type. In the following snippet the data type `String` is specified in anchors (< and >) after the `Vector` declaration, preceded by a period (`.`):

```
    var gestures:Vector.<String>;
```

 Each supported gesture is then traced to the output console.

Gesture Events and Event Handling

Via the Flash Player, the simple touch of a finger on a device's screen will trigger an event to be dispatched, which can be detected in AS3.

Setting the Input Mode for Gesture Events

To handle gesture events, you need to set the `Multitouch.inputMode` property to `MultitouchInputMode.GESTURE`. This will allow you to handle gestures recognized by the device, as in the following snippet:

```
    if(Multitouch.supportsGestureEvents)
    {
          Multitouch.inputMode = MultitouchInputMode.GESTURE;

          var gestures:Vector.<String> = Multitouch.supportedGestures;

          for(var i:int=0; i < gestures.length; i++)
          {
                 trace(gestures[i]);
          }
    }
```

Gesture Event Types and Properties

Once you've selected `MultitouchInputMode.GESTURE` as the *input mode*, three main gesture events can be dispatched depending on what gesture the user has initiated:

➤   `GestureEvent`: This gesture event consists of one
    event-type property, which is dispatched as
    `GestureEvent.GESTURE_TWO_FINGER_TAP` and represents
    a user-initiated two-finger tap. Figure 4-6 shows the
    two-finger-tap gesture; here fingers on each hand tap
    simultaneously.

FIGURE 4-6 The two-finger-tap gesture

➤ `PressAndTapGestureEvent`: This gesture event also has one event-type property, which is referenced as `PressAndTapGestureEvent.GESTURE_PRESS_AND_TAP` and represents the user-initiated press and tap. Figure 4-7 shows the press-and-tap gesture; here the left hand presses while the right hand taps simultaneously.

FIGURE 4-7 The press and tap gesture

➤ `TransformGestureEvent`: This gesture event has four event-type properties, which can be referenced as:

  ➤ `TransformGestureEvent.GESTURE_PAN` to represent the user-initiated pan gesture

  ➤ `TransformGestureEvent.GESTURE_ROTATE` to represent the user-initiated rotate gesture

  ➤ `TransformGestureEvent.GESTURE_SWIPE` to represent the user-initiated swipe gesture

  ➤ `TransformGestureEvent.GESTURE_ZOOM` to represent the user-initiated zoom gesture.

Figure 4-8 shows the rotate gesture. Here a finger on the right hand presses the screen, while a finger on the left hand simulates drawing an arc around the stationary finger on the right hand.

As with the touch events, each gesture event must be registered through `addEventListener()`. The following snippet shows how to handle a `GESTURE_TWO_FINGER_TAP` event:

FIGURE 4-8 The rotate gesture

```
if(Multitouch.supportsGestureEvents)
{
        Multitouch.inputMode = MultitouchInputMode.GESTURE;

        var g:Vector.<String> = Multitouch.supportedGestures;

        for(var i:int=0; i < g.length; i++)
        {
                if(gestures[i] == GestureEvent.GESTURE_TWO_FINGER_TAP)
                {
                        this.addEventListener(g[i], onTwoFingerTap);
                }
        }
}
```

Each of the three gesture event types returns objects that have properties setting them apart from single touch events.

Registering Gesture Events on Interactive Objects

Up to now the `MultitouchAndGestures.as` example tracks a single touch point and draws a shape to the screen when a single finger moves. Next, you look at how the pan gesture can be used to move each of the shapes drawn in the application, and in the following steps you combine the use of a timer with gesture events:

1. Begin by importing five new classes, `Stage`, `GesturePhase`, `TransformGestureEvent`, `Timer`, and `TimerEvent` classes (Listing 4-19).

LISTING 4-19: Importing the Timer and TimerEvent classes

```
package
{
        import flash.display.Sprite;
        import flash.display.Stage;
        import flash.events.GesturePhase;
        import flash.events.TimerEvent;
        import flash.events.TouchEvent;
        import flash.events.TransformGestureEvent;
        import flash.text.TextField;
        import flash.text.TextFieldAutoSize;
        import flash.ui.Multitouch;
        import flash.ui.MultitouchInputMode;
        import flash.utils.Timer;
```

2. Next, in the private variable declarations, define a `Timer` object called `idleTimer`, and a `String` variable called `currentTarget` (Listing 4-20).

LISTING 4-20: Declaring new class variables

```
public class MultitouchAndGestures extends Sprite
{
        private var coordinates:TextField;
        private var currentTarget:String;
        private var idleTimer:Timer;
        private var offsetX:Number;
        private var offsetY:Number;
        private var multitouch:TextField;
```

The purpose of the timer is to reset idle gesture movement, hence the name `idleTimer`. While the user's finger touch is currently handled as a touch point, the aim will be to use the pan gesture when a shape is touched, allowing it to be moved around. This will mean that the input mode will need to change from touch to gesture, and then revert back to touch after a period of inactivity, to allow more shapes to be drawn. The `currentTarget` is defined to hold the last shape touched.

3. In `MultitouchAndGestures()` instantiate `idleTimer`. The class constructor for `Timer` takes milliseconds as the first parameter and here should be set to `1000`, representing 1 second. You also need to add an event listener to the object that triggers an event handler called `onTimer()` when the timer has completed a cycle (Listing 4-21).

LISTING 4-21: Registering timer events via the class constructor in MultitouchAndGestures.as

```
public function MultitouchAndGestures()
{
        multitouch = new TextField();
        multitouch.autoSize = TextFieldAutoSize.LEFT;

        idleTimer = new Timer(1000);
```

```
idleTimer.addEventListener(TimerEvent.TIMER, onTimer);

switch(Multitouch.supportsTouchEvents)
{
```

4. Underneath the class constructor create four new stubs: onTimer(), initializeGestures(), initializeTimer(), and initializeTouch(). The onTimer() event handler should retrieve the TimerEvent object e; none of the other functions require parameters to be defined (Listing 4-22).

LISTING 4-22: Adding the onTimer(), initializeGestures(), initializeTimer(), and initializeTouch() method stubs in MultitouchAndGestures.as

```
private function onTimer(e:TimerEvent):void {}

private function initializeGestures():void {}

private function initializeTimer():void {}

private function initializeTouch():void {}
```

5. In onTimer(), to prevent further timer event calls from being made once the timer finishes a cycle, call the stop() method on idleTimer (Listing 4-23).

LISTING 4-23: Stopping the timer via the onTimer() method in MultitouchAndGestures.as

```
private function onTimer(e:TimerEvent):void
{
    idleTimer.stop();
}
```

6. Next, in initializeTimer(), set the delay property of idleTimer to 1000. This will effectively reset the countdown back to the beginning. Also check whether the timer is still counting down at all; if it is not running, restart it using the start() method (Listing 4-24).

LISTING 4-24: Starting the timer via the initializeTimer() method in MultitouchAndGestures.as

```
private function initializeTimer():void
{
    idleTimer.delay = 1000;

    if(!idleTimer.running)
        idleTimer.start();
}
```

Note that once stop() has been called on idleTimer the timer should no longer be running.

7. In the initializeTouch() function, set the input mode to touch point (Listing 4-25).

LISTING 4-25: Setting the input mode to touch point via the initializeTouch() method in MultitouchAndGestures.as

```
private function initializeTouch():void
{
    if(Multitouch.supportsTouchEvents)
        Multitouch.inputMode = MultitouchInputMode.TOUCH_POINT;
}
```

8. Returning to the onTimer() function after the timer has been stopped, make a call to initializeTouch() (Listing 4-26).

LISTING 4-26: Initializing touch points via the onTimer() method in MultitouchAndGestures.as

```
private function onTimer(e:TimerEvent):void
{
    idleTimer.stop();
    initializeTouch();
}
```

9. In the initializeGestures() function, set the input mode to gesture, then make a call to initializeTimer() (Listing 4-27).

LISTING 4-27: Setting the input mode to support gestures and initializing the timer via the initializeGestures() method in MultitouchAndGestures.as

```
private function initializeGestures():void
{
    if(Multitouch.supportsGestureEvents)
    {
        Multitouch.inputMode = MultitouchInputMode.GESTURE;
        initializeTimer();
    }
}
```

10. Returning to onTouch(), for the TOUCH_BEGIN event use the e.target property to determine whether a user's touch event is dispatched from the stage. Save the reference of the target e.target.name to currentTarget and then call initializeGestures() to set the input mode to gestures (Listing 4-28).

LISTING 4-28: Initializing gestures via the onTouch() method in MultitouchAndGestures.as

```
private function onTouch(e:TouchEvent):void
{
    var id:Number = e.touchPointID;
    var x:Number = e.stageX;
```

```
    var y:Number = e.stageY;

    switch(e.type)
    {
        case TouchEvent.TOUCH_BEGIN:
        {
            if(e.target is Stage)
            {
                drawLines(id, x, y);
                drawShape(id, x, y);

            } else {

                currentTarget = e.target.name;
                initializeGestures();
            }
        }
        break;
        case TouchEvent.TOUCH_MOVE:
        {
            moveLines(id, x, y);
            drawShape(id, x, y);
        }
        break;
        case TouchEvent.TOUCH_END:
        {
            removeLines(id);
        }
        break;
    }
}
```

11. In drawShape(), after the shape sprite been instantiated, use
Multitouch.supportedGestures to check whether the gesture pan is supported. Then call
addEventListener(), supplying the TransformGestureEvent.GESTURE_PAN event type
g as the first parameter and an event handler called onPan() as the second parameter. The
onPan() event handler should be added below the drawShape() function (Listing 4-29).

LISTING 4-29: Adding the pan gesture event to a shape via the drawShape() method in
MultitouchAndGestures.as

```
private function drawShape(id:Number, x:Number, y:Number):void
{
    var shape:Sprite;
    var shapeId:String = id.toString();

    if(!"stage.getChildByName(shapeId))
    {
        shape = new Sprite();
        shape.name = shapeId;

        for each(var g:String in Multitouch.supportedGestures)
```

continues

LISTING 4-29 *(continued)*

```
        {
                switch(g)
                {
                        case TransformGestureEvent.GESTURE_PAN:
                        {
                                shape.addEventListener(g, onPan);
                        }
                        break;
                }

                stage.addChild(shape);

        } else {

                shape = child as Sprite;
        }

        var width:Number = x-offsetX;
        var height:Number = y-offsetY;

        shape.graphics.clear();
        shape.graphics.lineStyle(2, 0x000000, 1.0);
        shape.graphics.beginFill(0x000000, 0.0);
        shape.graphics.drawRect(offsetX, offsetY, width, height);
        shape.graphics.endFill();
}

private function onPan(e:TransformGestureEvent):void {}
```

Handling Gesture Events

Lastly, take a look at how to use the data in a dispatched gesture event:

1. In the onPan() function use the GesturePhase.UPDATE event phase to reposition the shape that is currently in focus. You need to retrieve the shape using the currentTarget variable and the getChildByName() function. Then use the offsetX and offsetY properties of the TransformGestureEvent object e to reposition the shape, before calling initializeTimer() (Listing 4-30).

LISTING 4-30: Assigning the offsetX and offsetY properties to the shape via the onPan() method in MultitouchAndGestures.as

```
private function onPan(e:TransformGestureEvent):void
{
        var shape:Sprite = stage.getChildByName(currentTarget);

        switch(e.phase)
```

```
        {
                case GesturePhase.UPDATE:
                {
                        shape.x = shape.x + e.offsetX;
                        shape.y = shape.y + e.offsetY;

                        initializeTimer();
                }
                break;
        }
}
```

 NOTE *All the changes to the* `MultitouchAndGesture.as` *file from Listing 4-1 to Listing 4-30 should now have been saved to file. Returning to Device Central, you should now be able to emulate the pan gesture.*

2. In Device Central open the `MultitouchAndGestures.swf` file in the emulator.

3. Next draw a shape on screen. Press the Alt key and simultaneously left-click the mouse. You should see your first touch point, along with the coordinates at which the shape will be drawn (Figure 4-9). If you are using a Trackpad, you can simply create a touch point by pressing the Alt key on the keyboard while pressing on the Trackpad.

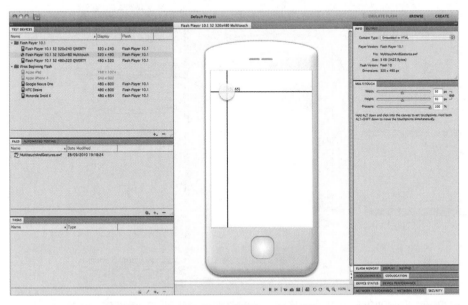

FIGURE 4-9 Adding the first touch point to the Multitouch and Gestures App in Device Central

4. With the Alt key and mouse button still pressed, drag the mouse to a new position on the stage. You should now have a shape drawn on the stage (Figure 4-10).

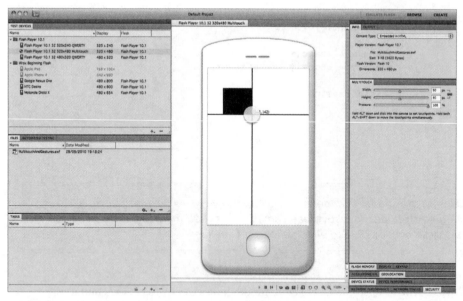

FIGURE 4-10 Drawing a shape in the Multitouch and Gestures App

5. Once the shape is drawn, with the cursor over the shape press the Alt key and simultaneously left-click the mouse to simulate another finger touch as before (Figure 4-11).

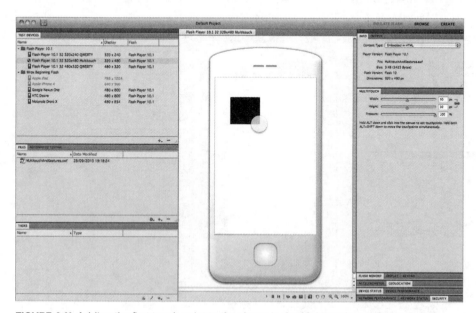

FIGURE 4-11 Adding the first touch point to the shape in the Multitouch and Gestures App

6. While the Alt key is still pressed and the first touch point is still visible, add a second touch point somewhere else on the shape, this time holding the Shift key (Figure 4-12).

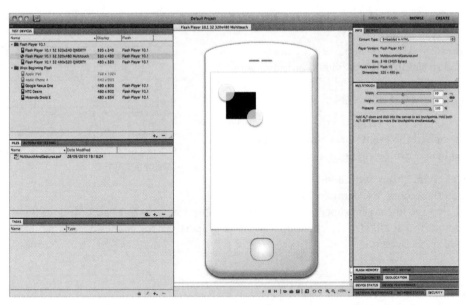

FIGURE 4-12 Adding the second touch point to the shape in the Multitouch and Gestures App

7. Finally, move the shape to the bottom right of the screen (Figure 4-13).

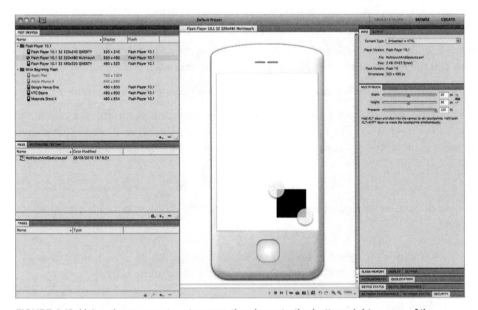

FIGURE 4-13 Using the pan gesture to move the shape to the bottom right corner of the stage in the Multitouch and Gestures App

UTILIZING THE MULTITOUCH PANEL IN DEVICE CENTRAL

In Device Central the Multitouch panel provides three settings that can be used to simulate touch points, including a user's finger coverage and the pressure applied by a finger when it interacts with the screen (Figure 4-14).

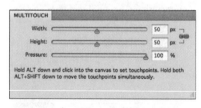

These properties directly correlate to the properties briefly mentioned for each of the event types covered in this chapter. The width and height can be changed along with the pressure.

FIGURE 4-14 The Multitouch panel in Device Central

I recommend experimenting with these properties in the `MultitouchAndGestures.as` example. For instance, you could try changing the line style properties of the horizontal and vertical lines according to the size of the touch point. You could also try changing the alpha property of the shapes depending on the pressure applied to the screen.

SUMMARY

Implementing multitouch requires paying a little more attention to how your applications will work when compared to using button-press events simply because there is more data to handle.

Over the course of the chapter you have created an example that demonstrates the new multitouch features of the Flash player. First you learned how to determine support for multitouch and the need to set the input mode for touch and gesture separately.

You also learned how to handle touch and gesture events, using the properties of touch events to generate shapes and the data returned by the pan gesture to interact with those shapes.

In the next chapter you'll take a closer look at developing for multiple devices and various screen sizes.

Before moving on to the next chapter, there are a few gesture events and properties not covered by the code examples in this chapter. The following set of exercises should allow you to explore these event types in more detail applying them to the example project.

EXERCISES

1. Apply the rotate gesture event `TransformGestureEvent.GESTURE_ROTATE` to rotate a shape once it has been drawn.

2. Add the press and tap gesture event `PressAndTapGestureEvent.GESTURE_PRESS_AND_TAP` to randomly change the color of a selected shape when the gesture is detected.

3. Use the swipe gesture event `TransformGestureEvent.GESTURE_SWIPE` to remove a shape from view.

4. Use the zoom gesture event `TransformGestureEvent.GESTURE_ZOOM` to increase the size of a shape.

▶ WHAT YOU LEARNED IN THIS CHAPTER

TOPIC	KEY CONCEPT
Multitouch input	Two categories of multitouch input can be detected in mobile flash applications: touch input and gesture input.
Determining touch input support	Use `Multitouch.supportsTouchEvents` to determine touch input support on a mobile device. This should return `true` when supported.
Setting the input mode for touch support	Use `MultitouchInputMode.TOUCH_POINT` to define the input mode for touch. Set the `Multitouch.inputMode` to `MultitouchInputMode.TOUCH_POINT` to initialize touch input.
Handling touch events	Register a `TouchEvent` type to handle touch input, using `addEventListener()` to register an interest in one of eight `TouchEvent` types.
Determining gesture input support	Use `Multitouch.supportsGestureEvents` to determine gesture support on a mobile device. Then use `Multitouch.supportedGestures` to determine exactly which gestures are supported.
Setting the input mode for touch support	Use `MultitouchInputMode.GESTURE` to define the input mode for gestures. Set the `Multitouch.inputMode` to `MultitouchInputMode.GESTURE` to initialize gestures.
Handling gesture events	Three distinct types of gesture event objects can be dispatched: `GestureEvent`, `PressAndTapGestureEvent`, and `TransformGestureEvent`. Each gesture event object has several event `type` properties. Register a particular gesture event type using `addEventListener()` to respond to gesture movements.
Using the Multitouch panel	In Device Central use the Multitouch panel to emulate a user's finger touch. Modify the size of a user's finger by setting the width and height of touch points. Set the degree of weight applied by the finger touch, by altering the pressure.

5

Developing for Multiple Screen Sizes

WHAT YOU WILL LEARN IN THIS CHAPTER:

➤ Understanding screen size and screen resolution

➤ Automatically scaling applications

➤ Adapting content to different stage sizes

➤ Handling changes in device orientation

➤ Utilizing MXML group containers

➤ Using states in a Flex mobile application

In this chapter you'll take a look at how to approach developing mobile applications that will adapt to more than one screen size.

In essence, the chapter focuses mainly on the design of the mobile application within the viewing window. For the majority of apps the logic and core should be the same, and so giving applications a consistent look is the order of the day.

First you'll get an understanding of screen resolution and the difference between measuring screen size by the number of pixels and measuring the screen size by physical distances.

Then you'll take a look at utilizing the stage to handle size changes in an application. You'll also examine how to determine the relative dimensions and sizes of assets, components, and fonts.

This chapter guides you through how to update an application when the device changes orientation between portrait and landscape. You'll then go through a series of techniques to position assets in the application using Flash Builder.

CONSIDERATIONS FOR MULTIPLE SCREEN SIZES

The screen size on a mobile handset is pretty much what determines the space available to you, and the viewing window for an application. Not all mobile devices have the same screen size, which poses potential issues in presenting a consistent look-and-feel across multiple devices.

The main goal of this chapter is to outline the techniques that will help you target and deploy applications to multiple devices. When coding for different screen sizes, the two main things you have to take into consideration are:

➤ **Screen resolution:** The total number of pixels a screen contains

➤ **Screen aspect ratio:** The measured width of a screen in relation to the height

In tackling the first point, you should consider whether an application will need to look different if it runs on a device with a higher or lower pixel density.

And with the screen aspect ratio, you must consider whether the application will need to run on a device where the full width of the screen needs to be longer or shorter than its measured height.

Both these factors affect the design or layout of a mobile application.

Pixel Density

Although pixels give a computational measurement of screen size, they don't represent the real physical measurements directly, in the way that centimeters or inches do. The number of dots per inch (DPI) or pixels per inch (PPI) is used to provide a way by which the number of inches on a screen can be calculated.

Table 5-1 lists some screen resolutions for comparison across different devices.

TABLE 5-1: A Comparison of Mobile Devices with Different Screen Resolutions

DEVICE	DISPLAY SIZE (INCHES)	SCREEN RESOLUTION (PIXELS)	PRIMARY ORIENTATION	DPI
Google Nexus One	3.7"	480w x 800h	Portrait	254
Google Nexus S	4"	480w x 800h	Portrait	235
Apple iPhone 4	3.5"	640w x 960h	Portrait	326
Apple iPad	9.7"	768w x 1024h	Portrait	132
BlackBerry PlayBook	7"	1024w x 600h	Landscape	170
Motorola Xoom	10.1"	1280w x 800h	Landscape	160

Take a look at the DPI column in Table 5-1. The first thing you should notice is the difference in screen display size, which varies depending on whether the mobile device is a tablet or smartphone.

Smartphone devices like the Google Nexus One, which has a screen resolution of 480 × 800 pixels, have a pixel density of 254 DPI, whereas the Apple iPhone 4 has a resolution of 640 × 960 pixels, with a pixel density of 326 DPI.

A tablet device like the BlackBerry PlayBook has a screen resolution of 1024 × 600 pixels, with a pixel density of 170 DPI, whereas the Apple iPad has a resolution of 768 × 1024 pixels, with a pixel density of 132 DPI.

What you can also take from the table is the fact that just because a device has a larger screen size doesn't mean it has a higher pixel density.

In Flash Builder you can view a number of device configurations and properties, including pixel density, in the Preferences panel (see Figure 5-1). To open this panel, select Flash Builder ⇨ Preferences . . . from the main menu.

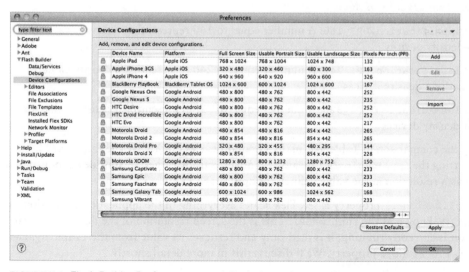

FIGURE 5-1: Flash Builder Preferences panel displaying numerous device configurations

Utilizing Device DPI

The device DPI can be utilized in a number of ways. You can let an application detect and handle differences in DPI across devices automatically, or you can programmatically code for those differences.

Scaling Applications with the Application DPI

When you create a Flex-based mobile application, you have the option of scaling the application to automatically address potential differences in pixel density when your application runs on different devices.

You do this by setting the `applicationDPI` property of the main application container, either inside your `<s:ViewNavigatorApplication>` or the `<s:TabbedViewNavigatorApplication>` tag, as shown in the following snippet:

```
<?xml version="1.0" encoding="utf-8"?>
<s:TabbedViewNavigatorApplication xmlns:fx="http://ns.adobe.com/mxml/2009"
                                   xmlns:s="library://ns.adobe.com/flex/spark"
                                   applicationDPI="240">

</s:TabbedViewNavigatorApplication>
```

This property can be set to one of three values: 160, 240 or 320. These three values are known as DPI Classification constants and are defined by three static properties of the `mx.core.DPIClassification` class:

➤   `DPIClassification.DPI_160`: A number equal to 160 representing a density value for low-density devices

➤   `DPIClassification.DPI_240`: A number equal to 240 representing a density value for medium-density devices

➤   `DPIClassidication.DPI_320`: A number equal to 320 representing a density value for high-density devices

As shown by the comparison in Table 5-1, many popular devices don't have the same screen resolution. Setting the `applicationDPI` means you are effectively targeting your development at a device that has a resolution at the value defined for `applicationDPI`.

When the `applicationDPI` property is set, Flex scales everything in the application in relation to another property, known as the `runtimeDPI`. This is the screen resolution of the device in which the application is currently running; it is read-only and retrieves its value from the `flash.system.Capabilities.screenDPI` property. We'll discuss this in more detail shortly.

When an app runs on a device that has a different `runtimeDPI` from the target `applicationDPI` value, it scales the content automatically. If the `applicationDPI` property is not set, no scaling occurs.

Consider the following scenarios:

If the `applicationDPI` is set to 160 and the target device has a DPI of 160, no scaling occurs. The scale is deemed to be a factor of 1, or 100%. If the target device has a DPI of 320, a scale factor of 2, or 200%, is applied. If a target device has a DPI of 240, a scale factor of 1.5, or 150%, is applied.

Scale factors can go up as well as down. So, if the applicationDPI is set to 320 and the target device has a DPI of 160, then a scale factor of 0.5, or 50%, is applicable.

Note that when you run an application in Flash Builder, the debug window uses a DPI of 240.

A device's runtimeDPI value will fall into one of three DPI Classification constants, which are mapped by default in Flash Builder to one of three associated ranges, as shown in Table 5-2.

TABLE 5-2: Device DPI to DPI Classification Constant Mappings

DEVICE DPI	DPI CLASSIFICATION
Less than 200 dpi	160 dpi
Between 201 dpi and 279 dpi	240 dpi
280 dpi and above	320 dpi

Using Table 5-2 as a guide, you can expect that when the applicationDPI property is set to 240, content running on a Google Nexus One won't scale, as its runtimeDPI, a value of 254, will fall into the 240 dpi classification, and hence a scale factor of 1.

From Table 5-2 and Table 5-1, you can also determine that the Apple iPad, BlackBerry PlayBook, and Motorola Zoom, each with DPI values of less than 200 dpi, will fall into the 160 dpi classification, whereas only the Apple iPhone 4 will fall into the high-density 320 dpi classification.

Setting Styles with the Application DPI

Using the Flex framework there is also support for applying styles based on the target OS and application DPI in CSS, by setting a @media rule in the <fx:Styles> declaration.

To do this, you can use a combination of the application-dpi and os-platform properties to selectively apply styles based on the device DPI and the target platform on which the application is running.

Like the applicationDPI property, the supported values for the application-dpi CSS property are 160, 240, and 320.

The os-platform CSS property is matched to the value of the first three letters of the flash .system.Capabilities.version property returned by the application running in Flash Player.

Set the os-platform property to one of the supported values:

➤ AND: To reference the Google Android platform

➤ IOS: To reference the Apple iOS platform

➤ QNX: To reference the BlackBerry Tablet OS platform

➤ MAC: To reference the Apple Macintosh platform

➤ WIN: To reference the Windows platform

➤ LNX: To reference the Linux platform

The @media rule supports the common operators and, or, and not.

The following code snippet shows how to set the default fontSize style property to 12 for the <s:Label> control, and also uses the @media rule to determine whether the application is running on an Apple iOS device and whether it uses 240 DPI to set the fontSize property to 10:

```
<?xml version="1.0" encoding="utf-8"?>
<s:ViewNavigatorApplication xmlns:fx="http://ns.adobe.com/mxml/2009"
                            xmlns:s="library://ns.adobe.com/flex/spark"
                            applicationDPI="160">
        <fx:Style>

                @namespace s "library://ns.adobe.com/flex/spark";

                s|Label
                {
                        fontSize:12;
                }

                @media (os-platform: "IOS") and (application-dpi: 240)
                {
                        s|Label
                        {
                                fontSize:10;
                        }
                }


        </fx:Style>

</s:ViewNavigatorApplication>
```

The following code snippet sets the backgroundColor property of an application running on the BlackBerry Tablet OS platform to #000000, when the device DPI is 160, but not on Android, nor iOS:

```
<?xml version="1.0" encoding="utf-8"?>
<s:ViewNavigatorApplication xmlns:fx="http://ns.adobe.com/mxml/2009"
                            xmlns:s="library://ns.adobe.com/flex/spark"
                            applicationDPI="160">
        <fx:Style>

                @namespace s "library://ns.adobe.com/flex/spark";

                @media (os-platform: "QNX") and (application-dpi: 160),
                        not (os-platform: "AND"),
                        not (os-platform: "IOS")
```

```
        {
                s|ViewNavigatorApplication
                {
                        backgroundColor:#000000;
                }
        }


        </fx:Style>

</s:ViewNavigatorApplication>
```

When setting styles, you can essentially override the scale factor applied to the application once you have set the `applicationDPI`.

Using the Screen DPI to Calculate Physical Measurements

Let's now turn to the `Capabilities.screenDPI` property, which you can use to retrieve the device's screen DPI and calculate the number of pixels for a particular physical measurement.

The screen size and DPI prove to be important factors when developing for multiple screens, because components' assets could in essence work perfectly on one device but be too small to read or tap on devices with higher resolutions.

When we refer to physical measurements, essentially what this means is that for the Google Nexus One, one inch is represented by 254 pixels, and on the BlackBerry PlayBook, one inch is 170 pixels.

Use the following `import` statement to use the `Capabilities` class:

```
import flash.system.Capabilities;
```

The following snippet draws a 2-inch × 1-inch rectangle on the stage. Targeting the Nexus One device, this is done by multiplying 254 by 2 to get the width at 508 pixels, and then using 267 pixels for the height of the rectangle.

```
var rectangle:Sprite = new Sprite();
rectangle.graphics.beginFill(0x000000);
rectangle.graphics.drawRect(0, 0, 508, 267)
rectangle.graphics.endFill();

addChild(rectangle);
```

For the BlackBerry PlayBook, however, the rectangle would actually be rendered as 3.14 × 3 inches, which is larger than the physical dimensions specified for the application. Also, if the application were to run on the Apple iPhone 4, the rectangle would be rendered as 1.64 inches.

If you were to put each of these values in order, you would expect to find that the higher resolution should display a bigger rectangle, with an increasing DPI number.

With the `Capabilities.screenDPI` property, you can ensure that the size of the rectangle is rendered to an exact size, regardless of the screen it's being drawn on, as shown by example in the following snippet:

```
var width:unit = Capabilities.screenDPI * 2;
var height:unit = width;

var rectangle:Sprite = new Sprite();
rectangle.graphics.beginFill(0x000000);
rectangle.graphics.drawRect(0, 0, width, height)
rectangle.graphics.endFill();

addChild(rectangle);
```

This code would now render a 2- × 1-inch rectangle on each device. Next let's take a look at how to adapt content to the stage size.

ADAPTING CONTENT TO STAGE SIZE

One of the main aims of multiple screen development is to enable an application to adapt itself to different screen sizes. This doesn't necessarily need to include every part of the application but some assets will have to be resized to make them more visible.

Using the StageScaleMode and StageAlign Classes

The `StageScaleMode` and `StageAlign` classes can be used together to provide values to set the scale mode property `stage.scaleMode` and the alignment property `stage.align` on the `Stage` object of an application.

The `StageScaleMode` class has the following static constants:

➤   `StageScaleMode.EXACT_FIT`: To specify that content in the application fills the visible area of the stage

➤   `StageScaleMode.NO_BORDER`: To ensure that content in the application fills the entire stage when the stage is scaled

➤   `StageScaleMode.NO_SCALE`: To prevent the content in the application from resizing and filling the entire stage when the stage is scaled

➤   `StageScaleMode.SHOW_ALL`: To maintain the aspect ratio of the content in the application when the stage is scaled

From the list, you see three settings that would at first glance appear to be ideal options for targeting multiple screen sizes. These are the `StageScaleMode.EXACT_FIT`, `StageScaleMode.SHOW_ALL`, and `StageScaleMode.NO_BORDER` constants, which would automatically resize content to fit the stage.

However, using `StageScaleMode.EXACT_FIT` can potentially distort content in the application, because the content isn't resized to maintain its aspect ratio.

With `StageScaleMode.NO_BORDER`, cropping may occur because the setting will maintain the aspect ratio. You can be sure that all content will be displayed only if the aspect ratio fits the size of the stage.

When using `StageScaleMode.SHOW_ALL`, borders can appear at either side of the application, which is done to maintain the aspect ratio of the content in the application while filling the area that the resized stage occupies.

None of the three options discussed are really viable for resizing content on mobile devices because each has constraints that programmatically are impractical to implement in an application. The only downside to using `StageScaleMode.NO_SCALE` is that the application will not resize any of the content when the stage is scaled. Scaling the stage down from the initial application means that cropping will occur if the application window is smaller than the content, whereas scaling up from the initial application content means that the stage of the application will get larger without adjusting the content, hence the content would look small.

These problems both can be rectified through listening to events triggered from the stage, for instance detecting when it resizes. This will be covered a little later.

The `StageAlign` class has the following static constants:

➤ `StageAlign.BOTTOM`: To align content in the application relative to the bottom of the stage

➤ `StageAlign.BOTTOM_LEFT`: To align content in the application relative to the bottom-left corner of the stage

➤ `StageAlign.BOTTOM_RIGHT`: To align content in the application relative to the bottom-right corner of the stage

➤ `StageAlign.LEFT`: To align content in the application relative to the left of the stage

➤ `StageAlign.RIGHT`: To align content in the application relative to the right of the stage

➤ `StageAlign.TOP`: To align content in the application relative to the top of the stage

➤ `StageAlign.TOP_LEFT`: To align content in the application relative to the top-left corner of the stage

➤ `StageAlign.TOP_RIGHT`: To align content in the application relative to the top-right corner of the stage

You need to set the `stage.scaleMode` property to `StageScaleMode.NO_SCALE` and the `stage.align` property to `StageAlign.TOP_LEFT` as shown in the following code snippet:

```
stage.scaleMode = StageScaleMode.NO_SCALE;
stage.align = StageAlign.TOP_LEFT;
```

This will actually prevent automatically scaling the application, allowing you to specify code to scale and lay out content in the application dynamically.

To dynamically scale and lay out content you need a mechanism by which the application recognizes the area which it occupies, so that in turn it can apply its own dimensions and position itself correctly. This can be achieved through the stage by handling the resize event.

Handling Stage Resize Events

The stage dispatches the `Event.RESIZE` event when the mobile application first initializes, and also when the device orientation changes. On the desktop and with Flash embedded in the browser the `Event.RESIZE` event is also dispatched when the window or embed container is resized.

Using `addEventListener()` you can assign `Event.RESIZE` to an event handler, as shown in the following code snippet:

```
stage.addEventListener(Event.RESIZE, onResize);
```

The `stage` object has two properties to return the width and height of the stage, through the `stage.stageWidth` and `stage.stageHeight` properties, respectively.

For the `event.target` property for the `Event.RESIZE` event is the `Stage` object where you can retrieve the width and height values. The `onResize()` event handler would need to include the code to perform the dynamic changes to the layout. When laying out content it's important to have a preconception of what assets may need to be resized and positioned.

You'll explore handling the stage resize event in more detail shortly.

Creating the Sprite Layout App Example

In this section you'll simply render the layout for an application using sprites to represent different proportions of the screen, and use portrait and landscape layouts to arrange and resize each sprite.

In Flash Builder you will need to create a new ActionScript Mobile Project called Sprite Layout App. This example will use AS3.

The two layouts for the application are shown in Figures 5-2 and 5-3.

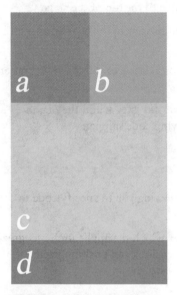

FIGURE 5-2: The portrait layout design for Sprite Layout App

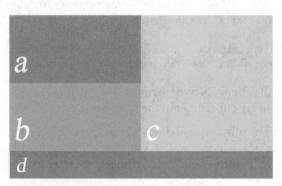

FIGURE 5-3: The landscape layout design for Sprite Layout App

Each layout contains four distinct parts, which will be referred to as *a*, *b*, *c*, and *d*. Referring to the diagram, *a* is the blue sprite, *b* is the green sprite, *c* is the yellow sprite, and *d* is the red sprite.

In the portrait layout (Figure 5-1) you can see that *a* and *b* are aligned together horizontally, both occupying half of the screen width, while *c* and *d* are vertically aligned underneath *a* and *b* and occupy the full width of the screen.

In the landscape layout (Figure 5-2) you see that *a* and *b* still occupy the screen width, but this time they are vertically aligned. Also in the landscape layout, *c* now occupies half the screen width and is aligned to the top right of the stage, while *d* still occupies the full width of the screen at the bottom.

Defining the ActionScript Mobile Project Settings

Following are a few of the settings that you will need to ensure are defined for the project:

➤ **Name:** Set the Name for the project to **SpriteLayoutApp**.

➤ **Application ID:** Set the Application ID to **com.wrox.ch5.SpriteLayoutApp**.

Building Sprite Layout App

The following steps will guide you through creating the example that changes the arrangement of items depending on whether it's in a portrait layout or landscape layout.

1. In Flash Builder create the Sprite Layout App project (Figure 5-4).

2. In `SpriteLayoutApp.as`, define four private `static` constants of type `int` to represent a color for each of the blocks, and also add four private variables to represent each of the sprites a, b, c, and d. Then in the class constructor, set the `stage.align` property to `StageAlign` `.TOP_LEFT` and the `stage.scaleMode` to `StageScaleMode.NO_SCALE`, to ensure that the `StageAlign` and `StageScaleMode` classes are imported (Listing 5-1).

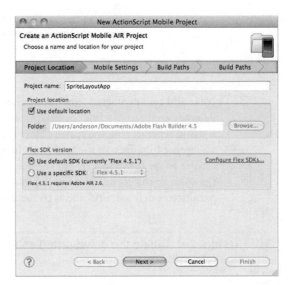

FIGURE 5-4: The New ActionScript Mobile Project dialog for Sprite Layout App

LISTING 5-1: Declaring static variables for the colors blue, green, red, and yellow, and private variables for the sprites a, b, c, and d in SpriteLayoutApp.as

```
package
{
    import flash.display.Sprite;
    import flash.display.StageAlign;
```

continues

LISTING 5-1 *(continued)*

```
import flash.display.StageScaleMode;

public class SpriteLayoutApp extends Sprite
{
        private static const BLUE:int = 0x3399FF;
        private static const GREEN:int = 0x99CC00;
        private static const YELLOW:int = 0xFFCC00;
        private static const RED:int = 0xFF3333;

        private var a:Sprite;
        private var b:Sprite;
        private var c:Sprite;
        private var d:Sprite;

        public function SpriteLayoutApp()
        {
                super();

                stage.align = StageAlign.TOP_LEFT;
                stage.scaleMode = StageScaleMode.NO_SCALE;
        }
    }
}
```

3. Next add two protected functions called drawSprites() and drawRectangle(). For drawRectangle() define four parameters for the method. The first parameter should be id, a string representing the sprite object's id and name properties. The second should be width, an integer to represent the width of the sprite. The third parameter should be height, an integer to set the height of the sprite object, and then lastly color, also an integer to set the color of the sprite. Then in drawRectangle() create a new sprite object using the parameters defined, and add it to the application (Listing 5-2).

LISTING 5-2: Adding the drawSprite() and drawRectangle() function calls in SpriteLayoutApp.as

```
public function SpriteLayoutApp()
{
    super();

    stage.align = StageAlign.TOP_LEFT;
    stage.scaleMode = StageScaleMode.NO_SCALE;
}

protected function drawSprites():void {}

protected function drawRectangle(id:String, w:int, h:int, color:int):void
```

```
{
        var sprite:Sprite = new Sprite();
        sprite.name = id;
        sprite.graphics.beginFill(color);
        sprite.graphics.drawRect(0, 0, w, h);
        sprite.graphics.endFill();

        addChild(sprite);
}
```

4. In `drawSprites()` make four calls to `drawRectangle()`, one for each sprite, assigning a different color for each. Then in the constructor of `SpriteLayoutApp`, make a call to `drawSprites()` (Listing 5-3).

LISTING 5-3: Initializing sprites a, b, c, and d through the drawSprites() and drawRectangle() functions in SpriteLayoutApp.as

```
public function SpriteLayoutApp()
{
        super();

        stage.align = StageAlign.TOP_LEFT;
        stage.scaleMode = StageScaleMode.NO_SCALE;

        drawSprites();
}

protected function drawSprites():void
{
        drawRectangle("a", 1, 1, BLUE);
        drawRectangle("b", 1, 1, GREEN);
        drawRectangle("c", 1, 1, RED);
        drawRectangle("d", 1, 1, YELLOW);
}

protected function drawRectangle(id:String, w:int, h:int, color:int):void
{
        var sprite:Sprite = new Sprite();
        sprite.name = id;
        sprite.graphics.beginFill(color);
        sprite.graphics.drawRect(0, 0, w, h);
        sprite.graphics.endFill();

        addChild(sprite);
}
```

5. Next register the `Event.RESIZE` event with `stage`, and define the private function called `onResize()` as the event handler (Listing 5-4).

LISTING 5-4: Assigning Event.RESIZE to the event handler function onResize() in SpriteLayoutApp.as

```
public function SpriteLayoutApp()
{
        super();

        stage.align = StageAlign.TOP_LEFT;
        stage.scaleMode = StageScaleMode.NO_SCALE;
        stage.addEventListener(Event.RESIZE, onResize);

        drawSprites();
}

private function onResize(e:Event):void {}
```

6. In `onResize()` use a reference to the stage called `stageObj` to assign the `Stage` `.stageWidth` and the `Stage.stageHeight` properties from the `Event` object to two new functions, `sizeComponents()` and `layoutComponents()` (Listing 5-5).

LISTING 5-5: Supplying the stageWidth and stageHeight properties as arguments to the sizeComponents() and layoutComponents() functions via onResize() in SpriteLayoutApp.as

```
private function onResize(e:Event):void
{
        var w:int = Stage(e.target).stageWidth;
        var h:int = Stage(e.target).stageHeight;

        sizeComponents(w, h);
        layoutComponents(w, h);
}

private function sizeComponents(stageWidth:int, stageHeight:int):void {}

private function layoutComponents(stageWidth:int, stageHeight:int):void {}
```

7. Under the `onResize()` method add a new function called `getSprite()` to return one of the sprites based on its `id` property (Listing 5-6).

LISTING 5-6: Adding the getSprite() function to retrieve a sprite in SpriteLayoutApp.as

```
private function onResize(e:Event):void
{
        var w:int = Stage(e.target).stageWidth;
        var h:int = Stage(e.target).stageHeight;

        sizeComponents(w, h);
        layoutComponents(w, h);
}

public function getSprite(id:String):Sprite
{
        return this.getChildByName(id) as Sprite;
}
```

8.   In `sizeComponents()` set the width of sprites a and b to half the stage width. Then set the `height` property on both sprites to one third (1/3) of the full screen height (Listing 5-7).

LISTING 5-7: Setting the width and height of sprites a and b via the sizeComponents() function in SpriteLayoutApp.as

```
protected function sizeComponents(stageWidth:int, stageHeight:int):void
{
    a = this.getSprite("a");
    a.width = stageWidth/2;
    a.height = 1/3 * stageHeight;

    b = this.getSprite("b");
    b.width = stageWidth/2;
    b.height = 1/3 * stageHeight;
}
```

9.   In `layoutComponent()`, set the x and y coordinates of sprite a to 0. And then set the y position of sprite b to 0 and the x position to where sprite a ends. This should be calculated by retrieving the x and `width` properties of sprite a (Listing 5-8).

LISTING 5-8: Setting the x and y positions of sprites a and b via the layoutComponents() function in SpriteLayoutApp.as

```
protected function layoutComponents(stageWidth:int, stageHeight:int):void
{
    a = this.getSprite("a");
    a.x = 0;
    a.y = 0;

    b = this.getSprite("b");
    b.x = a.x + a.width;
    b.y = 0;
}
```

10.   If you run the application you should now see the two sprites adjacent to each other (Figure 5-5).

11.   Next, in `sizeComponents()`, set the `width` property on sprites c and d to be equal to the full width of the stage. Then for sprite d set the height equal to one-sixth of the stage height and exactly half the height of sprites a and b. Then for sprite c set the `height` property to be the remainder of the space available in view (Listing 5-9).

FIGURE 5-5: Sprites a and b in the portrait layout for SpriteLayoutApp

LISTING 5-9: Setting the width and height of sprites c and d via the sizeComponents() function in SpriteLayoutApp.as

```
protected function sizeComponents(stageWidth:int, stageHeight:int):void
{
        a = this.getSprite("a");
        a.width = stageWidth/2;
        a.height = 1/3 * stageHeight;

        b = this.getSprite("b");
        b.width = stageWidth/2;
        b.height = 1/3 * stageHeight;

        c = this.getSprite("c");
        c.width = stageWidth;
        c.height = stageHeight - (1/3 * stageHeight) - (1/6 * stageHeight);

        d = this.getSprite("d");
        d.width = stageWidth;
        d.height = 1/6 * stageHeight;
}
```

12. In `layoutComponents()` set the x property of sprites c and d to 0. Set the y property of sprite c to where sprite b ends. Then set the y property of sprite d to the full height of the stage, less the height of the sprite (Listing 5-10).

LISTING 5-10: Setting the x and y positions of sprites c and d via the layoutComponents() function in SpriteLayoutApp.as

```
protected function layoutComponents(stageWidth:int, stageHeight:int):void
{
        a = this.getSprite("a");
        a.x = 0;
        a.y = 0;

        b = this.getSprite("b");
        b.x = a.x + a.width;
        b.y = 0;

        c = this.getSprite("c");
        c.x = 0;
        c.y = b.y + b.height;

        d = this.getSprite("d");
        d.x = 0;
        d.y = stageHeight - d.height;
}
```

13. If you run the application you should now see each of the sprites arranged correctly as shown earlier in the Portrait view (Figure 5-6).

FIGURE 5-6: Sprites a, b, c, and d in the portrait layout for Sprite Layout App

Next take a look at how the code will change for a landscape mode.

14. In `sizeComponents()` wrap the current code in an `if` statement to ensure that the code executes when `stageHeight` is greater than `stageWidth` (Listing 5-11).

LISTING 5-11: Determining whether the stageWidth property is less or greater than the stageHeight property via the sizeComponents() function in SpriteLayoutApp.as

```
protected function sizeComponents(stageWidth:int, stageHeight:int):void
{
        if(stageWidth < stageHeight)
        {
                a = this.getSprite("a");
                a.width = stageWidth/2;
                a.height = 1/3 * stageHeight;

                b = this.getSprite("b");
                b.width = stageWidth/2;
                b.height = 1/3 * stageHeight;

                c = this.getSprite("c");
                c.width = stageWidth;
                c.height = stageHeight - (1/3 * stageHeight) - (1/6 * stageHeight);

                d = this.getSprite("d");
                d.width = stageWidth;
                d.height = 1/6 * stageHeight;

        } else if(stageWidth > stageHeight) {

        }
}
```

15. Next determine what happens when `stageWidth` is greater than `stageHeight`. Set the `width` property on sprites a, b, and c to equal half the width of the stage, and then for sprite d set the `width` to the full stage width. For sprite d set the `height` property to one-sixth of the full stage. Then for sprites a and b set the `height` property to equal half the stage height minus the `height` of sprite d. For sprite d set the height to equal one-sixth of the stage height. And then for sprite c set the `height` to be the remainder of the space available in view (Listing 5-12).

LISTING 5-12: Setting the width and height of sprites a, b, c, and d when the stageWidth property is greater than the stageHeight property via the sizeComponents() function in SpriteLayoutApp.as

```
protected function sizeComponents(stageWidth:int, stageHeight:int):void
{
        if(stageWidth < stageHeight)
        {
```

continues

LISTING 5-12 *(continued)*

```
                a = this.getSprite("a");
                a.width = stageWidth/2;
                a.height = 1/3 * stageHeight;

                b = this.getSprite("b");
                b.width = stageWidth/2;
                b.height = 1/3 * stageHeight;

                c = this.getSprite("c");
                c.width = stageWidth;
                c.height = stageHeight - (1/3 * stageHeight) - (1/6 * stageHeight);

                d = this.getSprite("d");
                d.width = stageWidth;
                d.height = 1/6 * stageHeight;

        } else if(stageWidth > stageHeight) {

                a = this.getSprite("a");
                a.width = stageWidth/2;
                a.height = stageHeight/2 - (1/6 * stageHeight)/2;

                b = this.getSprite("b");
                b.width = stageWidth/2;
                b.height = stageHeight/2 - (1/6 * stageHeight)/2;

                c = this.getSprite("c");
                c.width = stageWidth/2;
                c.height = stageHeight - (1/6 * stageHeight);

                d = this.getSprite("d");
                d.width = stageWidth;
                d.height = 1/6 * stageHeight;
        }
}
```

16. Similarly in `layoutComponents()` wrap the current code in an `if` statement to ensure that the code executes when `stageHeight` is greater than `stageWidth`. Then add the *else if* portion of the `if()` statement to determine what happens when `stageWidth` is greater than `stageHeight`. Here set the x property on sprites a, b, and d to 0. For sprite c set the x property to half the `stageWidth`. Then set the y property on sprites a and c to 0. Then for sprite b set the y property to where the height of sprite b ends. For sprite d set the y property to the full height of the stage, less the `height` of the sprite (Listing 5-13).

LISTING 5-13: Setting the x and y positions for sprites a, b, c, and d when the stageWidth property is greater than the stageHeight property via the layoutComponents() function in SpriteLayoutApp.as

```
protected function layoutComponents(stageWidth:int, stageHeight:int):void
{
    if(stageWidth < stageHeight)
    {
        a = this.getSprite("a");
        a.x = 0;
        a.y = 0;

        b = this.getSprite("b");
        b.x = a.x + a.width;
        b.y = 0;

        c = this.getSprite("c");
        c.x = 0;
        c.y = b.y + b.height;

        d = this.getSprite("d");
        d.x = 0;
        d.y = stageHeight - d.height;

    } else if(stageWidth > stageHeight) {

        a = this.getSprite("a");
        a.x = 0;
        a.y = 0;

        b = this.getSprite("b");
        b.x = 0
        b.y = a.y + a.height;

        c = this.getSprite("c");
        c.x = a.x + a.width;
        c.y = 0;

        d = this.getSprite("d");
        d.x = 0;
        d.y = stageHeight - d.height;
    }
}
```

17. Run the project once again. You will see the portrait layout when it launches in the adl window.

To see the landscape layout, use the adl menu and select Device ➪ Rotate Right (Figure 5-7).

The Landscape view should now be displayed (Figure 5-8).

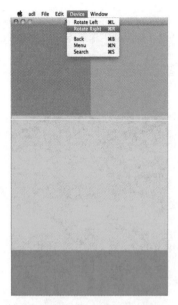

FIGURE 5-7: Using the adl menu to rotate the device in Sprite Layout App

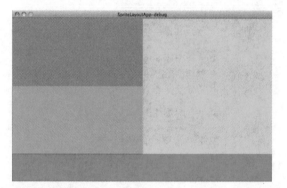

FIGURE 5-8: Sprites a, b, c, and d in the landscape layout for Sprite Layout App

There are a number of things going on in this project. First, to give an appreciation of the differences in layout, the app simply draws four sprites to the screen, then uses two functions to address resizing and aligning assets.

Resizing Assets

When the stage initializes, the resize event handler `onResize()` calls two functions, `sizeComponents()` followed by `layoutComponents()`. Each method is passed two arguments from the `Stage` object, `Stage.stageWidth` and `Stage.stageHeight`.

Both arguments are used to calculate the sizes of each of the sprites added to the view in `SpriteLayoutApp`.

Of course, the sizing of each sprite in this case is totally dependent on the design of the layout. For instance, both sprites a and b needed to occupy half the full width of the stage, and their heights are calculated to be a third of the height of the stage. Sprite c occupies the full stage width and calculates the vertical space left, taking into consideration the height of sprite d, which in turn occupies one-sixth of the full height of the stage.

When the screen is resized, all the measurements will be relative to the `Stage` object's `stageWidth` and `stageHeight` properties. And so on different screens with various pixel densities, the sprites will occupy the same space.

When creating Flex mobile applications, it is recommended that you use the `systemManager .screen.width` and `systemManager.screen.height` properties to retrieve the device's width and height, respectively, while an application is running. This method is employed when you build the Flex example later.

Aligning Assets

To align the sprites correctly a number of techniques have been employed.

First, sprite a is *absolutely* positioned. Because sprite a will always be in the top left-hand corner of the screen, its x and y properties are set to 0. Sprites b and c both apply *absolute* and *relative* positioning, as their positioning can be calculated by using the positions of other assets, in particular sprite a. So the position is relative with respect to setting the y properties, and absolute with respect to setting the x properties.

For sprite b, the y position is hard-coded to 0, while its x position is calculated based on the position and width of sprite a. For sprite c, the x position is hard-coded to 0, while its y position is calculated based on the height of sprite a.

Finally, for sprite d a slightly different approach was taken to calculate its y position. In the design for the layout the sprite is sitting at the very bottom of the stage. Thus, the y value for sprite d is calculated by subtracting the height of the actual sprite from the full stage height.

HANDLING DEVICE ORIENTATION

Next take a look at how you can receive notifications for an update in device orientation. These events are triggered when a user manually changes the orientation of a device, between landscape and portrait.

In the AIR Application Descriptor file, one of the settings found in the `<initialWindow>` node is the `<autoOrients>` property, as shown in the following snippet:

```
<autoOrients>true</autoOrients>
```

This tells the mobile application whether to allow auto orientation. Here it is set to `true`, and so the application's content can rotate. When this is set to `false`, the application will be prevented from rotating its content, and, in turn, will stay in its initial aspect ratio. So, if an application is initialized with the stage width set less than the stage height, that is, portrait, it will remain like this even when a user rotates the device.

When the `<autoOrient>` setting is set to `true`, the user can rotate a device, which will have an impact on the application's design. Retrieving the device's width and height, you have the best option for laying out items precisely, especially when the stage resizes.

Some applications may also need to know what the device's screen orientation is to determine how the application needs to lay out the particular assets it contains.

Two classes must be used to detect device orientation changes: `StageOrientation` and `StageOrientationEvent`.

Using the StageOrientation Class

The StageOrientation class has several constants that contain possible values that describe a device's orientation. The following list details the possible options:

➤ StageOrientation.DEFAULT: The default stage orientation.

➤ StageOrientation.ROTATED_LEFT: The stage has been rotated left.

➤ StageOrientation.ROTATED_RIGHT: The stage has been rotated right.

➤ StageOrientation.UNKNOWN: An unknown stage orientation.

➤ StageOrientation.UPSIDE_DOWN: The stage has been turned upside down.

The device's orientation can be retrieved from the Stage object's read-only property deviceOrientation, and when an application launches, this will be set to StageOrientation .DEFAULT.

Using the StageOrientationEvent Class

The StageOrientationEvent class has two event types:

➤ StageOrientationEvent.ORIENTATION_CHANGE: The stage orientation has changed.

➤ StageOrientationEVENT.ORIENTATION_CHANGING: The stage is in the process of changing orientation.

To detect when the deviceOrientation property is updated, you need to register an event listener for the StageOrientationEvent.ORIENTATION_CHANGE event type on the Stage object.

TRY IT OUT Handling Device Orientation Changes

The following steps will guide you through how to display device orientation changes in the Sprite Layout App.

1. Above the constructor for SpriteLayoutApp.as, add a new private variable called spriteOrientation of TextField type (Listing 5-14).

Available for download on Wrox.com

LISTING 5-14: Adding a TextField component to display the stage orientation in SpriteLayoutApp.as

```
private static const BLUE:int = 0x3399FF;
private static const GREEN:int = 0x99CC00;
private static const YELLOW:int = 0xFFCC00;
private static const RED:int = 0xFF3333;

private var a:Sprite;
private var b:Sprite;
private var c:Sprite;
private var d:Sprite;

private var stageOrientation:TextField;
```

2. Under `drawSprites()` add a protected function called `addTxt()`, to initialize `stageOrientation`. Assign it a new `TextFormat` and then add it to the stage (Listing 5-15).

LISTING 5-15: Adding the addTxt() method in SpriteLayoutApp.as

```
protected function drawSprites():void
{
        drawRectangle("a", 1, 1, BLUE);
        drawRectangle("b", 1, 1, GREEN);
        drawRectangle("c", 1, 1, RED);
        drawRectangle("d", 1, 1, YELLOW);
}

protected function addTxt():void
{
        var tF:TextFormat = new TextFormat();

        stageOrientation = new TextField();
        stageOrientation.setTextFormat(tF);
        stageOrientation.text = "";

        addChild(stageOrientation);
}
```

3. In the constructor for `SpriteLayoutApp.as` following the `drawSprites()`, make a call to `addTxt()` (Listing 5-16).

LISTING 5-16: Calling addTxt() via the SpriteLayoutApp class constructor in SpriteLayoutApp.as

```
public function SpriteLayoutApp()
{
        super();

        stage.align = StageAlign.TOP_LEFT;
        stage.scaleMode = StageScaleMode.NO_SCALE;
        stage.addEventListener(Event.RESIZE, onResize);

        drawSprites();
        addTxt();
}
```

4. Next add an event listener for the `StageOrientationEvent.ORIENTATION_CHANGE` event type, and assign it to a new private function called `onOrientationChange()`. Then in `onOrientationChange()`, assign the `StageOrientationEvent` object's `deviceOrientation` property to the `text` property on `stageOrientation` (Listing 5-17).

LISTING 5-17: Assigning StageOrientationEvent.ORIENTATION_CHANGE to the event handler function onOrientationChange() in SpriteLayoutApp.as

```
public function SpriteLayoutApp()
{
        super();

        stage.align = StageAlign.TOP_LEFT;
        stage.scaleMode = StageScaleMode.NO_SCALE;
        stage.addEventListener(Event.RESIZE, onResize);
        stage.addEventListener( StageOrientationEvent.ORIENTATION_CHANGE,
                                onOrientationChange );

        drawSprites();
        addTxt();
}

private function onOrientationChange(e:StageOrientationEvent):void
{
        stageOrientation.text = e.target.deviceOrientation;
}
```

5. Run the project using either a *device* or *desktop* run configuration. When the Sprite Layout App is initialized you see each of the sprites arranged as before.

When you use a device run configuration, rotate the device and you will see the deviceOrientation property displayed.

When you use a desktop run configuration you can use the adl menu to simulate rotating the device physically. Select Device ➪ Rotate Left to rotate the device to the left, or select Device ➪ Rotate Right to rotate the device to the right.

The result of rotating the device right is shown in Figure 5-9.

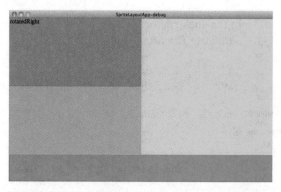

FIGURE 5-9: The deviceOrientation property being displayed in the landscape layout design for Sprite Layout App

USING LAYOUTS IN FLEX

As mentioned in Chapter 1, the Flex framework provides a lot of functionality when it comes to laying out components and resizing elements in an application.

In this section you'll take a look at applying the design of the layout in portrait and landscape using elements of the Flex framework, and create a second project in Flash Builder called Sprite Layout Flex App.

The layout created in the Sprite Layout App project can quite easily be replicated using a combination of the MXML declarations, containers, and components, including <s:layout>, <s:VerticalLayout>, <s:HorizontalLayout>, <s:HGroup>, <s:VGroup>, and <s:Group>.

Aligning Items in Group Containers

As mentioned earlier, each of the group containers <s:Group>, <s:HGroup>, and <s:VGroup> allows nesting of visual assets within an application and effectively designating the flow of items.

Nesting items in a <s:HGroup> container allows items to be aligned horizontally, and in the following snippet you will see two sprites, represented by the <s:Graphic> tags, horizontally aligned:

```
<s:HGroup>

    <s:Graphic>
        <s:Rect width="150" height="150">
            <s:fill>
                <s:solidColor color="0x3399FF">
            </s:fill>
        </s:Rect>
    </s:Graphic>

    <s:Graphic>
        <s:Rect width="150" height="150">
            <s:fill>
                <s:solidColor color="0x99CC00">
            </s:fill>
        </s:Rect>
    </s:Graphic>

</s:HGroup>
```

Each sprite is rendered with a width and height of 150 pixels. The <s:Graphic> element nests a series of elements. The first <s:Rect> draws a rectangle and is the equivalent of the Graphics .drawRectangle() method used for rendering the sprites earlier. Within the <s:Rect> a number of style properties can be defined; here the <s:fill> declaration nests a <s:solidColor>, the color of the sprite.

When nesting items in a <s:VGroup> container you can place items vertically, and in the following snippet you'll see an example of the same two sprites, each with a different color assigned, aligned vertically:

```
<s:VGroup>

    <s:Graphic>
        <s:Rect width="150" height="150">
            <s:fill>
                <s:solidColor color="0x3399FF">
            </s:fill>
```

```
            </s:Rect>
        </s:Graphic>

        <s:Graphic>
            <s:Rect width="150" height="150">
                <s:fill>
                    <s:solidColor color="0x99CC00">
                </s:fill>
            </s:Rect>
        </s:Graphic>

    </s:VGroup>
```

A number of attributes in the `<s:HGroup>` and `<s:VGroup>` containers can affect the layout rendering, including:

➤ `direction`: Sets the directional flow of items in a container

➤ `gap`: Assigns spacing between each item

➤ `paddingBottom`: Assigns padding to the bottom of the container

➤ `paddingLeft`: Assigns padding to the left of the container

➤ `paddingRight`: Assigns padding to the right of the container

➤ `paddingTop`: Assigns padding to the top of the container

➤ `verticalAlign`: Vertically aligns items within the container

➤ `horizontalAlign`: Horizontally aligns items within the container.

Setting the `direction` property allows you to define how the items in the containers should be rendered. Specifying `ltr` means that the container will render items from left to right; specifying `rtl` means items will be rendered from right to left. The following snippet demonstrates reversing the default flow of items in the `<s:HGroup>` container, which by default renders items from left to right:

```
<s:HGroup direction="rtl">

    <s:Graphic>
        <s:Rect width="150" height="150">
            <s:fill>
                <s:solidColor color="0x3399FF">
            </s:fill>
        </s:Rect>
    </s:Graphic>

    <s:Graphic>
        <s:Rect width="150" height="150">
            <s:fill>
                <s:solidColor color="0x99CC00">
            </s:fill>
```

```
            </s:Rect>
        </s:Graphic>

    </s:HGroup>
```

Setting the gap property on the container allows you to set the spacing between each item. This is a pixel measurement. The gap property represents the vertical gap set between items in a <s:VGroup> container, and the horizontal gap for items in a <s:HGroup> container.

In the following snippet the vertical gap for <s:VGroup> is set to 10 pixels:

```
<s:VGroup gap="10">

    <s:Graphic>
        <s:Rect width="150" height="150">
            <s:fill>
                <s:solidColor color="0x3399FF">
            </s:fill>
        </s:Rect>
    </s:Graphic>

    <s:Graphic>
        <s:Rect width="150" height="150">
            <s:fill>
                <s:solidColor color="0x99CC00">
            </s:fill>
        </s:Rect>
    </s:Graphic>

</s:VGroup>
```

Applying the <s:HGroup> and <s:VGroup> Containers in the Portrait Layout of Sprite Layout App

Returning to the Sprite Layout App, remember that both sprites a and b in the Portrait view need to be horizontally aligned, and so they can be placed in a <s:HGroup> container, as shown in the following snippet:

```
<s:HGroup gap="10">

    <s:Graphic>
        <s:Rect id="a" width="150" height="150">
            <s:fill>
                <s:solidColor color="0x3399FF">
            </s:fill>
        </s:Rect>
    </s:Graphic>

    <s:Graphic>
        <s:Rect id="b" width="150" height="150">
            <s:fill>
                <s:solidColor color="0x99CC00">
```

```
                        </s:fill>
                    </s:Rect>
            </s:Graphic>

    </s:HGroup>
```

Because sprite c needs to be placed underneath sprites a and b, these items can all be placed in a `<s:VGroup>` container, nesting the `<s:HGroup>` containing sprites a and b, as shown in the following snippet:

```
<s:VGroup gap="10">

    <s:HGroup gap="10">

            <s:Graphic>
                <s:Rect id="a" width="150" height="150">
                    <s:fill>
                            <s:solidColor color="0x3399FF">
                    </s:fill>
                </s:Rect>
            </s:Graphic>

            <s:Graphic>
                <s:Rect id="b" width="150" height="150">
                    <s:fill>
                            <s:solidColor color="0x99CC00">
                    </s:fill>
                </s:Rect>
            </s:Graphic>

    </s:HGroup>

    <s:Graphic>
        <s:Rect id="c" width="150" height="150">
            <s:fill>
                    <s:solidColor color="0xFFCC00">
            </s:fill>
        </s:Rect>
    </s:Graphic>

</s:VGroup>
```

Both sprites c and d also are vertically aligned in the Portrait view, and so they can be aligned in the same `<s:VGroup>` container:

```
<s:VGroup gap="10">

    <s:HGroup gap="10">

            <s:Graphic>
                <s:Rect id="a" width="150" height="150">
                    <s:fill>
                            <s:solidColor color="0x3399FF">
                    </s:fill>
```

```
            </s:Rect>
        </s:Graphic>

        <s:Graphic>
            <s:Rect id="b" width="150" height="150">
                <s:fill>
                        <s:solidColor color="0x99CC00">
                </s:fill>
            </s:Rect>
        </s:Graphic>

    </s:HGroup>

    <s:Graphic>
        <s:Rect id="c" width="150" height="150">
            <s:fill>
                    <s:solidColor color="0xFFCC00">
            </s:fill>
        </s:Rect>
    </s:Graphic>

    <s:Graphic>
        <s:Rect id="d" width="150" height="150">
            <s:fill>
                    <s:solidColor color="0xFF3333">
            </s:fill>
        </s:Rect>
    </s:Graphic>

</s:VGroup>
```

The main problem with nesting the items in `<s:HGroup>` and `<s:VGroup>` containers is that if and when the layout needs to change, whether it is through resizing or changes in device orientation, each of the items will be aligned incorrectly. When using the group containers there's no easy way to change the alignment at run time.

For instance sprites a and b, which are nested in the `<s:HGroup>`, will not be vertically aligned when the orientation changes to the Landscape view. Also, sprite c will remain nested in the `<s:VGroup>` and so will not be horizontally aligned in the Landscape view. For this you will need to utilize the `<s:layout>` declaration.

Using Layout Declarations within Containers

An alternative approach to laying out items in a view is to use `<s:Group>` containers and specify a `<s:layout>` declaration.

The following snippet demonstrates how you can use the `<s:HorizontalLayout>` declaration to specify that elements should be arranged horizontally, without using a `<s:HGroup>` container:

```
<s:Group>

    <s:layout>
        <s:HorizontalLayout/>
```

```
        </s:layout>

        <s:Graphic>
            <s:Rect width="150" height="150">
                <s:fill>
                    <s:solidColor color="0x3399FF">
                </s:fill>
            </s:Rect>
        </s:Graphic>

        <s:Graphic>
            <s:Rect width="150" height="150">
                <s:fill>
                    <s:solidColor color="0x99CC00">
                </s:fill>
            </s:Rect>
        </s:Graphic>

    </s:Group>
```

In the following snippet, the `<s:VerticalLayout>` declaration is being applied to a `<s:Group>` container:

```
<s:Group>

    <s:layout>
        <s:VerticalLayout/>
    </s:layout>

    <s:Graphic>
        <s:Rect width="150" height="150">
            <s:fill>
                <s:solidColor color="0x3399FF">
            </s:fill>
        </s:Rect>
    </s:Graphic>

    <s:Graphic>
        <s:Rect width="150" height="150">
            <s:fill>
                <s:solidColor color="0x99CC00">
            </s:fill>
        </s:Rect>
    </s:Graphic>

</s:Group>
```

Using States to Change the Layout of a Container at Run Time

Different layouts can be applied in applications with the help of states, and using the `<s:State>` declaration. Consider the portrait and Landscape views of Sprite Layout App. To define these as individual states you specify them in the `<fx:Declarations>` block of a view, as shown in the following snippet:

```
<fx:Declarations>
      <s:State name="portrait">
      <s:State name="landscape">
</fx:Declarations>
```

In the context of layouts, the <s:State> declaration allows you to apply a state for any particular <s:layout> declaration in a view. In the following snippet the items nested in the <s:Group> container will be vertically aligned when the portrait state is active in the view, but horizontally aligned when the landscape state is active:

```
<s:Group>

      <s:layout.portrait>
            <s:VerticalLayout/>
      </s:layout.portrait>

      <s:layout.landscape>
            <s:HorizontalLayout/>
      </s:layout.landscape>

      <s:Graphic>
            <s:Rect width="150" height="150">
                  <s:fill>
                        <s:solidColor color="0x3399FF">
                  </s:fill>
            </s:Rect>
      </s:Graphic>

      <s:Graphic>
            <s:Rect width="150" height="150">
                  <s:fill>
                        <s:solidColor color="0x99CC00">
                  </s:fill>
            </s:Rect>
      </s:Graphic>

</s:Group>
```

Notice here that in order to specify the state in which a layout should be applied, the state name, preceded by a period (.), is added after the layout. Thus, referring to the preceding code snippet, <s:layout.portrait> allows rendering the <s:VerticalLayout> container in the portrait state, and <s:layout.landscape> allows rendering the <s:HorizontalLayout> in the landscape state.

To set the state of the application you need to set the currentState property of the view. In the following snippet you see that the landscape state is set for the application:

```
currentState = "landscape";
```

In the next section you'll take a look at creating the Sprite Layout Flex App, which demonstrates the use of states in this context.

TRY IT OUT   Using Group Containers to Create the Sprite Layout Flex App

The following steps will guide you through re-creating the Sprite Layout App, this time using Flex and the Flash Debug Perspective. First take a look at utilizing breakpoints in the Source view:

1. In Flash Builder create a new Flex Mobile project and call it `SpriteLayoutFlexApp` (Figure 5-10).

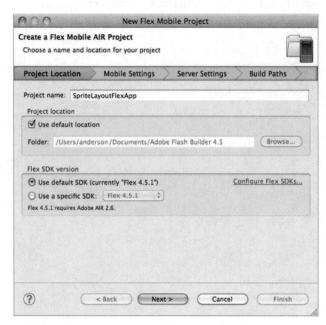

FIGURE 5-10: Defining the Sprite Layout Flex App project in Flash Builder

2. In `SpriteLayoutFlexAppHome.mxml`, set the `actionBarVisible` property of the view to `false` and the `tabBarVisible` property to `false`. Then assign the `onCreationComplete()` stub to the `creationComplete` property. Also define each of the colors for the sprites (Listing 5-18).

Available for download on Wrox.com

LISTING 5-18: Setting the actionBarVisible and tabBarVisible properties, defining variables for the colors in SpriteLayoutFlexAppHome.mxml

```xml
<?xml version="1.0" encoding="utf-8"?>
<s:View xmlns:fx="http://ns.adobe.com/mxml/2009"
        xmlns:s="library://ns.adobe.com/flex/spark"
        actionBarVisible="false"
        tabBarVisible="false"
```

```
        creationComplete="onCreationComplete()"
        title="Home">

    <fx:Script>
        <![CDATA[

                private static const BLUE:int = 0x3399FF;

                private static const GREEN:int = 0x99CC00;

                private static const YELLOW:int = 0xFFCC00;

                private static const RED:int = 0xFF3333;

                protected function onCreationComplete():void {}

        ]]>
    </fx:Script>
</s:View>
```

3. In `onCreationComplete()` add an event listener for the `Event.ADDED_TO_STAGE` event, assigning `onAddedToStage()` as the event handler. Then in `onAddedToStage()` assign the `StageOrientationEvent.ORIENTATION_CHANGE` event to the stage, with the method stub `onOrientationChange()` as the event handler (Listing 5-19).

LISTING 5-19: Adding event handlers for the ADDED_TO_STAGE and the ORIENTATION_CHANGE events in SpriteLayoutFlexAppHome.mxml

```
protected function onCreationComplete():void
{
    this.addEventListener(Event.ADDED_TO_STAGE, onAddedToStage);
}

private function onAddedToStage(e:Event):void
{
    e.target.stage.addEventListener( StageOrientationEvent.ORIENTATION_CHANGE,
                                    onOrientationChange );
}

private function onOrientationChange(e:StageOrientationEvent):void {}
```

4. Following the closing `<fx:Script>` tag, add a `<s:Group>` container with the two `<s:Rect>` sprites for a and b (Listing 5-20).

LISTING 5-20: Defining `<s:Rect>` a and b components and adding them to a `<s: Group>` container in SpriteLayoutFlexAppHome.mxml

```
<fx:Script>
    <![CDATA[
```

continues

LISTING 5-20 *(continued)*

```
                    private static const BLUE:int = 0x3399FF;

                    private static const GREEN:int = 0x99CC00;

                    private static const YELLOW:int = 0xFFCC00;

                    private static const RED:int = 0xFF3333;

                    private function onCreationComplete():void {}

          ]]>
    </fx:Script>

    <s:Group>

        <s:Graphic>
            <s:Rect id="a">
                    <s:fill>
                            <s:solidColor color="{BLUE}">
                    </s:fill>
            </s:Rect>
        </s:Graphic>

        <s:Graphic>
            <s:Rect id="b">
                    <s:fill>
                            <s:solidColor color="{GREEN}">
                    </s:fill>
            </s:Rect>
        </s:Graphic>

    </s:Group>
```

5. Add the <s:Rect> for sprite c to the view and nest it within a <s:Group> container (Listing 5-21).

LISTING 5-21: Defining <s:Rect> c and adding it to a <s:Group> container in SpriteLaypoutFlexAppHome.mxml

```
<s:Group>

    <s:Group>

        <s:Graphic>
            <s:Rect id="a">
                    <s:fill>
                            <s:solidColor color="{BLUE}">
                    </s:fill>
            </s:Rect>
```

```
            </s:Graphic>

            <s:Graphic>
                <s:Rect id="b">
                    <s:fill>
                        <s:solidColor color="{GREEN}">
                    </s:fill>
                </s:Rect>
            </s:Graphic>

        </s:Group>

        <s:Graphic>
            <s:Rect id="c">
                <s:fill>
                    <s:solidColor color="{YELLOW}">
                </s:fill>
            </s:Rect>
        </s:Graphic>

    </s:Group>
```

6. Add the `<s:Rect>` for sprite d to the view and nest it within a `<s:Group>` container (Listing 5-22).

Available for download on Wrox.com

LISTING 5-22: Defining <s:Rect> d and adding it to a <s:Group> container in SpriteLayoutFlexAppHome.mxml

```
<s:Group>

    <s:Group>

        <s:Group>

            <s:Graphic>
                <s:Rect id="a">
                    <s:fill>
                        <s:solidColor color="{BLUE}">
                    </s:fill>
                </s:Rect>
            </s:Graphic>

            <s:Graphic>
                <s:Rect id="b">
                    <s:fill>
                        <s:solidColor color="{GREEN}">
                    </s:fill>
                </s:Rect>
            </s:Graphic>

        </s:Group>

        <s:Graphic>
```

continues

LISTING 5-22 *(continued)*

```
                        <s:Rect id="c">
                                <s:fill>
                                        <s:solidColor color="{YELLOW}">
                                </s:fill>
                        </s:Rect>
                </s:Graphic>

        </s:Group>

        <s:Graphic>
                <s:Rect id="d">
                        <s:fill>
                                <s:solidColor color="{RED}">
                        </s:fill>
                </s:Rect>
        </s:Graphic>

    </s:Group>
```

7. Underneath each opening `<s:Group>` tag, add a `<s:layout>` declaration with a nesting `<s:VerticalLyout>`. Set the gap property on the `<s:VerticalLayout>` to 0 (Listing 5-23).

LISTING 5-23: Adding `<s:layout>` declarations to the view in SpriteLayoutFlexAppHome.mxml

```
<s:Group>

        <s:layout>
                <s:VerticalLayout gap="0"/>
        </s:layout>

        <s:Group>

                <s:layout>
                        <s:VerticalLayout gap="0"/>
                </s:layout>

                <s:Group>

                        <s:layout>
                                <s:VerticalLayout gap="0"/>
                        </s:layout>

                        <s:Graphic>
                                <s:Rect id="a">
                                        <s:fill>
                                                <s:solidColor color="{BLUE}">
                                        </s:fill>
                                </s:Rect>
```

```
                            </s:Graphic>

                            <s:Graphic>
                                    <s:Rect id="b">
                                            <s:fill>
                                                    <s:solidColor color="{GREEN}">
                                            </s:fill>
                                    </s:Rect>
                            </s:Graphic>

                    </s:Group>

                    <s:Graphic>
                            <s:Rect id="c">
                                    <s:fill>
                                            <s:solidColor color="{YELLOW}">
                                    </s:fill>
                            </s:Rect>
                    </s:Graphic>

            </s:Group>

            <s:Graphic>
                    <s:Rect id="d">
                            <s:fill>
                                    <s:solidColor color="{RED}">
                            </s:fill>
                    </s:Rect>
            </s:Graphic>

    </s:Group>
```

8. Next add two `<s:State>` declarations to the view within the `<fx:Declarations>` blocks called portrait and landscape (Listing 5-24).

LISTING 5-24: Defining the portrait and landscape states for the view in SpriteLayoutFlexAppHome.mxml

```xml
<?xml version="1.0" encoding="utf-8"?>
<s:View xmlns:fx="http://ns.adobe.com/mxml/2009"
        xmlns:s="library://ns.adobe.com/flex/spark"
        actionBarVisible="false"
        tabBarVisible="false"
        creationComplete="onCreationComplete()"
        title="Home">

    <fx:Declarations>
            <s:State name="portrait"/>
            <s:State name="landscape"/>
    </fx:Declarations>
```

9. For each of the `<s:layout>` definitions specify the `portrait` state, updating the MXML tags to `<s:layout.landscape>` (Listing 5-25).

LISTING 5-25: Updating the `<s:layout>` declaration in SpriteLayoutFlexAppHome.mxml

```
<s:Group>

    <s:layout.portrait>
        <s:VerticalLayout gap="0"/>
    </s:layout.portrait>

    <s:Group>

        <s:layout.portrait>
            <s:VerticalLayout gap="0"/>
        </s:layout.portrait>

        <s:Group>

            <s:layout.portrait>
                <s:VerticalLayout gap="0"/>
            </s:layout.portrait>

            <s:Graphic>
                <s:Rect id="a">
                    <s:fill>
                        <s:solidColor color="{BLUE}">
                    </s:fill>
                </s:Rect>
            </s:Graphic>
```

10. Copy the `sizeComponents()` function that was completed in Listing 5-12, the earlier project, into `SpriteLayoutFlexAppHome.mxml`. You will need to remove each of the `getSprite()` calls (Listing 5-26).

LISTING 5-26: Adding the sizeComponents() method in SpriteLayoutFlexAppHome.mxml

```
protected function sizeComponents(stageWidth:int, stageHeight:int):void
{
    if(stageWidth < stageHeight)
    {
        a.width = stageWidth/2;
        a.height = 1/3 * stageHeight;

        b.width = stageWidth/2;
        b.height = 1/3 * stageHeight;

        c.width = stageWidth;
```

```
            c.height = stageHeight - (1/3 * stageHeight) - (1/6 * stageHeight);

            d.width = stageWidth;
            d.height = 1/6 * stageHeight;

    } else if(stageWidth > stageHeight) {

            a.width = stageWidth/2;
            a.height = stageHeight/2 - (1/6 * stageHeight)/2;

            b.width = stageWidth/2;
            b.height = stageHeight/2 - (1/6 * stageHeight)/2;

            c.width = stageWidth/2;
            c.height = stageHeight - (1/6 * stageHeight);

            d.width = stageWidth;
            d.height = 1/6 * stageHeight;
    }
}
```

11. In the `onAddedToStage()` and `onOrientationChange()` methods, make a call to `sizeComponents()`, supplying the `systemManager.screen.width` and `systemManager.screen.height` properties as arguments (Listing 5-27).

LISTING 5-27: Calling the sizeComponents() method from within onAddedToStage() and onOrientationChange() in SpriteLayoutFlexAppHome.mxml

```
private function onAddedToStage(e:Event):void
{
    e.target.stage.addEventListener( StageOrientationEvent.ORIENTATION_CHANGE,
                                     onOrientationChange );

    sizeComponents(systemManager.screen.width, systemManager.screen.height);
}

private function onOrientationChange(e:StageOrientationEvent):void
{
    sizeComponents(systemManager.screen.width, systemManager.screen.height);
}
```

12. Next add three more `<s:layout>` declarations to the view for when the application state changes to landscape. Underneath each of the existing `<s:layout.portrait>` declarations, add a `<s:layout.landscape>` declaration. In the outermost `<s:Group>` container, the layout should be defined as a `<s:VerticalLayout>`. The other two declarations should be `<s:HorizontalLayout>`. Again set the `gap` property to `0` (Listing 5-28).

LISTING 5-28: Adding <s:layout.landscape> layout declarations in
SpriteLayoutFlexAppHome.mxml

```
<s:Group>

        <s:layout.portrait>
            <s:VerticalLayout gap="0"/>
        </s:layout.portrait>

        <s:layout.landscape>
            <s:VerticalLayout gap="0"/>
        </s:layout.landscape>

    <s:Group>

            <s:layout.portrait>
                <s:VerticalLayout gap="0"/>
            </s:layout.portrait>

            <s:layout.landscape>
                <s:HorizontalLayout gap="0"/>
            </s:layout.landscape>

        <s:Group>

                <s:layout.portrait>
                    <s:VerticalLayout gap="0"/>
                </s:layout.portrait>

                <s:layout.landscape>
                    <s:HorizontalLayout gap="0"/>
                </s:layout.landscape>

                <s:Graphic>
                    <s:Rect id="a">
                        <s:fill>
                            <s:solidColor color="{BLUE}">
                        </s:fill>
                    </s:Rect>
                </s:Graphic>

                <s:Graphic>
                    <s:Rect id="b">
                        <s:fill>
                            <s:solidColor color="{GREEN}">
                        </s:fill>
                    </s:Rect>
                </s:Graphic>

        </s:Group>
```

13. Last, set the `currentState` property of the view to `portrait` when the `stageWidth` is less than the `stageHeight`, and set it to landscape when the `stageWidth` is more than the `stageHeight` (Listing 5-29).

> **LISTING 5-29: Setting the currentState property on the view via the sizeComponents() method in SpriteLayoutFlexAppHome.mxml**

```
protected function sizeComponents(stageWidth:int, stageHeight:int):void
{
    if(stageWidth < stageHeight)
    {
        currentState = "portrait";

        a.width = stageWidth/2;
        a.height = 1/3 * stageHeight;

        b.width = stageWidth/2;
        b.height = 1/3 * stageHeight;

        c.width = stageWidth;
        c.height = stageHeight - (1/3 * stageHeight) - (1/6 * stageHeight);

        d.width = stageWidth;
        d.height = 1/6 * stageHeight;

    } else if(stageWidth > stageHeight) {

        currentState = "landscape";

        a.width = stageWidth/2;
        a.height = stageHeight/2 - (1/6 * stageHeight)/2;

        b.width = stageWidth/2;
        b.height = stageHeight/2 - (1/6 * stageHeight)/2;

        c.width = stageWidth/2;
        c.height = stageHeight - (1/6 * stageHeight);

        d.width = stageWidth;
        d.height = 1/6 * stageHeight;
    }
}
```

14. Run the Sprite Layout Flex App using the desktop run configuration.

You should see the Portrait view (Figure 5-11) and Landscape view (Figure 5-12) exactly as defined in the design of the application.

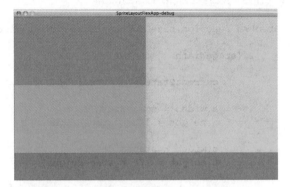

FIGURE 5-11: Sprites a, b, c, and d in the portrait layout for Sprite Layout Flex App

FIGURE 5-12: Sprites a, b, c, and d in the landscape layout for Sprite Layout Flex App

The main benefit to using the state approach with the `<s:layout>` declaration and the `<s:Group>` containers is that less ActionScript code is required to make the changes to the arrangement of items.

You can also visually see what items should be visible and in which state when you view the States view in the Source view of the Flash Perspective in Flash Builder. In Figure 5-13 you will see the default Source view, which displays the code for all states.

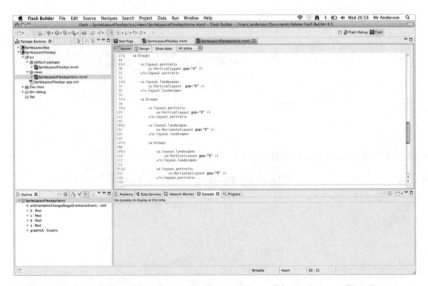

FIGURE 5-13: Displaying all states in the Source view of Sprite Layout Flex App

In Figure 5-14 you will see the Portrait view source, which displays only the MXML that is applicable to the Portrait view.

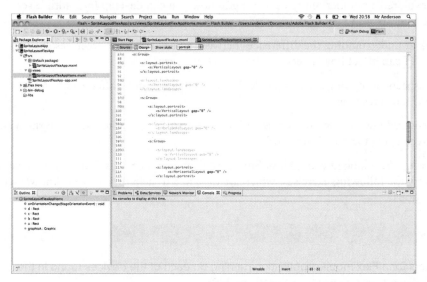

FIGURE 5-14: Displaying the portrait state in the Source view of Sprite Layout Flex App

Lastly in Figure 5-15 you will see the Landscape Source view, which displays only the MXML that is applicable to the application when the landscape state is active.

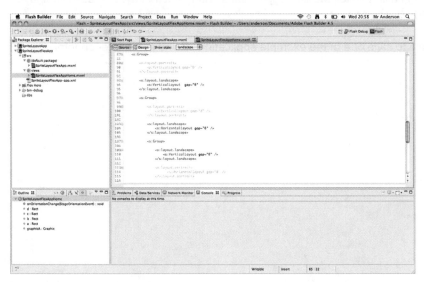

FIGURE 5-15: Displaying the landscape state in the Source view of Sprite Layout Flex App

All in all, states provide a neat feature in the Flash Builder IDE to allow you to develop for multiple screen sizes without the need to provide excessive code.

SUMMARY

In this chapter you explored a number of topics relating to how you can develop for multiple screen sizes using both ActionScript and Flex.

First you took a look at understanding the differences between screen size and screen resolution, and how the screen DPI can affect how assets are drawn to the screen.

You also examined aspects of the stage and in particular how content can be affected by changes in device orientation and stage resizing.

Finally the chapter covered how to combine states with layouts to arrange sprites based on the width and height of the screen using the Flex framework.

In the next chapter you take a look at using Flash Builder to debug applications. Before you move on to the next chapter, try the following exercises, which are designed to help further your knowledge of debugging applications.

EXERCISES

1. List the scale factors for a Flex mobile application running on each of the devices found in the Flash Builder preferences, using `applicationDPI` of 240.

2. In an ActionScript Mobile Project, create a new layout for a project and implement it using sprites.

3. Replicate your design using a Flex Mobile Project, substituting each of the sprites in your layout for a Flex-based MXML component.

4. Use the `@media` rule to style one of the example applications found in the later chapters.

▶ WHAT YOU LEARNED IN THIS CHAPTER

TOPIC	KEY CONCEPT
Using the stage	Use `StageScaleMode.NO_SCALE` and `StageAlign.TOP_LEFT` to define the scale mode and alignment of content in the mobile application. Use `Stage.stageWidth` and `Stage.stageHeight` to retrieve the width and height of the device's screen in pixels.
Utilizing Application DPI	Use the `applicationDPI` property to automatically scale an application, using one of three DPI Classification constants: `160`, `240`, or `320`.
Setting styles based on Application DPI	Use the `@media` rule, `application-dpi`, and `os-platform` properties to set styles based on a device's DPI. Use `AND` for Android, `IOS` for Apple iOS, and `QNX` for BlackBerry PlayBook, when styling against mobile platforms.
Utilizing capabilities	Use `Capabilities.ScreenDPI` to retrieve the number of dots per inch available across multiple devices.
Detecting stage resize	Use `StateOrientationEvent.CHANGE` to detect when the stage has resized.
Using application states	Define states for a view using the `<s:State name="STATE_NAME">` within the `<fx:Declarations>`, where `STATE_NAME` is the name of the state being defined.
Defining states on layouts	Use `<s:layout.STATE_NAME>` to define the state of a `<s:layout>` declaration.

Debugging Applications

WHAT YOU WILL LEARN IN THIS CHAPTER:

➤ Setting breakpoints in source code and using the Breakpoints panel

➤ Using the Flash Debug Perspective in Flash Builder

➤ Utilizing the Variables panel

➤ Global error handling

➤ Handling uncaught errors

➤ Using Try...Catch statements

➤ Stepping through source code

In this chapter you'll take a closer look at using Flash Builder to debug applications using the Flash Debug Perspective.

Flash Builder offers debugging capabilities that allow you to find bugs within your application. The Debug panel allows you to stop and start the mobile application to find problems, or to examine or substitute values for variables.

This chapter covers example code that intentionally introduces a bug from the outset. You then go through a series of tools and techniques to identify and fix the issue using the Debug Perspective in Flash Builder.

SETTING BREAKPOINTS

In this section you create the Debugging App project in Flash Builder and take a look at setting breakpoints for specific lines in source code.

Setting Breakpoints

The following steps will guide you through using the Flash Debug Perspective. First take a look at utilizing breakpoints in the Source view.

1. In Flash Builder create a new Flex Mobile project and call it Debugging App (Figure 6-1).

FIGURE 6-1: New Flex Mobile Project panel for the Debugging App in Flash Builder

2. In `DebuggingAppHome.mxml`, set the `title` property of the view to `Debugging App`. Add a `<s:VGroup>` container with the `paddingLeft`, `paddingRight`, and `paddingTop` properties set to 20. Within the container add a `<s:Label>` and `<s:Button>` component to the view, setting the `id` property on the `<s:Label>` component to `testLabel`, and the `id` property on the `<s:Button>` component to `testButton`. Also set the `label` property on the `<s:Button>` component to `Test onClick()` (Listing 6-1).

Available for download on Wrox.com

LISTING 6-1: Adding the <s:Button> and <s:Label> components to a <s:VGroup> container in DebuggingAppHome.mxml

```
<?xml version="1.0" encoding="utf-8"?>
<s:View xmlns:fx="http://ns.adobe.com/mxml/2009"
        xmlns:s="library://ns.adobe.com/flex/spark"
        title="Debugging App">

    <s:VGroup paddingLeft="20"
              paddingRight="20"
              paddingTop="20">

        <s:Label id="testLabel"/>

        <s:Button id="testButton"
```

```
                              label="Test onClick()"/>

            </s:VGroup>

        </s:View>
```

3. Next add a `<fx:Script>` block with a new `protected` function defined called `onClick()`. Then assign the function to the `<s:Button>` component's `click` property (Listing 6-2).

> **LISTING 6-2: Adding the onClick() method to the <fx:Script> declaration in DebuggingAppHome.mxml**

```xml
<?xml version="1.0" encoding="utf-8"?>
<s:View xmlns:fx="http://ns.adobe.com/mxml/2009"
        xmlns:s="library://ns.adobe.com/flex/spark"
        title="Debugging App">

    <fx:Script>
        <![CDATA[

            protected function onClick():void {}

        ]]>
    </fx:Script>

    <s:VGroup>

        <s:Label id="testLabel"/>

        <s:Button id="testButton"
                  label="Test onClick()"
                  click="onClick()"/>

    </s:VGroup>

</s:View>
```

4. Within `onClick()` add a local variable called `labelStr` of `String` type. Then create a `for` loop that increments the variable `i`. Within the loop add an `if` statement to set `labelStr` to label text is set when `i` is equal to 5. Following the `for` loop, assign the `labelStr` variable to the `text` property on the `<s:Label>` component, using the `String.toLowerCase()` method (Listing 6-3).

> **LISTING 6-3: Creating the for loop and if statement within the onClick() in DebuggingAppHome.mxml**

```
protected function onClick():void
{
    var labelStr:String;
    var i:int;

    for(i=0; i<=4; i++)
```

continues

LISTING 6-3 *(continued)*

```
{
        if(i==5)
        {
                labelStr = "label text is set.";
        }
}

testLabel.text = labelStr.toLowerCase();
}
```

Note here that the `for` loop is only incremented to 4.

5. Next add two breakpoints. Add the first breakpoint on the first line of the for loop declaration, by double-clicking the space next to the line number. Then add the second breakpoint on the line that assigns the text to `labelStr`. The breakpoints should be set on lines 14 and 18 (Figure 6-2).

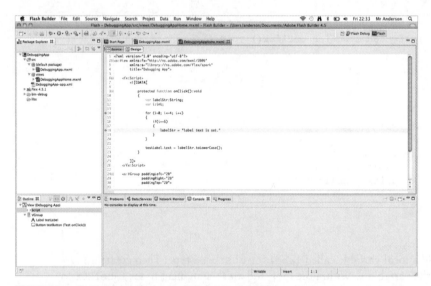

FIGURE 6-2: Setting breakpoints in DebuggingAppHome.mxml

 NOTE *By default Flash Builder doesn't display line numbers. If there are no line numbers displayed in the IDE, to view them you must enable them in the Text Editor Preferences panel. Bring up the context menu in the source view of DebuggingAppHome.mxml, then Select ➪ Preferences . . . to display the Preferences panel. Finally toggle the Show Line Numbers checkbox, click Apply, then OK.*

6. Next run the project using a Debug configuration. Select Run ➪ Debug (Figure 6-3).

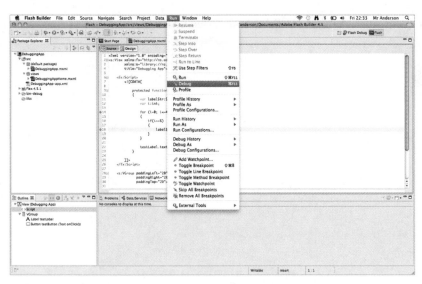

FIGURE 6-3: Launching the project with a Debug configuration

7. In the Debug Configurations panel that opens, create a configuration for launching the application called Debugging App on Desktop. Enter Debugging App as the project, leave `src/DebuggingApp` `.mxml` as the application file, choose Google Android as the target platform, and select Desktop and Google Nexus One as the launch method. Click Apply, and then click Debug to launch the project in a debugging session (Figure 6-4).

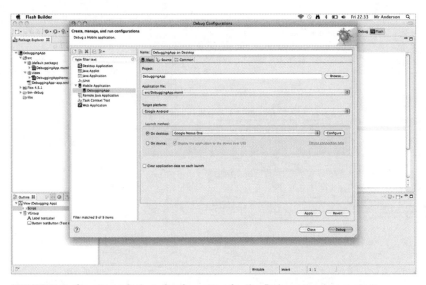

FIGURE 6-4: Creating a Debug Configuration for the Debugging App project

8. In the adl window that opens, click the Test onClick() button (Figure 6-5).

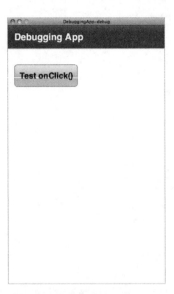

FIGURE 6-5: The Debugging
App project

When you click the button you will be asked to switch to the Flash Debug Perspective. This is
automatically opened when a breakpoint has been reached. Click Yes to continue (Figure 6-6).

FIGURE 6-6: Confirm Perspective Switch dialog in Flash Builder

The debugging session will pause the current thread of the application at this stage, which is focused on the onClick() function (Figure 6-7).

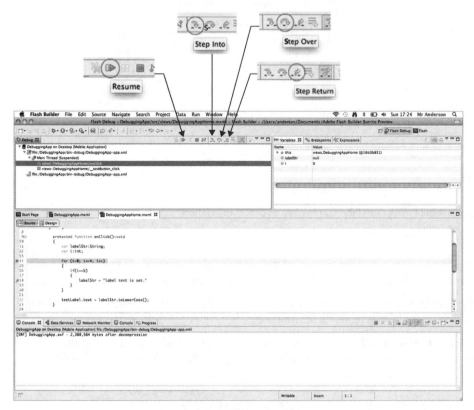

FIGURE 6-7: The current thread of the application being displayed in the Debug panel. Note the Step Over and other buttons.

 NOTE When the application reaches a breakpoint, the application is paused, and the current line highlighted in the source code is the line that is about to be executed by the compiler. You can use the Step Over button in the Debug panel (Figure 6-7) to progress through the app and move onto the next line. Some of the other buttons shown on the panel will be referred to later in this chapter.

9. Take a look at the Variables panel in the Flash Debug panel. In the list of variable names, look for the labelStr. The value of the labelStr should be set to null. Also look for the variable i; this value should be set to 0 (Figure 6-8).

FIGURE 6-8: The list of variables available in the current thread of the application, displayed in the Variables panel

Note that the first breakpoint is only reached because of the conditional `if` statement. One lesson to learn is that breakpoints are reached only when the line of code that the breakpoint is set on is about to be executed.

10. The application is currently paused in this debugging session. Resume the application by clicking the Resume button in the Debug panel or pressing F8.

Notice that the breakpoint on the conditional `for` loop statement is reached again. Look at the value of variable `i` in the Variables panel; this should now be highlighted in yellow, and the value should be set to `1` (Figure 6-9).

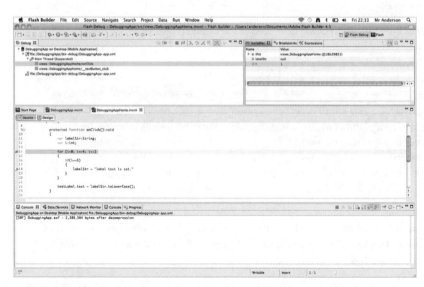

FIGURE 6-9: Checking the value of variable i in the Variables panel for the first time

11. Next click the Step Over button in the Debug panel or press F6, twice, to increment through the for loop. Check the value of variable i in the Variables panel once again. This time the value set for i will be 2 (Figure 6-10).

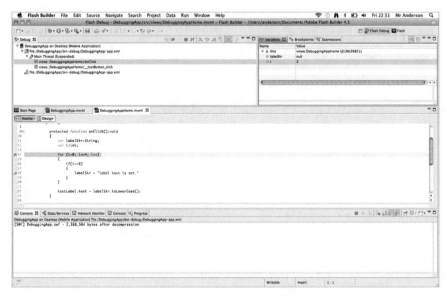

FIGURE 6-10: Checking the value of variable i in the Variables panel for the second time

12. Next disable the first breakpoint. Select the Breakpoints panel in the Flash Debug perspective, which should be next to the Variables panel. Then select the breakpoint that references the conditional if statement and unselect the checkbox (Figure 6-11).

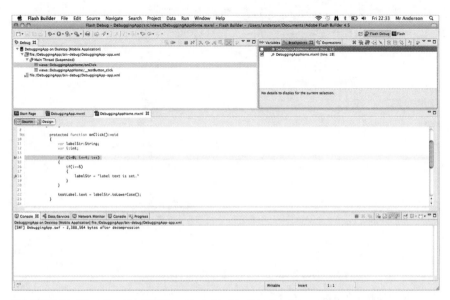

FIGURE 6-11: Disabling the first breakpoint in the Breakpoints panel

Once you have disabled the first breakpoint, the line in the source code that assigns the text to the variable `labelStr` should still have a breakpoint in place and enabled. If you double-click one of the breakpoints in the Breakpoints panel you should see the line of code highlighted in the Source view (Figure 6-12).

FIGURE 6-12: Selecting a line of code in Source view that has the breakpoint, from within the Breakpoints panel

You can toggle the breakpoint by double-clicking it in the Breakpoints panel or via the context menu (Figure 6-13).

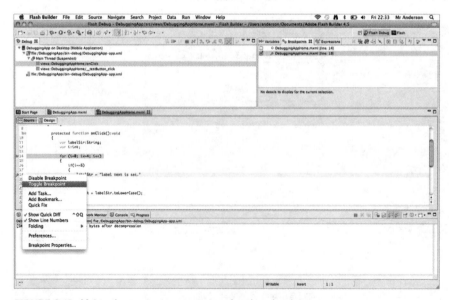

FIGURE 6-13: Using the context menu to toggle a breakpoint

13. Next resume the application once more.

You will notice that the application throws an error on the line that assigns the `labelStr` variable to the `text` property on the `<s:Label>` component. This error is highlighted in both the Debug and Console panels (Figure 6-14).

FIGURE 6-14: An application error being displayed in the Debug and Console panels

14. If you take a look in the Variables panel, you should see that variable `i` is set to `5` (Figure 6-15).

FIGURE 6-15: Checking the value of variable i in the Variables panel for the third time

Note that because the conditional statement within the for loop is only set to execute when i is less than or equal to 4, the last iteration it makes is incrementing the variable i from 4 to 5.

How It Works

You've reached a point where there is a minor error in the source code. Using the current logic, the application throws an error on the line that assigns the labelStr variable to the text property on the <s:Label> component.

If you remember, the for loop defined reaches only a count of 4 on the variable i and never reaches 5. Thus the line within the conditional if statement that requires i to equal 5 is never executed, and labelStr remains as null. You cannot assign a null value to the text property of a <s:Label> component, because it is expecting a String object.

Knowing the reason for the error at this stage shouldn't distract you from the underlying exercise, which is to teach you how to use breakpoints and the Debug panel.

GLOBAL ERROR HANDLING

The Flash Player 10.1 runtime API introduced a new class that handles errors at a global level. Here you'll take a brief look at how to handle errors using the UncaughtErrorEvent class.

The UncaughtErrorEvent class has just one event type constant, UncaughtErrorEvent .UNCAUGHT_ERROR.

To capture errors on a global level you need to retrieve the loaderInfo object. This is accessible only when the mobile application has fully loaded, and so using the Flex framework loaderInfo is obtainable only when the applicationComplete event has been dispatched at the root of the application <s:ViewNavigatorApplication>.

Once you've retrieved the loaderInfo object, you use the following code to capture an error:

```
var err:UncaughtErrorEvents = loaderInfo.uncaughtErrorEvents;
err.addEventListener(UncaughtErrorEvent.UNCAUGHT_ERROR, onUncaughtError);
```

In the next section you'll take a look at implementing the UncaughtErrorEvent in the Debugging App project.

HANDLING UNCAUGHT ERRORS

So far you have learned how to set breakpoints, and how to read variables during the debugging session. Now take a look at handling the error introduced to the project using Watch expressions.

TRY IT OUT Handling Uncaught Errors

The following steps will take you through handling the error introduced in the Debugging App project using the `UncaughtErrorEvent` class.

1. Return to the Flash Perspective in the Debugging App project. In `DebuggingApp.mxml`, add a protected function called `onAppComplete()`, and then assign the function to the `applicationComplete` property in the attributes for opening the `<s:ViewNavigatorApplication>` tag (Listing 6-4).

Available for download on Wrox.com

LISTING 6-4: Adding the onAppComplete() method to the <fx:Script> declaration in DebuggingApp.mxml

```
<?xml version="1.0" encoding="utf-8"?>
<s:ViewNavigatorApplication xmlns:fx="http://ns.adobe.com/mxml/2009"
                             xmlns:s="library://ns.adobe.com/flex/spark"
                             firstView="views.DebuggingAppHome"
                             applicationComplete="onAppComplete()">

        <fx:Script>
                <![CDATA[

                        protected function onAppComplete():void {}

                ]]>
        </fx:Script>

</s:ViewNavigatorApplication>
```

2. In `onAppComplete()` add the code to handle any uncaught errors in the application, using the `loaderInfo` object. Add a stub for the `private function` called `onUncaughtError()`, defining the parameter `e` as an `UncaughtErrorEvent` type, and assign it to the `UncaughtErrorEvent.UNCAUGHT_ERROR` event type via `addEventListener()` (Listing 6-5).

Available for download on Wrox.com

LISTING 6-5: Assigning the UncaughtErrorEvent.UNCAUGHT_ERROR event to the onUncaughtError() method in DebuggingApp.mxml

```
protected function onAppComplete():void
{
        var err:UncaughtErrorEvents = loaderInfo.uncaughtErrorEvents;
        err.addEventListener(UncaughtErrorEvent.UNCAUGHT_ERROR, onUncaughtError);
}

private function onUncaughtError(e:UncaughtErrorEvent):void {}
```

3. In `onUncaughtError()` assign the error message on the `UncaughtErrorEvent` object to the text property on `testLabel`. Use the `UncaughtErrorEvent.error` property to determine the object type; if the error is an `Error` object, assign the `Error.message` property to `msg` (Listing 6-6).

LISTING 6-6: Retrieving the Error.message property via the onUncaughtError() method in DebuggingApp.mxml

```
private function onUncaughtError(e:UncaughtErrorEvent):void
{
        var msg:String;

        if(e.error is Error)
        {
                msg = Error(e.error).message;
        }
}
```

4. Launch the DebuggingApp project, again using the Debug configuration. Set a breakpoint on the opening if statement in onUncaughtError() on line 20, and then step through. You should see the error message caught by the unhandled error assigned to the msg variable in the Variables panel (Figure 6-16).

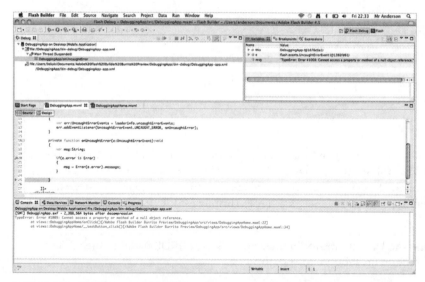

FIGURE 6-16: Handling an uncaught error and assigning the Error.message property to the msg variable in the Variables panel

How It Works

In this example you are simply writing the code to determine what happens should your application throw a runtime error.

If you recall, the line within the conditional if statement, which requires i to equal 5, is never executed, and labelStr remains null, so when it is assigned to the text property on the <s:Label> component, the application will show an error.

The error invoked bubbles up to the root of the application, and because it doesn't have any listeners assigned to it to handle the error, it effectively becomes an uncaught error, dispatching the UncaughtErrorEvent_UNCAUGHT_ERROR event.

In `onUncaughtError()` you see one type of error event being handled. This could have been an `IOErrorEvent` that failed to load an image, in which case `onUncaughtError()` would need to be modified to look like the following:

```
private function onUncaughtError(e:UncaughtErrorEvent):void
{
    var msg:String;

    if(e.error is Error)
    {
        msg = Error(e.error).message;

    } else if(e.error is IOErrorEvent) {

        msg = IOErrorEvent(e.error).text;
    }
}
```

Note here that `IOErrorEvent` details its error message via the `IOErrorEvent.text` property.

While the DebuggingApp project now demonstrates handling an uncaught error at the global level, the line of code with the potential error should ideally be wrapped in a Try...Catch block.

Next, you'll take a look at how you use Try...Catch statements.

TRY...CATCH STATEMENTS

To aid in preventing your mobile applications from either crashing or presenting runtime errors to users, a Try...Catch block should be used in source code where possible.

Try...Catch statements effectively test a block of code to see if it contains errors at run time.

For developers it is not always explicit where or when a Try...Catch block should be used, but in general these statements can be applied to code wherever there is an uncertainty about a particular variable assignment or a particular function call. The structure of the Try...Catch statement means that you can provide an alternative outcome in the catch portion of the Try...Catch block.

Now take a look at using a Try...Catch block in the Debugging App project.

TRY IT OUT   Using a Try...Catch Statement

The following steps will take you through using the Try...Catch statement in the Debugging App project.

1. In `DebuggingAppHome.mxml`, wrap the assignment of the `labelStr` variable to `testLabel.text` in a Try...Catch statement to handle when the application throws an `Error` object (Listing 6-7).

**LISTING 6-7: Adding the Try...Catch statement to the onClick() method in
DebuggingAppHome.mxml**

```
protected function onClick():void
{
        var labelStr:String;
        var i:int;

        for(i=0; i<=4; i++)
        {
                if(i==5)
                {
                        labelStr = "label text is set.";
                }
        }

        try
        {
                testLabel.text = labelStr.toLowerCase();

        } catch(e:Error)
        {

        }
}
```

2. In the Catch block, simply assign the text Error was caught! to the text property on the
   <s:Label> component testLabel (Listing 6-8).

**LISTING 6-8: Defining the code to execute in the Catch block in the onClick() method in
DebuggingAppHome.mxml**

```
protected function onClick():void
{
        var labelStr:String;
        var i:int;

        for(i=0; i<=4; i++)
        {
                if(i==5)
                {
                        labelStr = "label text is set.";
                }
        }

        try
        {
                testLabel.text = labelStr.toLowerCase();

        } catch(e:Error)
```

```
                    {
                        testLabel.text = "Error was caught!";
                    }
            }
```

3. Launch the Debugging App project, once again using the Run configuration.

This time when the application launches and you click the Test onClick() button, you'll see the text Error was caught! written in the <s:Label> component (Figure 6-17).

How It Works

Having established exactly where the application error occurs through using the breakpoints earlier, the Try...Catch block was strategically placed to handle the null exception on the assignment to the text property on <s:Label>. The application will still attempt to assign labelStr even though it is still null; however, if an error is thrown, it will be caught in the Catch portion of the Try...Catch statement. Here the Catch statement simply defines what should be done if this error is caught.

FIGURE 6-17: Catching an error using the Try...Catch statement in the Debugging App project

STEPPING THROUGH CODE

In this section you'll finally take a look at how to fix the error in the Debugging App project.

If you recall, an error occurs because the conditional if statement, which requires i to equal 5, is never executed, and labelStr remains null. So when it is assigned to the text property on the <s:Label> component the application errors.

Step through code is a term used to describe examining source code, usually line by line. In Flash Builder the Debug panel provides the tools to step through each line of code, allowing you to see what happens before and after a line of code has been executed.

TRY IT OUT **Stepping through Code in the Debugging Session**

The following steps will take you through fixing the error in the code example about handling the error introduced in the Debugging App project, using the UncaughtErrorEvent class.

1. First, return to the for loop in onClick() and increase the number of iterations from 4 to 5 (Listing 6-9).

LISTING 6-9: Updating the number of iterations in the for loop in the onClick() method in DebuggingAppHome.mxml

```
protected function onClick():void
{
        var labelStr:String;
        var i:int;

        for(i=0; i<=5; i++)
        {
                if(i==5)
                {
                        labelStr = "label text is set.";
                }
        }

        try
        {
                testLabel.text = labelStr.toLowerCase();

        } catch(e:Error)
        {

                testLabel.text = "The Error was caught!";
        }
}
```

2. Launch the Debugging App project again, this time using the Debug configuration. Ensure that only a single breakpoint is in place in the application, where the text is assigned to the labelStr variable in DebuggingAppHome.mxml.

> **NOTE** *When you add additional lines of code, breakpoints will move with the line of code that has the breakpoint assigned. In this example the breakpoint should remain on line 18.*

This time when the application launches it will pause at the breakpoint. If you take a look in the Variables panel, you will see that the variable i is set to 5, and the labelStr variable is set to null. What is more significant here is that now the breakpoint has reached the line where the text is assigned to the labelStr variable within the if statement (Figure 6-18).

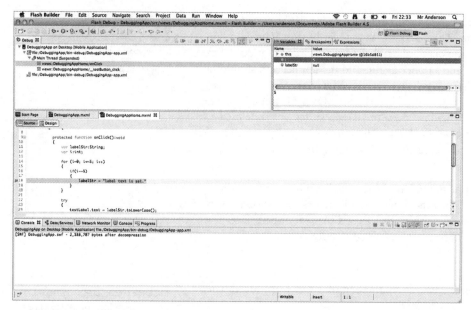

FIGURE 6-18: Checking the value of variable i and labelStr in the Variables panel

3. Move off the current line in the code by clicking the Step Over button. Look in the Variables panel once again, and you will now see that the labelStr variable is set to label text is set (Figure 6-19).

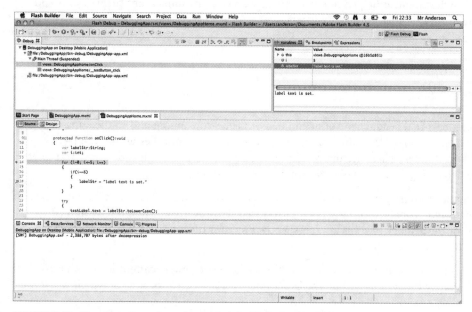

FIGURE 6-19: Checking the value of variable labelStr in the Variables panel

4. Move out of the `for` loop in `onClick()` by clicking the Step
Return button. Then click the Step Over button. The next line
highlighted is the opening bracket of the `try` declaration. Click
the Step Over button once again, and the application should fall
on the line where `labelStr` is assigned to `testLabel.text`,
inside the `try` statement. Click the Step Over button again. The
next line highlighted is where the `catch` statement is defined.
Click the Step Over button for the final time, and you will notice
that the debugger skips the line assigning the text `Error was`
`caught!` to `testLabel.text`.

5. Resume the application by clicking the Resume button in the
Debug panel. When the application launches, you should see that
the `<s:Label>` component is assigned the text `label text is`
`set`. Eureka! The bug is now fixed (Figure 6-20).

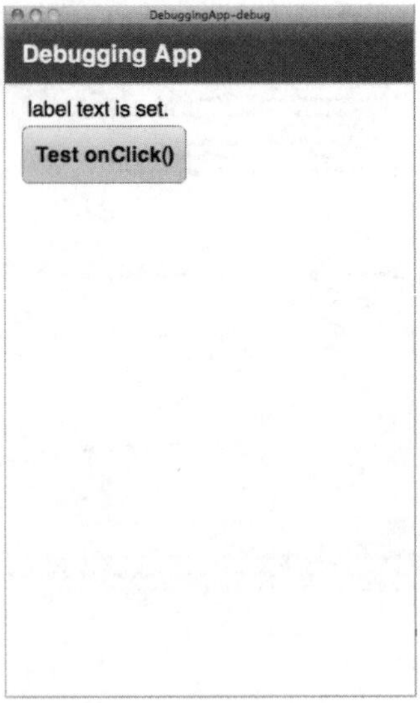

How It Works

The aim of this exercise was to fix the bug that was introduced when
the Debugging App was created.

FIGURE 6-20: Debugging App
now displaying "label text is set"

Stepping through code allows you to see what you're looking for in the
application at a granular level by examining each line of code and also to monitor the variables in the
application.

The hard work was actually finding the bug. That was done through a combination of techniques that
included using breakpoints, watching variables, and stepping through code. The `UncaughtErrorEvent`
class and the Try...Catch statement helped to ensure there won't be any unpleasant surprises for end
users if they run the project on their mobile handsets.

SUMMARY

Software bugs can be a real headache. And it can be both time-consuming and challenging to find
them in source code. The art of catching errors, whether major or minor, lies within the Debug
Perspective of Flash Builder, where setting breakpoints and stepping through code allow you to
perform precise debugging sessions while the application is running.

While the Debugging App project only introduced one error, one could argue that with more careful
coding the error would probably not have been introduced. However, you should have gained
an appreciation for the armory of tools and perspectives at your disposal in Flash Builder, which
ultimately helped to isolate and fix the error.

The `UncaughtErrorEvent` object is useful in situations where you simply cannot locate an error in
the code; unfortunately it doesn't give you the exact line where the error occurred, which would be
useful.

Also, the Try...Catch statement proves to be vital in wrapping code in blocks to catch potential errors, also allowing you to define an alternative track through the code when an error is caught.

In the next chapter you'll take a look at working with files and the filesystem. But before you move on to that chapter, try the following exercises, which are designed to help further your knowledge of debugging applications.

EXERCISES

1. Set another breakpoint in the Debugging App project, this time at the line where the `loaderInfo` object is used in `DebuggingApp.mxml`. Launch the project using the Debug configuration and take note of the values for each property in the object.

2. Introduce another error in the code that concerns loading an image, and see if you can use the techniques delivered in this chapter to isolate and handle the `IOErrorEvent`.

3. Revisit Chapter 5 and pick out three areas in which to apply the Try...Catch statement.

▶ **WHAT YOU LEARNED IN THIS CHAPTER**

TOPIC	KEY CONCEPT
Setting breakpoints in source code	Set a line breakpoint in the Source view of Flash Builder by double-clicking the space next to the line number or right-clicking to use the context menu.
Using the Breakpoints panel	Use the Breakpoints panel to see the lists of all line breakpoints that have been set across all files in the application.
	Enable a breakpoint by selecting a checkbox or disable a breakpoint by unselecting a checkbox.
	Double-click a breakpoint to automatically go to that line in the Source view.
Using the Variables panel	Use the Variables panel to see a list of all the variable names and assigned values while the application is running.
Using the Debug panel	Use the Debug panel to see where the current thread of the application is paused.
	Use the Step Into, Step Over, and Step Return buttons to navigate your way in, around, out, and over lines of code and functions while the application is running in the debugging session (see Figure 6-7).
Stepping through source code	To examine each line of code as the application is running, step through code using the Debug panel.
Global error handling	Use the `UncaughtErrorEvents` object on `loaderInfo` to register an interest in the `UncaughtErrorEvent.UNCAUGHT_ERROR` event.
	Add the event listener for `UncaughtErrorEvent.UNCAUGHT_ERROR` in the main application `<s:ViewNavigatorApplication>` once the `applicationComplete` event is triggered.
Adding Try...Catch Blocks	Write AS3 code within the Try block to catch potential errors.
	Code within the Catch block executes when the code in the Try block throws an error.

7

Working with the Filesystem

WHAT YOU WILL LEARN IN THIS CHAPTER:

➤ Creating File and FileStream objects

➤ Resolving file object paths

➤ Modifying files and directories

➤ Using browse dialogs

This chapter takes a look at the AIR File System API in depth, again using Flash Builder to take you through related examples. These will help you to build applications that can create or utilize existing data on a user's mobile device, whether that data is an MP3 file found in the device's native media library, or an image file referenced from the photo gallery.

The key aspect of the API is getting to understand the filesystem, learning how to resolve paths to files, and containing folders on the device. This chapter looks at all this in depth.

 WARNING *For security reasons the AIR File System API is restricted for use in non-browser Flash applications. Bear this in mind if you intend to create browser-based Flash mobile applications. In addition, Google Android and BlackBerry Tablet OS devices require users to grant usage of certain security levels when using the API.*

Over the course of this chapter you'll construct a simple example running the majority of features.

READING FROM THE FILESYSTEM

To utilize the filesystem within your Flash mobile applications on a mobile device using AIR, you first need to familiarize yourself with the core classes involved in the API, and pay particular attention to how one points to files and directories in the filesystem.

The File and FileStream Classes

The `File` and `FileStream` classes are the key classes that you can use to gain access to the filesystem data on the mobile device using AIR. Both files are located in the `flash.filesystem` package.

To use the `File` class in an ActionScript Mobile project, you need to import the class using the following statement:

```
import flash.filesystem.File;
```

Similarly, to use the `FileStream` class in an AS project, you need to import the class using the following statement:

```
import flash.filesystem.FileStream;
```

Using Flash Builder with the Flex framework and AIR doesn't require you to import the class in this way. The Files Explorer project therefore doesn't have either of these statements. Bear this in mind when you create your other projects.

The `File` class provides reference points to information about files and file directories, also giving you the methods to create, modify, and delete files or file directories. The `FileStream` class provides you with the methods to open, read, write, and modify files on the filesystem.

The File Object

A `File` object has a number of properties that should uniquely distinguish it from another file object on the filesystem. These properties include:

- ➤ `url`: An absolute reference to a file object on the device
- ➤ `nativePath`: A reference to the file object's path on the device
- ➤ `name`: A string representing the file object's name
- ➤ `creationDate`: A string containing the creation date of the file object, relative to GMT
- ➤ `modificationDate`: A string detailing the last time the file object was modified
- ➤ `exists`: A Boolean that indicates whether the file object exists
- ➤ `size`: A number returning the actual size of the file object
- ➤ `spaceAvailable`: A string representing the total space available on the filesystem in which the file object resides
- ➤ `creator`: A string representing the creator of the file object
- ➤ `type`: A string returning the type of file object

➤ `extension`: A string returning the file extension of the file object

➤ `isDirectory`: A Boolean that indicates whether or not the file object reference is a directory

➤ `isHidden`: A Boolean that indicates whether or not the file object is hidden

➤ `isPackage`: A Boolean that indicates whether or not the file object is a package

➤ `parent`: Returns a reference to a file object in which the current file or directory resides

You should be familiar with the majority of these properties as entities on your home computer. The modification date is a property of a file used frequently to see when a file was last saved. Looking at the properties, you can easily identify a file object by its name, whether it is a file or a directory, its size, the creation or modification dates, and URL paths.

Next take a look at the different ways in which you can create file objects using AIR.

Creating File Objects from the URL Path

The `nativePath` and `url` properties of the file object are references that point to a file object's location on the mobile device.

There are three URL schemes that are supported which can be used to create file objects via the `File` class constructor: `app:/`; `app-storage:/`; and `file://`.

In the following code snippet the `file://` URL scheme is used to create a `File` object fileObj that attempts to point to Notes, a folder contained in the Documents directory on the filesystem:

```
var fileObj:File = new File("file:///documents/notes");
```

The way this file object is created could potentially pose a few problems for cross-platform compatibility and running the app on devices with different mobile operating systems. How does the mobile application know that the Documents or Notes directories exist on a device? And is the file path URL format recognized by the device?

If you don't know whether the file object created is present on the device, you can use the `File.exists` property of the `File` object to determine whether a particular file or directory exists — but this is only once the URL path of the file object has been set, again pointing to a potential issue with the URL format. To address differences in URL formats, you can use static properties of the file class to retrieve generic locations on devices, and as you'll see it provides an alternative way to create a file object by referencing a specific location on the device.

Creating File Objects from Static Locations

On a laptop or PC you may be familiar with commonly used file spaces such as Documents and Applications for Mac OS, or My Documents and Programs on a Windows machine. Simply put, these are quick access references to file directories that have certain document types. In essence these are familiar short names given to potentially complex filesystem references.

On mobile devices, users are less familiar with locations such as these, and generally come across physical file directory paths only when using applications designed for this. Applications such as

Finder for Mac OS and File Explorer on Windows are designed for large screens, allowing a user to explore whole filesystems, which on mobile devices would be harder to navigate.

The `File` class has five static properties that you can use to reference commonly used file locations:

➤ `File.applicationStorageDirectory`: Returns a file object pointing to a storage directory that is unique to the AIR application installed on a device

➤ `File.applicationDirectory`: Returns a file object pointing to the location where the application is installed on the device

➤ `File.desktopDirectory`: Returns a file object pointing to an equivalent of the Desktop directory found on Mac OS and Windows machines

➤ `File.documentsDirectory`: Returns a file object pointing to an equivalent of a user's Documents directory found on Mac OS and Windows machines

➤ `File.userDirectory`: Returns a file object pointing to an equivalent of the Users directory found on Mac OS and Windows machines

The file objects returned by these properties can be used to avoid potential issues like the ones encountered when specifying a hard-coded file-path URL. Each of the file references is pretty much static and can be referenced universally across different platforms using AIR.

Table 7-1 lists example `url` values returned by each static property on an Android mobile device running Gingerbread 2.3.4

TABLE 7-1: Example URL Property Values Returned on an Android Device

PROPERTY	VALUE
`File.applicationDirectory.url`	`app:/`
`File.applicationStorageDirectory.url`	`app-storage:/`
`File.desktopDirectory.url`	`file:///mnt/sdcard`
`File.documentsDirectory.url`	`file:///mnt/sdcard`
`File.userDirectory.url`	`file:///mnt/sdcard`

From the table you'll see that the Android device returns three distinct file object `url` values.

WARNING *Note that you cannot write to files or directories that have paths that use the* `app:` *URL scheme. Nor can you delete or create files or folders that have paths that use the scheme, as modifying content in the application directory is considered a bad practice, and for security reasons, it is usually blocked by the OS.*

Resolving the Reference Path of a File Object

On Google Nexus One, an Android device running Gingerbread 2.3.4, the `File.desktopDirectory`, `File.documentsDirectory`, and `File.userDirectory` each returns a file object that points to the `file:///mnt/sdcard` location. To ensure that a file object points to a particular location, you must use the `resolvePath()` method to refine the target path.

In the following snippet the file object is pointing to the `file:///mnt/sdcard/notes` directory using the `File.documentsDirectory` as the initial reference point:

```
var fileObj:File = File.documentsDirectory.resolvePath("notes");
```

For the file object created, `fileObj`, if the Notes directory existed, then `fileObj.exists` would be set to `true`. Using the `resolvePath()` method essentially sets the target path for the file object, whether it exists or not. This is important for creating new files and folders, as you'll see later.

While the `url` property of a file object gives a precise value to a location, the `nativePath` property gives the full path to the file object as represented in the host operating system.

Next take a look at using the `nativePath` property of the file object in the example project.

Creating a Files Explorer App Example

You will need to set up a new Flex Mobile Project in Flash Builder.

Defining the Flex Mobile Project Settings

The following lists a few of the familiar settings you will need to ensure are defined for the project:

➤ **Name:** Set the Name for the project to **FilesExplorerApp.**

➤ **Application ID:** Set the Application ID to **com.wrox.ch7.FilesExplorerApp.**

➤ **Application Template:** Set the Application Template to a View-Based Application, setting the initial view title to **FilesExplorerAppHome.**

Targeting Mobile Devices on Different Platforms

This example project can run on each of the mobile platforms supporting AIR, including Apple iOS, Google Android, and BlackBerry Tablet OS. For Google Android and BlackBerry Tablet OS, a number of permissions need to be set to allow the application to utilize the device's filesystem, whereas for Apple iOS, no permissions need to be defined specifically.

Defining Google Android Permissions

For the AIR Application Descriptor file generated with the project in Flash Builder, `FilesExplorerApp-app.xml`, ensure the `android.permission.WRITE_EXTERNAL_STORAGE` permission is included as a manifest addition for the Google Android platform, as shown in the following code snippet:

```
<android>
  <manifestAdditions>
    <![CDATA[
```

```
        <manifest>
          <uses-permission android:name="android.permission.WRITE_EXTERNAL_STORAGE"/>
        </manifest>
      ]]>
    </manifestAdditions>
  </android>
```

Defining BlackBerry Tablet OS Permissions

For BlackBerry Tablet OS applications, you need to specify the `access_shared` permission, to allow the application to write to the mobile device. Ensure this is set in the `blackberry-tablet.xml` file, as shown in the following code snippet:

```
<?xml version="1.0" encoding="UTF-8"?>
<qnx>
    <author>jganderson</author>
    <authorId>gYAAgFbt6rihu</authorId>
    <category>core.media</category>
    <buildId>1</buildId>
    <platformVersion>1.0.0.0</platformVersion>
    <permission>access_shared</permission>
</qnx>
```

Defining Apple iOS Settings

There are no permissions that need to be defined for the Apple iOS platform.

Creating Run and Debug Configurations

You can elect to run this project on the desktop or directly on your mobile device. For consistency, this chapter uses a Google Nexus One as the connected device.

Building the Files Explorer App

In this section, you begin building the Files Explorer App project in Flash Builder, first taking a look at the `nativePath` property of the `File` object.

TRY IT OUT   Displaying the Native Path of a File Object

For the Files Explorer App project, follow the next steps to add a label to the main view that shows the current filesystem directory.

1. As shown in Listing 7-1, the main application file, `FilesExplorerApp.mxml`, has a similar MXML markup as covered in earlier chapters, with the exception of the `firstView` attribute's value, which is set to `views.FilesExplorerAppHome` (Listing 7-1).

LISTING 7-1: The FilesExplorerApp.mxml application file for the Files Explorer project

```
<?xml version="1.0" encoding="utf-8"?>
<s:ViewNavigatorApplication xmlns:fx="http://ns.adobe.com/mxml/2009"
                     xmlns:s="library://ns.adobe.com/flex/spark"
                     firstView="views.FilesExplorerAppHome">
```

```
        <fx:Declarations>
                <!-- Non-visual elements (e.g., services, value objects) -->
        </fx:Declarations>

    </s:ViewNavigatorApplication>
```

2. Replace the `<fx:Declarations>` with an `<fx:Style>` declaration. Inside the `<fx:Style>` declaration, specify s as the spark namespace. Then define three style declarations for the View, Label, and List components that will be used in the application. For the `<s:View>` components, define the `backgroundColor` property as #999999, and `color` property as #393839. For the `<s:Label>` components, define the `fontSize` as 18. Then for the `<s:List>` components, define the `alternativeItemColors` property as #CCCCCC and #EEEEEE, define the `selectionColor` property as `yellow`, `fontSize` property as 22, and `color` property as #393839 (Listing 7-2).

LISTING 7-2: Setting the styles via the `<fx:Style>` declaration in FilesExplorerApp.mxml

```
<?xml version="1.0" encoding="utf-8"?>
<s:ViewNavigatorApplication xmlns:fx="http://ns.adobe.com/mxml/2009"
                            xmlns:s="library://ns.adobe.com/flex/spark"
                            firstView="views.FilesExplorerAppHome">
    <fx:Style>

        @namespace s "library://ns.adobe.com/flex/spark";

        s|View
        {
            backgroundColor:#999999;
            color:#393839;
        }

        s|Label
        {
            fontSize:22;
        }

        s|List
        {
            alternatingItemColors: #CCCCCC, #EEEEEE;
            selectionColor:yellow;
            fontSize:22;
            color:#393839;
        }

    </fx:Style>

</s:ViewNavigatorApplication>
```

3. Modify the `FilesExplorerAppHome.mxml` file, setting the `title` property to `Files Explorer`. Then within a `<fx:Script>` declaration, add a private method called `exit()` to quit the application, calling `NativeApplication.nativeApplication.exit()`. Add a protected method stub called `readDir()` and assign it to the view's `creationComplete` attribute. Finally, add an `<s:layout>` declaration container for the view, defining the `<s:VerticalLayout>` (Listing 7-3).

LISTING 7-3: The FilesExplorerAppHome.mxml view for the Files Explorer project

```xml
<?xml version="1.0" encoding="utf-8"?>
<s:View xmlns:fx="http://ns.adobe.com/mxml/2009"
        xmlns:s="library://ns.adobe.com/flex/spark"
        creationComplete="readDir()"
        title="Files Explorer">

    <fx:Script>
        <![CDATA[
            protected function readDir():void {}

            private function exit():void
            {
                    NativeApplication.nativeApplication.exit();
            }
        ]]>
    </fx:Script>

    <s:layout>
        <s:VerticalLayout/>
    </s:layout>

</s:View>
```

4. Add a `<s:Button>` component with the label `Quit` to a `<s:navigationContent>` declaration.
    Assign the view's `exit()` method to the `click` property on the `<s:Button>` component. Under
    the `<s:navigationContent>` definition add a new `<s:Label>` component to the main view in
    `FilesExplorerAppHome.mxml`. Set the `id` property of the label to `currentDir`, the `width` property to
    100%, and the `height` to 60. Then set the `paddingLeft` property to 10, the `paddingTop` property to 15,
    and the `text` to read `Current Directory`. The vertical alignment needs to be set to `Middle` (Listing 7-4).

LISTING 7-4: Adding `<s:Button>` and `<s:Label>` components to the view in
FilesExplorerAppHome.mxml

```xml
<fx:Script>
    <![CDATA[
        protected function readDir():void {}

        private function exit():void
        {
                NativeApplication.nativeApplication.exit();
        }
    ]]>
</fx:Script>

<s:layout>
    <s:VerticalLayout/>
</s:layout>

<s:navigationContent>
```

```
        <s:Button label="Quit"
                  click="exit()"/>
    </s:navigationContent>

    <s:Label id="currentDirectory"
             text="Current Directory"
             paddingLeft="10"
             paddingTop="15"
             width="100%"
             height="60"
             verticalAlign="middle"/>
```

5. Next, above the `readDir()` stub, declare a private variable called `selectedDir` that has the `File` type (Listing 7-5).

LISTING 7-5: Defining the private variable to reference the selected directory in FilesExplorerAppHome.mxml

```
<fx:Script>
    <![CDATA[
        private var selectedDirectory:File;

        protected function readDir():void {}

        private function exit():void
        {
            NativeApplication.nativeApplication.exit();
        }
    ]]>
</fx:Script>
```

6. Within the `onCreationComplete()` method, assign the `documentsDirectory` property of the `File` class to `selectedDirectory`. Then using the `selectedDirectory` file object, set the text property of the new label to the `nativePath` (Listing 7-6).

LISTING 7-6: Setting the text to the native path in FilesExplorerAppHome.mxml

```
<fx:Script>
    <![CDATA[
        private var selectedDirectory:File;

        protected function readDir():void
        {
            selectedDirectory = File.documentsDirectory;
            currentDirectory.text = selectedDirectory.nativePath;
        }

        private function exit():void
        {
            NativeApplication.nativeApplication.exit();
        }
    ]]>
</fx:Script>
```

7. Run the project using the device run configuration. Using an Android device you should see the native path of the file object device displayed in the application beneath the header (Figure 7-1).

FIGURE 7-1: Displaying the current directory in the Files Explorer App running on Android 2.3.4

TRY IT OUT   Listing the Files of a Directory

Next take a look at how to display the contents of a directory.

1. First add a new `<s:List>` component to the directories view in `FilesExplorerAppHome.mxml`, directly beneath the `<s:Label>` component. Set the id property to `dirList`, set the `width` property to 100%, the `height` property to 85%, the `fontFamily` property to `Arial`, and the `contentBackgroundColor` to `#B6B3B3` (Listing 7-7).

LISTING 7-7: Adding a `<s:List>` component to the view in FilesExplorerAppHome.mxml

```
<s:Label id="currentDirectory"
         text="Current Directory"
         paddingLeft="10"
         paddingTop="15"
         width="100%"
         height="60"
```

```
                verticalAlign="middle"/>

    <s:List id="dirList"
            width="100%"
            height="85%"
            fontFamily="Arial"
            contentBackgroundColor="#B6B3B3"/>
```

2. Within the `readDir()` method, declare a new array called `docsDirectory`, then assign the `getDirectoryListing()` method on the `selectedDirectory` file object to the array (Listing 7-8).

LISTING 7-8: Retrieving the directory listing in FilesExplorerAppHome.mxml

```
protected function readDir():void
{
        selectedDirectory = File.documentsDirectory;
        currentDirectory.text = selectedDirectory.nativePath;

        var docsDirectory:Array = selectedDirectory.getDirectoryListing();
}
```

3. Next populate the List component with the file objects retrieved in `docsDirectory` using the `name` property for the label of each row. You will need to instantiate the `dataProvider` on the List component and then use the `addItem()` function to define the label representing each file object (Listing 7-9).

LISTING 7-9: Populating the <s:List> component with the file object name property in FilesExplorerAppHome.mxml

```
protected function readDir():void
{
        selectedDirectory = File.documentsDirectory;
        currentDirectory.text = selectedDir.nativePath;

        var docsDirectory:Array = selectedDirectory.getDirectoryListing();

        var fileObj:File;
        dirList.dataProvider = new ArrayCollection();

        for(var i:int = 0; i < docsDirectory.length; i++)
        {
                fileObj = docsDirectory[i];
                dirList.dataProvider.addItem({ label: fileObj.name });
        }
}
```

4. Run the project using the device configuration. Using an Android device, you should now see the contents of the Documents directory for the device displayed beneath its native path as in Figure 7-2.

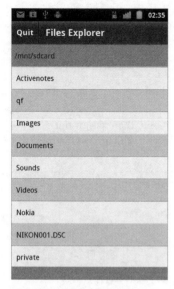

FIGURE 7-2: Displaying the contents of the Documents directory in the Files Explorer App running on Android 2.3.4

Next modify the list so that only folders are displayed.

5. In the `for` loop, use the `isDirectory` property on the file object to determine whether the reference is an actual directory and not a file (Listing 7-10).

LISTING 7-10: Filtering the List component with directories only in FilesExplorerAppHome.mxml

```
for(var i:int = 0; i < docsDirectory.length; i++)
{
        fileObj = docsDirectory[i];

        if(fileObj.isDirectory)
            dirList.dataProvider.addItem({ label: fileObj.name });

}
```

6. Run the project again using the device configuration. Using an Android device, you should now see that only folders are visible in the list (Figure 7-3).

FIGURE 7-3: Displaying only folders contained in the Documents directory in the Files Explorer App running on Android 2.3.4

How It Works

Within `readDir()` the `getDirectoryListing()` method is what provides the array of file objects from the `selectedDirectory` file object to the `docsDirectory` array. This object points to the reference Documents Directory on the mobile device. The `length` property on `docsDirectory` returns the number of file objects in the array. This is used in the `for` loop to iterate through each file object and display its `name` property in the List component `dirList`.

The `dirData` is used to hold only file objects that are known to be directories; using the `isDirectory` property all the files are filtered out of the array.

Next take a look at navigating between each directory.

7. Add an array called `dirData` to the private variable list (Listing 7-11).

LISTING 7-11: Defining a new private Array object to store file objects in FilesExplorerHome.mxml

```
<fx:Script>
    <![CDATA[
            private var dirData:Array;
            private var selectedDirectory:File;
```

8. Within the `readDir()` method ensure `dirData` gets populated with each of the file objects retrieved (Listing 7-12).

LISTING 7-12: Storing data in the Array object in FilesExplorerAppHome.mxml

```
protected function readDir():void
{
        selectedDirectory = File.documentsDirectory;
        currentDirectory.text = selectedDirectory.nativePath;

        var docsDirectory:Array = selectedDirectory.getDirectoryListing();

        var fileObj:File;
        dirData = [];
        dirList.dataProvider = new ArrayCollection();

        for(var i:int = 0; i < docsDirectory.length; i++)
        {
                fileObj = docsDirectory[i];

                if(fileObj.isDirectory)
                {
                        dirData.push(fileObj);
                        dirList.dataProvider.addItem({ label: fileObj.name });
                }
        }
}
```

9. Next update the `<s:List>` component. Set the `selectionColor` property to `#00A2FF`, the `selectedIndex` property to a default of `0`, and the `click` property to the `readDir()` event (Listing 7-13).

LISTING 7-13: Setting a selection color, the selected index, and click event handler for the `<s:List>` component in FilesExplorerAppHome.mxml

```
<s:List id="dirList"
        width="100%"
        height="85%"
        fontFamily="Arial"
        contentBackgroundColor="#B6B3B3"
        selectionColor="#00A2FF"
        selectedIndex="0"
        click="readDir()"/>
```

10. Next modify the `readDir()` method to allow for other file directories to be read. You need to utilize the `selectedIndex` property of the List component (Listing 7-14.)

LISTING 7-14: Setting the selected directory from the data stored in the data array in FilesExplorerAppHome.mxml

```
protected function readDir():void
{
        if(dirData)
        {
                selectedDirectory = dirData[dirList.selectedIndex];
```

```
    } else {

        selectedDirectory = File.documentsDirectory;
    }

    currentDirectory.text = selectedDirectory.nativePath;

    var docsDirectory:Array = selectedDirectory.getDirectoryListing();

    var fileObj:File;
    dirData = [];
    dirList.dataProvider = new ArrayCollection();

    for(var i:int = 0; i < docsDirectory.length; i++)
    {
        fileObj = docsDirectory[i];

        if(fileObj.isDirectory)
        {
            dirData.push(fileObj);
            dirList.dataProvider.addItem({ label: fileObj.name });
        }
    }
}
```

11. Run the project as it is. You will now be able to select a directory view showing any subfolders it contains. Figure 7-4 shows a folder being highlighted.

Figure 7-5 shows the screen on the device when the folder has been selected. You will also notice that the native path is updated in the display.

FIGURE 7-4: Navigating to sub-folders in the Files Explorer App running on Android 2.3.4

FIGURE 7-5: Displaying the contents of the Images directory in the Files Explorer App running on Android 2.3.4

**RUNNING THE FILES EXPLORER APP ON APPLE IOS
AND BLACKBERRY TABLET OS DEVICES**

For the Files Explorer App running on an Apple iPhone 4, the initial file directory opened by the application will consist of the following URL path:

```
/var/mobile/Applications/<ID>/Documents
```

Here the `<ID>` value represents a unique value generated for the application by the device and could vary from iPhone to iPhone.

For the Files Explorer App running on a BlackBerry PlayBook, the initial file directory will consist of the following path:

```
/accounts/1000/appdata/com.wrox.ch7.FilesExplorerApp.debug.test<ID>/
shared/documents
```

Similarly, the `<ID>` value here also represents a value generated for the application by the device and could vary from PlayBook to PlayBook.

Next take a look at navigating back to the previous directory. For this you need to use the `parent` property of the file object.

12. After the `readDir()` method, add an empty stub for a new protected method called `setParentDir()`. Then above the `for` loop statement in `readDir()`, make a call to `setParentDir()` as shown in Listing 7-15.

LISTING 7-15: Adding a method to call the parent directory in FilesExplorerAppHome.mxml

```
protected function readDir():void
{
    if(dirData)
    {
        selectedDirectory = dirData[dirList.selectedIndex];

    } else {

        selectedDirectory = File.documentsDirectory;
```

```
        }

        currentDirectory.text = selectedDirectory.nativePath;

        var docsDirectory:Array = selectedDirectory.getDirectoryListing();

        var fileObj:File;
        dirData = [];
        dirList.dataProvider = new ArrayCollection();

        setParentDir();

        for(var i:int = 0; i < docsDirectory.length; i++)
        {
                fileObj = docsDirectory[i];

                if(fileObj.isDirectory)
                {
                        dirData.push(fileObj);
                        dirList.dataProvider.addItem({ label: fileObj.name });
                }
        }
    }

    protected function setParentDir():void {}
```

13. In `setParentDir()` add the `parent` file object to the List component using the `addItem()` method. Use square brackets and two dots `[..]` to denote the parent directory. You also need to ensure that the parent is saved to the directory data array (Listing 7-6).

LISTING 7-16: Adding the parent file directory to the <s:List> component in FilesExplorerAppHome.mxml

```
protected function setParentDir():void
{
        var fileObj:File = selectedDirectory.parent;

        if(fileObj)
        {
                dirData.push(fileObj);
                dirList.dataProvider.addItem({label:"[..]"});
        }
}
```

14. Run the project as it is. You will now be able to select a directory and return to the parent directory by selecting `[..]` (Figure 7-6).

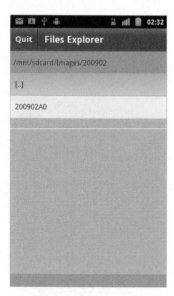

FIGURE 7-6: Navigating to the parent directory in the Files Explorer App running on Android 2.3.4

MODIFYING FILES AND FILESYSTEMS

So far you've learned how to read the filesystem of a mobile device using AIR. In this section you take a look at modifying the filesystem objects.

Creating New Files and Directories

To create files and folders on the mobile device, you need to use a combination of the `File`, `FileStream`, and `FileMode` classes.

Using the FileMode Class

The `FileMode` class is found in the `flash.filesystem` package. When creating ActionScript Mobile projects, you need to import the class through the following statement:

```
import flash.filesystem.FileMode;
```

When creating a Flex Mobile project in Flash Builder, you don't need to import the class.

The `FileMode` class provides four static constants. These are flags to define what a `FileStream` object should do with a `File` object it receives via the `FileStream.open()` method. At least one of these properties needs to be supplied as the second parameter in the `open()` method:

➤ `FileMode.WRITE`: To write new data to a file object instance

➤ `FileMode.UPDATE`: To update an existing file object instance

➤ `FileMode.APPEND`: To append data to a file object instance

➤ `FileMode.READ`: To read data from a file object instance

The following sections demonstrate how each of the `FileMode` properties can be used to read and write strings to a text file using the `FileStream.readUTFBytes()` and `FileStream.writeUTFBytes()` methods.

Writing to a File

To *write*, *update*, and *append* a file, you use the `writeUTFBytes()` method on a `FileStream` object, supplying the text you want to add to the file as an argument.

In the following code snippet the `FileStream` object `fs` opens a text `File` object called `story.txt`, resolving a path located in the documents directory. The file stream opens the file and then writes the string "A long time ago," which is 15 characters, and then closes the file stream:

```
var fileObj:File = File.documentsDirectory.resolvePath("story.txt");

var fs:FileStream = new FileStream();
fs.open(fileObj, FileMode.WRITE);
fs.writeUTFBytes("A long time ago");
fs.close();
```

Updating the Contents of a File

In the following code snippet the `story.txt` file is updated:

```
var fileObj:File = File.documentsDirectory.resolvePath("story.txt");

var fs:FileStream = new FileStream();
fs.open(fileObj, FileMode.UPDATE);
fs.position = 15;
fs.writeUTFBytes(" in a galaxy far, far away.... ");
fs.close();
```

Notice that the `FileStream.position` property on the `FileStream` object is set to 15. This property represents the current position in the file stream, and has been set so that the existing text in the file is kept and isn't overridden when new text is supplied to the `FileStream.writeUTFBytes()` method. Following on from the previous code snippet the file should read "A long time ago." When the update is applied the file should now read "A long time ago in a galaxy far, far away...."

Similarly, appending to a file using the `FileMode.APPEND` flag in `FileStream.open()` updates the file, but adds whatever is supplied to the `FileStream.writeUTFBytes()` method to the end of the file. The following code snippet appends the string "STAR WARS" to the `story.txt` file:

```
var fileObj:File = File.documentsDirectory.resolvePath("story.txt");

var fs:FileStream = new FileStream();
```

```
fs.open(fileObj, FileMode.APPEND);
fs.writeUTFBytes("STAR WARS");
fs.close();
```

Reading the Contents of a File

To *read* the contents of an existing text file, you need to use the `FileStream.readUTFBtyes()` method by supplying a reference to the `bytesAvailable` property on the file stream object.

In the following snippet the `story.txt` file is read:

```
var fileObj:File = File.documentsDirectory.resolvePath("story.txt");

var fs:FileStream = new FileStream();
fs.open(fileObj, FileMode.READ);
fs.readUTFBytes(fs.bytesAvailable);
fs.close();
```

Here the `FileStream` object `fs` is again passed a reference to the `File` object `fileObj`, which points to the `story.txt` file. The `FileMode.READ` flag is also passed to the `FileStream.open()` method.

If you've followed each of the previous code snippets, the `story.txt` file should read "A long time ago, in a galaxy far, far away. . . . STAR WARS."

Creating a New File Directory

Creating a new file directory simply requires calling the `createDirectory()` method on the file object. The path to the new folder needs to be resolved using the `resolvePath()` method, as shown in the following snippet:

```
var fileDir:File = File.desktopDirectory.resolvePath("untitled folder");
fileDir.createDirectory();
```

In this snippet the "untitled folder" is created in the Desktop directory.

Moving Files from One Directory to Another

To move a file from one location on the device to another, you need to utilize two file objects. The first file object should point to the originating location, and the second should point to where you want to move the file. You call the `moveTo()` method on the first file object, supplying the second file object as the parameter as shown in the following snippet:

```
var originalFile:File = File.documentsDirectory.resolvePath("story.txt");

var newDir:File = File.applicationStorageDirectory.resolvePath("story.txt");

originalFile.moveTo(newDir);
```

Here the `story.txt` file is moved from the documents directory to the application's storage directory on the device.

The text supplied to `resolvePath()` for the second file object is what defines either the new filename if you are moving a file, or the directory.

Moving a Folder

To move a file directory also requires the use of the `moveTo()` method on the file object. In the following snippet the `originalDir` file object, which points to the "untitled folder" on the desktop, is moved to the `destinationDir` file object, which points to a folder called "shapes" in the documents directory.

```
var originalDir:File = File.desktopDirectory.resolvePath("untitled folder");

var destinationDir:File = File.documentsDirectory.resolvePath("shapes");

originalDir.moveTo(destinationDir);
```

Here the `moveTo()` method is called on `originalDir`, which is the file object representing the directory that you want to move. The `destinationDir` file object is supplied as the parameter for the `moveTo()` method.

Copying Files and Directories

Copying a file or a directory also requires two file objects. To copy a file, you need to call the `copyTo()` method, as shown in the following snippet:

```
var file:File = File.applicationStorageDirectory.resolvePath("story.txt");

var newFile:File = File.documentsDirectory.resolvePath("story copy.txt");

file.copyTo(newFile);
```

In the following snippet the `originalDir` file object, which now points to the "shapes" folder in the documents directory, is copied and a new file directory `newDir` is created called "shapes copy" via the `copyTo()` method.

```
var originalDir:File = File.documentsDirectory.resolvePath("shapes");

var newDir:File = File.documentsDirectory.resolvePath("shapes copy");

originalDir.copyTo(newDir);
```

The `copyTo()` method is called on `originalDir`, which is the file object representing the directory that you want to copy. The `newDir` file object is supplied as the parameter for `copyTo()`.

Deleting a File from a Location

Removing a file from the filesystem on the mobile device first requires that a file exists. In the following snippet the `story copy.txt` file is removed from the documents directory via the `deleteFile()` method:

```
var fileObj:File = File.documentsDirectory.resolvePath("story copy.txt");

if(fileObj.exists)
        fileObj.deleteFile();
```

Deleting File Directories

To remove a directory from the filesystem, you call the `File.deleteDirectory()` method on a `File` object. Again, you need to ensure that the `resolvePath()` returns the correct file directory location.

```
var fileDir:File = File.documentsDirectory.resolvePath("stories");

if(fileDir.exists)
        fileDir.deleteDirectory();
```

TRY IT OUT   Creating New Files and Folders

Returning to the Files Explorer project, add two new options to the main view, *new folder* and *new file*. These options will be created to demonstrate exactly how the functions perform.

1.   First update the view in `FilesExplorerAppHome.mxml` to include the horizontal group layout component `<s:HGroup>`, placing it directly beneath the List component `dirList`. Set the id property of the component to `buttonContainer`, set the `width` to `100%`, set the `horizontalAlign` to `center`, and then set `paddingLeft` and `paddingTop` to `10` (Listing 7-17).

LISTING 7-17: Adding a horizontal group component to the view in FilesExplorerAppHome.mxml

```
<s:List id="dirList"
        width="100%"
        height="85%"
        fontFamily="Arial"
        contentBackgroundColor="#B6B3B3"
        selectionColor="#00A2FF"
        selectedIndex="0"
        click="readDir()"/>

<s:HGroup id="buttonContainer"
        width="100%"
        horizontalAlign="center"
        paddingTop="10"
        paddingBottom="10">

</s:HGroup>
```

2.   Next add two new `<s:Button>` components. Set the id property to `folderBtn` and the `label` property to `New Folder` on the first button. Then on the second button set the id property to `fileBtn` and `label` to `New File`. Both `height` properties of the components should be set to `55` and their `fontSize` properties should be set to `24`, (Listing 7-18).

LISTING 7-18: Adding two new <s:Button> components to the horizontal group component in FilesExplorerAppHome.mxml

```
<s:HGroup id="buttonContainer"
          width="100%"
          horizontalAlign="center"
          paddingTop="10"
          paddingBottom="10">

    <s:Button id="folderBtn"
              label="New Folder"
              height="55"
              fontSize="24"/>

    <s:Button id="fileBtn"
              label="New File"
              height="55"
              fontSize="24"/>

</s:HGroup>
```

3. Next create the `FolderView.mxml` view. In the Package Explorer panel highlight the Views Package folder. Then select File ➪ New ➪ MXML Component. In the New MXML Component pop-up window that opens, before clicking the Finish button, ensure that the Package field is set to `views`, the Name field to `Folder`, the Layout field to `spark.layouts.VerticalLayout`, and the Based On field to `spark.components.View` (Figure 7-7). After clicking Finish, the `FolderView` `.mxml` file is created in the Views folder of the Package Explorer panel.

FIGURE 7-7: Creating the FolderView MXML component for the Files Explorer App

4. Next modify the `FolderView.mxml` to include four new components. In `FolderView.mxml` modify the `title` property of the view component to read `Create a new Folder...` and set the `creationComplete` property to `onCreationComplete`. In the `<s:VerticalLayout>` container set the `paddingLeft` and `paddingTop` to 10. The `<fx:Script>` declaration should be added to include the `onCreationComplete()` stub. Directly beneath the `<s:layout>` declaration add two `<s:Label>` components. On the first label, set the `id` to `currentDirectory` and the `text` property to `Current Directory`. On the second `<sLabel>`, set the `text` property to `Folder name:`, and set the `width` and `height` on both labels to `100%` and 60, respectively. Add a `<s:TextInput>` component to the view, setting the `id` property on the component to `directoryName`, width to 450, and `contentBackgroundColor` to #605E5E. Finally, add a `<s:Button>` component setting the `label` to `Create Folder`, height to 55, and `fontSize` to 24 (Listing 7-19).

LISTING 7-19: Creating the FolderView.mxml view for the Files Explorer App project

```xml
<?xml version="1.0" encoding="utf-8"?>
<s:View xmlns:fx="http://ns.adobe.com/mxml/2009"
        xmlns:s="library://ns.adobe.com/flex/spark"
        creationComplete="onCreationComplete()"
        title="Create a new Folder...">

    <fx:Script>
        <![CDATA[
            protected function onCreationComplete():void {}
        ]]>
    </fx:Script>

    <s:layout>
        <s:VerticalLayout paddingLeft="10"
                          paddingTop="10"/>
    </s:layout>

    <s:Label id="currentDirectory"
             text="Current Directory"
             width="100%"
             height="58"
             verticalAlign="middle"/>

    <s:Label width="152"
             height="55"
             text="Folder name:"
             textAlign="left"
             verticalAlign="middle"/>

    <s:TextInput id="directoryName"
                 width="450"
                 contentBackgroundColor="#605E5E"/>

    <s:Button label="Create Folder"
              height="55"
              fontSize="24"/>

</s:View>
```

5. Next create the `FileView.mxml` component for the project. Add a new MXML component, this time setting the Name field to `FileView`. After clicking the Finish button, the `FileView.mxml` file should appear in the Package Explorer panel.

6. Next modify the File view to include four new components. In `FileView.mxml` modify the `title` property of the view to read `Create a new File...` and set the `creationComplete` property to `onCreationComplete`. The `<fx:Script>` declaration should be added to include the `onCreationComplete()` stub. In the `<s:VerticalLayout>` container set the `paddingLeft` and `paddingTop` to 10. Directly beneath the `<s:layout/>` component add two `<s:Label>` components. On the first label set the `id` to `currentDirectory` and the `text` property to `Current Directory`; on the second label set the `text` property to `File name:` and set the `width` and `height` on both labels to 100% and 60, respectively. Add a `<s:TextInput>` component to the view, setting the `id` property of the component to `fileName`, `width` to 450, and `contentBackgroundColor` to #605E5E. Add a second label component with the `text` property set to `File Content:` and then a `<s:TextArea>` component with an `id` property set to `fileContent`. Then finally add a `<s:Button>` component setting the `label` to `Create File`, the `height` to 55, and the `fontSize` property to 24. The basic structure for the File view is very similar to the Folder view. Listing 7-20 highlights the subtle differences.

LISTING 7-20: Creating the FileView.mxml file for the Files Explorer App project

```xml
<?xml version="1.0" encoding="utf-8"?>
<s:View xmlns:fx="http://ns.adobe.com/mxml/2009"
        xmlns:s="library://ns.adobe.com/flex/spark"
        creationComplete="onCreationComplete()"
        title="Create a new File...">

    <fx:Script>
        <![CDATA[
            protected function onCreationComplete():void {}
        ]]>
    </fx:Script>

    <s:layout>
        <s:VerticalLayout paddingLeft="10"
                          paddingTop="10"/>
    </s:layout>

    <s:Label id="currentDirectory"
             text="Current Directory"
             width="100%"
             height="58"
             verticalAlign="middle"/>

    <s:Label width="152"
             height="55"
             text="File name:"
             textAlign="left"
```

continues

LISTING 7-20 *(continued)*

```
                          verticalAlign="middle"/>

        <s:TextInput id="fileName"
                     width="450"
                     contentBackgroundColor="#605E5E"/>

        <s:Label width="203"
                 height="55"
                 text="File Content:"
                 textAlign="left"
                 verticalAlign="middle"/>

        <s:TextArea id="fileContent"
                    width="450"
                    height="209"
                    contentBackgroundColor="#605E5E"
                    verticalAlign="top"/>

        <s:Button label="Create File"
                  height="55"
                  fontSize="24"/>

    </s:View>
```

7. Next modify the `FolderView.mxml` and `FileView.mxml` files. Add a private `File` type variable called `selectedDirectory`, then in the `onCreationComplete()` function, set the `text` property on the `currentDirectory` label component to the `nativePath` property on `selectedDirectory`. Under the closing `<fx:Script>` tag, add a `<s:Button>` component to the `<s:navigationContent>` declaration, to navigate back to the `FilesExplorerAppHome.mxml` view. Add a private function called `back()` that calls the `navigator.pushView()` method of the view, passing a reference to `views.FilesExplorerAppHome` and the `selectedDirectory` file object (Listing 7-21).

LISTING 7-21: Displaying the nativePath and adding a back button in FolderView.mxml and FileView.mxml

```
<fx:Script>
    <![CDATA[
        private var selectedDirectory:File;

        protected function onCreationComplete():void
        {
            selectedDirectory = data as File;
            currentDirectory.text = selectedDirectory.nativePath;
        }

        private function back():void
        {
            navigator.pushView( views.FilesExplorerAppHome,
                                selectedDirectory );
```

```
                }
            ]]>
        </fx:Script>

        <s:navigationContent>
            <s:Button label="Back"
                        click="back()"/>
        </s:navigationContent>
```

8. In `FolderView.mxml` add a protected function called `createFolder()` under
    `onCreationComplete()`. In this method use the `selectedDirectory` file object to create a
    new file object with the `resolvePath()` method. First retrieve the value set on the text input
    component `directoryName`. If the text doesn't return a value or is left blank, create a directory
    with the path of `untitled folder`. Should text be set on the Text Input field, use the text
    returned. Create the new folder by calling the `createDirectory()` method on the `newDir` file
    object (Listing 7-22).

LISTING 7-22: Adding a method to create a new directory in the FolderView.mxml file

Available for
download on
Wrox.com

```
protected function onCreationComplete():void
{
        selectedDirectory = data as File;
        currentDirectory.text = selectedDirectory.nativePath;
}

protected function createFolder():void
{
        var directoryName:String = directoryName.text;
        var newDir:File;

        if(!directoryName || directoryName == "")
        {
                newDir = selectedDirectory.resolvePath("untitled folder");

        } else {

                newDir = selectedDirectory.resolvePath(directoryName);
        }

        newDir.createDirectory();
}
```

9. Next make a call to the `createFolder()` method via the Create Folder button (Listing 7-23).

LISTING 7-23: Assigning the createFolder() method to a click event in FolderView.mxml

Available for
download on
Wrox.com

```
<s:Button label="Create Folder"
            click="createFolder()"
            height="55"
            fontSize="24"/>
```

10. Next return to the File view. In `FileView.mxml` add a protected function called `createFile()` below `onCreationComplete()`. Use the `text` property on the Text Input field `fileName` along with `.txt` to generate a filename string. Then use the `resolvePath()` method on the `selectedDirectory` to generate a new file object `fileObj` (Listing 7-24).

LISTING 7-24: Adding the createFile() method to create a new file in FileView.mxml

```
protected function onCreationComplete():void
{
        selectedDirectory = data as File;
        currentDirectory.text = selectedDirectory.nativePath;
}

protected function createFile():void
{
        var nameStr:String = fileName.text + ".txt";
        var fileObj:File = selectedDirectory.resolvePath(nameStr);
}
```

11. Next use the newly created file object to create the new file through a `FileStream` object called `fs`. Use `FileMode.WRITE` as the file mode to pass to the `open()` method of the file stream object along with the file object. Then use the `text` property on the `fileContent` component to write to the file via `writeUTFBytes()`. Finally call the `close()` method on the file stream object (Listing 7-25).

LISTING 7-25: Creating the file stream in FileView.mxml

```
protected function createFile():void
{
        var nameStr:String = fileName.text + ".txt";
        var fileObj:File = selectedDirectory.resolvePath(nameStr);

        var fs:FileStream = new FileStream();
        fs.open(fileObj, FileMode.WRITE);
        fs.writeUTFBytes(fileContent.text);
        fs.close();
}
```

12. Next make a call to the `createFile()` method via the Create Folder button (Listing 7-26).

LISTING 7-26: Assigning the createFile() method to a click event in FileView.mxml

```
<s:Button label="Create File"
          click="createFile()"
          height="55"
          fontSize="24"/>
```

13. Finally update the `FilesExplorerAppHome.mxml` view. Above the `exit()` method create two new functions to display the new views. Add the private `folderView()` method to show the Folder view, then the `fileView()` method to show the File view. You need to call the `pushView()` method on the `navigator` property in each of the methods, supplying the respective view component along with the `selectedDirectory` file object as the data for the view (Listing 7-27).

LISTING 7-27: Navigating to the new views in FilesExplorerAppHome.mxml

```
private function fileView():void
{
        navigator.pushView(views.FileView, selectedDirectory);
}

private function folderView():void
{
        navigator.pushView(views.FolderView, selectedDirectory);
}

private function exit():void
{
        NativeApplication.nativeApplication.exit();
}
```

14. Next make a call to each of the view methods from their respective buttons. Set the `click` event on `folderBtn` to `folderView()` and for `fileBtn` set it to `fileView()` (Listing 7-28).

LISTING 7-28: Assigning folderView() and fileView() methods to click events in FilesExplorerAppHome.mxml

```
<s:HGroup id="buttonContainer"
          width="100%"
          horizontalAlign="center">

    <s:Button id="folderBtn"
              label="New Folder"
              click="folderView()"
              height="55"
              fontSize="24"/>

    <s:Button id="fileBtn"
              label="New File"
              click="fileView()"
              height="55"
              fontSize="24"/>

</s:HGroup>
```

15. Run the project. You will now see two buttons defined underneath the current directory label and the List component — the first to create a new folder and the second to create a new file (Figure 7-8).

16. Click the New Folder button. This takes you to the Folder view and displays the directory selected from the main view and a Text field that allows you to specify a name for the new folder (Figure 7-9).

FIGURE 7-8: The New Folder and New File buttons in the Files Explorer App running on Android 2.3.4

FIGURE 7-9: Creating a new folder called "archive" in the Files Explorer App running on Android 2.3.4

17. Enter a name for the folder, then click the Create Folder button. This should generate the new folder in the directory selected from the original list. Then click the Back button in the action bar to go back to the main view. In the main view you now should see the new folder created (Figure 7-10).

18. Next select the new folder you have just created, then click the New File button. This takes you to the File view and displays the directory selected from the main view. It also displays a Text field that allows you to specify a name for the new file and a Text field that allows you to enter text for the file. Enter a name for the file, then add some content to the text area. Then click the Create File button. This should generate the new file in the directory selected from the original list. Figure 7-11 shows the `FileView.mxml` file.

FIGURE 7-10: Displaying the new "archive" folder in the Files Explorer App running on Android 2.3.4

FIGURE 7-11: Creating a new file in the Files Explorer App running on Android 2.3.4

UTILIZING BROWSE DIALOGS

For AIR on Android, three *browse* methods on the `File` object allow you to reference image, video, and audio files using the mobile device's native window dialog:

➤ `browseForOpen()`: To select a single file

➤ `browseForOpenMultiple()`: To select multiple files

➤ `browseForSave()`: To select a file to save to

On an Android mobile device, the browse dialog allows the user to select only from audio, image, and video files, as shown in Figure 7-12.

FIGURE 7-12: Displaying the browse dialog to open files in the Files Explorer App running on Android 2.3.4

WARNING *On iOS, the browse APIs are not supported.*

Opening a Single File

Using the browseForOpen() method on a File object, you can present the user with a *browse for open* file dialog on the mobile device, which will allow you to reference a file in the application.

The browseForOpen() method takes two parameters. The first parameter is a title to be displayed in the dialog, and the second is an optional file filter that can be used to filter the types of files a user can select for opening.

The following snippet shows how a FileFilter object called audioFilter is defined to display all MP3 file types, before the browseForOpen() method is called on the File object fileDir:

```
var audioFilter:FileFilter;
audioFilter = new FileFilter("audio", "*.mp3");

var fileDir:File = File.applicationStorageDirectory;
fileDir.addEventListener(Event.SELECT, onSelect);
fileDir.browseForOpen("Select a file...", [audioFilter]);
```

In the constructor of the file filter the string audio is supplied as a description along with *.mp3, a string representing the MP3 file extension. The browseForOpen() method is given two parameters. The first is the string Select a file..., and the second is an array of FileFilter objects, though here only the mediaFilter object is supplied.

In the example, addEventListener() is called on fileDir to register Event.SELECT, an event that is fired when a user selects an item in the browse dialog. The handler for the event defined as onSelect() returns a file object reference to the file selected in the target property of the Event object e.

Opening Multiple Files

Using the browseForOpenMultiple() method on a File object, you can present the user with a browse file dialog to open and save files. Instead of Event.SELECT being fired when a user selects a media file from the browse dialog, the FileListEvent.SELECT_MULTIPLE event is triggered. The handler for the event returns an array of File objects in the target property instead of just a single file.

The following code snippet demonstrates how to use a browse dialog to select multiple files:

```
var fileDir:File = File.documentsDirectory;
fileDir.addEventListener(FileListEvent.SELECT_MULTIPLE, onSelect);
fileDir.addEventListener(Event.CANCEL, onCancel);
fileDir.browseForOpenMultiple("Select files...");
```

In this example addEventListener() is called on the File object fileDir to handle the SELECT_MULTIPLE event. In addition, the Event.CANCEL event is also handled by an onCancel() when the user clicks Cancel.

Take a look at browse dialogs in more detail.

TRY IT OUT Opening Multiple Image Files

Over the next few steps you'll try utilizing `browseForOpenMultiple()` by loading multiple images selected from a browse dialog directly into a mobile application.

1. Under the `exit()` method in `FilesExplorerAppHome.mxml`, add another protected function called `selectMedia()` that takes a single `File` object called `fileObj` as a parameter. In `selectMedia()` define a `FileFilter` object called `jpgFilter`, which filters the jpeg extension `*.jpg` (Listing 7-29).

LISTING 7-29: Defining a FileFilter object for selectMedia() in FilesExplorerAppHome.mxml

```
private function exit():void
{
        NativeApplication.nativeApplication.exit();
}

protected function selectMedia(fileObj:File):void
{
        var jpgFilter:FileFilter;
        jpgFilter = new FileFilter("JPEG Files", "*.jpg");
}
```

2. Add an empty stub method called `onSelect()` that takes a single parameter, `Event` object e. In `selectMedia()` register an interest for the `FileListEvent.SELECT_MULTIPLE` event on `fileObj`, using `onSelect()` as the event handler. Then finally call the `browseForOpenMultiple()` method, supplying a title for the browse dialog and `jpgFilter` as the single file filter (Listing 7-30).

LISTING 7-30: Adding the SELECT_MULTIPLE event to the File object and calling the browseForOpenMultiple() method in FilesExplorerAppHome.mxml

```
private function exit():void
{
        NativeApplication.nativeApplication.exit();
}

protected function selectMedia(fileObj:File):void
{
        var jpgFilter:FileFilter;
        jpgFilter = new FileFilter("JPEG Files", "*.jpg");

        fileObj.addEventListener(FileListEvent.SELECT_MULTIPLE, onSelect);
        fileObj.browseForOpenMultiple("Select 2 image files...", [jpgFilter]);
}

private function onSelect(e:Event):void {}
```

3. In the `onSelect()` event handler, the event object triggered by the `SELECT_MULTIPLE` event type is passed to the method. Navigate to the `ImagesView` view using the `navigator.pushView()` method, but only when the event object is of the `FileListEvent` type. The first parameter of

the `pushView()` method should be the Images view; the second parameter should be the `files` property returned by the event `e`, (Listing 7-31).

LISTING 7-31: Navigating to the Images view in onSelect() in FilesExplorerAppHome.mxml

```
private function onSelect(e:Event):void
{
        if(e is FileListEvent)
        {
                navigator.pushView(views.ImagesView, FileListEvent(e).files);
        }
}
```

4. Add a `<s:Button>` to the view in `FilesExplorerAppHome.mxml` to call the `selectMedia()` method (Listing 7-32).

LISTING 7-32: Adding a horizontal group component containing the Open multiple media button in FilesExplorerAppHome.mxml

```
<s:HGroup id="buttonContainer"
          width="100%"
          horizontalAlign="center">

    <s:Button height="55"
             label="Open multiple media"
             click="selectMedia(selectedDirectory)"
             fontSize="24"/>

</s:HGroup>


<s:HGroup id="buttonContainer"
          width="100%"
          horizontalAlign="center">

    <s:Button id="folderBtn"
             label="New Folder"
             height="55"
             fontSize="24"/>

    <s:Button id="fileBtn"
             label="New File"
             height="55"
             fontSize="24"/>

</s:HGroup>
```

5. Next create a new view for the project called `ImagesView` in the Views package. Add an `onCreationComplete()` event handler method stub in the `<fx:Script/>` declaration and assign it to the `creationComplete` property of the view component. Then add a title to the View Selected Files (Listing 7-33).

LISTING 7-33: Assigning values to the title and creationComplete in ImagesView.mxml

```xml
<?xml version="1.0" encoding="utf-8"?>
<s:View xmlns:fx="http://ns.adobe.com/mxml/2009"
        xmlns:s="library://ns.adobe.com/flex/spark"
        title="Selected files..."
        creationComplete="onCreationComplete()">

    <fx:Script>
        <![CDATA[
            protected function onCreationComplete():void {}
        ]]>
    </fx:Script>

</s:View>
```

6. Next under `onCreationComplete()` add a private method called `back()` to return to the `FilesExplorerAppHome` view, and add the call to a button in the `<s:navigationContent>` declaration (Listing 7-34).

LISTING 7-34: Adding a <s:Button> to navigate back in ImagesView.mxml

```xml
<?xml version="1.0" encoding="utf-8"?>
<s:View xmlns:fx="http://ns.adobe.com/mxml/2009"
        xmlns:s="library://ns.adobe.com/flex/spark"
        title="Selected files..."
        creationComplete="onCreationComplete()">

    <fx:Script>
        <![CDATA[
            protected function onCreationComplete():void {}

            private function back():void
            {
                navigator.pushView(views.FilesExplorerAppHome);
            }
        ]]>
    </fx:Script>

    <s:navigationContent>
        <s:Button label="Back"
                  click="back()"/>
    </s:navigationContent>

</s:View>
```

7. Under the `<s:navigationContent>` component add a vertical group component `<s:VGroup>`, with `paddingLeft` and `paddingTop` set to 10. Within the vertical group add two `<s:Image>` components, with their id properties set to `img0` and `img1` (Listing 7-35).

LISTING 7-35: Adding a vertical group of <s:Image> components to the view in ImagesView.mxml

```
<s:navigationContent>
      <s:Button label="Back"
                   click="back()"/>
</s:navigationContent>

<s:VGroup paddingTop="10"
          paddingLeft="10">

    <s:Image id="img0"/>

    <s:Image id="img1"/>

</s:VGroup>
```

8. After `onCreationComplete()`, add another private method stub called `displayImage()` that accepts two parameters: `url`, a string representing the path to the image; and `img`, an `Image` type referencing the image component in which to display. Set the `source` property of the image object `img` to the `url` value passed to the method (Listing 7-36).

LISTING 7-36: Setting the source on the image object in ImagesView.mxml

```
protected function onCreationComplete():void {}

protected function displayImage(url:String, img:Image):void
{
      img.source = url;
}
```

9. Lastly in `onCreationComplete()` cast the `data` object retrieved in the view to an `Array` variable called `selectedFiles`. Add a `File` type variable `fileObj`. Then iterate through the `selectedFiles` array and call the `displayImage()` method supplying `fileObj.url`, and a reference to the image component id using `this["img" + i]` (Listing 7-37).

LISTING 7-37: Calling the displayImage() method via onCreationComplete() in ImagesView.mxml

```
protected function onCreationComplete():void
{
      var selectedFiles:Array = data as Array;
      var fileObj:File;

      for (var i:int = 0; i < 2; i++)
      {
```

```
            fileObj = selectedFiles[i];

            if(fileObj.exists)
                  displayImage(fileObj.url, this["img" + i]);
        }
    }
```

10. Now run the project as it is. Click the Open Multiple Media button. You will see the browse dialog appear, as shown in Figure 7-13.

FIGURE 7-13: Browsing for multiple image files in the Files Explorer App running on Android 2.3.4

 NOTE *The text supplied as the* `title` *parameter for the* `browseForOpenMultiple()` *and* `browseForOpen()` *methods does not appear in the browse dialog on a Google Nexus One running Android 2.3.4. In Figure 7-13 and Figure 7-14 you will see Upload appear as the title.*

11. In the browse dialog, select Image Files, then choose two image files (Figure 7-14).

12. Click OK. The `ImagesView.mxml` view will open and show the images you selected (Figure 7-15).

FIGURE 7-14: Selecting the flash.jpg and air.jpg files in the Files Explorer App running on Android 2.3.4

FIGURE 7-15: Displaying the selecting images in the Files Explorer App running on Android 2.3.4

Saving a Single File to a Location

The `browseForSave()` method presents a dialog containing a list of files, and allows a user to save a file to a location on the mobile device.

The following snippet shows how to call `browseForSave()`:

```
var fileDir:File = File.applicationStorageDirectory;
fileDir.addEventListener(Event.SELECT, onSelect);
fileDir.browseForSave("Save file...");
```

As with `browseForOpen()`, `Event.SELECT` needs to be registered with the file object to handle when the user selects the OK button to confirm saving the file (Figure 7-16).

FIGURE 7-16: Saving to a directory using the browse dialog in the Files Explorer App running on Android 2.3.4

NOTE *The text supplied as the* `title` *parameter for the* `browseForSave()` *method doesn't appear in the browse dialog on a Google Nexus One running Android 2.3.4. In Figure 7-16 you will see Download appear as the title, and not Save File as highlighted in the snippet.*

SUMMARY

Over the course of this chapter you have learned how to utilize the AIR File System API using a combination of Flash, Flex, and AIR to build the Files Explorer project.

The `File` and `FileStream` classes are the key aspects of the AIR File System API, and can be used in a number of ways to read, write, and modify aspects of any existing filesystem via a Flash application, including: listing the files and folders of a directory; creating text files; and selecting media files to open on the device.

In the next chapter you'll use aspects of the AIR File System API to work with app data, focusing more on the application storage directory.

Before moving on to the next chapter, you can integrate a number of functions covered in this chapter into the Files Explorer project. The following set of exercises should allow you to explore these event types and appreciate gestures in more detail.

EXERCISES

1. Use a checkbox in the `FilesExplorerAppHome.mxml` view to toggle between displaying files and folders in the List component.

2. Use a button in `FilesExplorerAppHome.mxml` to read a `.txt` text file highlighted in the List component.

3. In the `FileView.mxml` add an option to delete a file.

4. In the `FolderView.mxml` add an option to move a folder to another directory.

5. Modify the List component used in `FilesExplorerAppHome.mxml` to display the creation date, size, space available, and (for a file) the file extension.

▶ WHAT YOU LEARNED IN THIS CHAPTER

TOPIC	KEY CONCEPT
Creating file objects	Use one of three URL schemes to create a file object: `app:/`; `app-storage:/`; and `file://`.
Creating file objects from static locations	Use one of five static properties to reference a file object, including: `File.applicationDirectory` `File.applicationStorageDirectory` `File.documentsDirectory` `File.desktopDirectory`, and `File.userDirectory`
Resolving file object paths	Use `resolvePath()` on a file object to refine a target path.
Writing to files	Use the `FileStream` and `FileMode` objects to write to a file. Set the file mode to `FileMode.WRITE` when opening a file stream to write to a file. Use `writeUTFBytes()` to write content to a file.
Modifying files and directories	Use `moveTo()` on the file object to move to a file path. Use `copyTo()` on the file object to make a duplicate of the file object. Use `deleteFile()` to remove a file. Use `deleteDirectory()` to remove a folder.
Using browse dialogs	Use `browseForOpen()` to open a single file and use `browseForOpenMultiple()` to open multiple files. Use `browseForSave()` to save a file object to the mobile device.

8

Working with Data

WHAT YOU WILL LEARN IN THIS CHAPTER:

- ➤ Implementing network detection
- ➤ Handling changes in network availability
- ➤ Monitoring URL requests
- ➤ Exploring SQLite operations
- ➤ Utilizing databases and tables

In this chapter you'll build a Flex mobile example utilizing SQLite, and incorporate the concept of saving Formula 1 racing team data to a database. If you don't know much about Formula 1, don't worry; you'll just be referencing a database of basic team data.

The data created by the application will be modifiable on the mobile device, so you will be able to create a team and add drivers, update the values, and remove them from the database, directly from the app.

SQL provides an avenue for creating mobile applications with self-contained data using Adobe AIR. You need to take a number of steps to open a database stored on the device and you should take a look at these first.

You'll begin in this chapter by implementing network detection, and learning how you can retrieve data over an available Internet network.

DETECTING CHANGES IN NETWORK AVAILABILITY

It's important to have a backup when working with online data services. It's also useful for the user to know what the status is when a network service changes.

Retrieving Data with URLRequest

You request remote data via an HTTP URL path through using the `URLRequest` and `URLLoader` classes. Both classes are found in the `flash.net` package and need to be imported in ActionScript mobile projects, as shown in the following snippet:

```
import flash.net.URLRequest;
import flash.net.URLLoader;
```

Because they are part of the same package, they can also be imported using the star notation, indicating that all classes within that package should be imported into the document:

```
import flash.net.*;
```

The following snippet shows a request for remote data, using two variables — a `URLRequest` object called `urlRequest`, and a `URLLoader` object called `urlLoader`:

```
var urlRequest:URLRequest;
urlRequest = new URLRequest("http://localhost/wrox/ch8/data.txt");

var urlLoader:URLLoader;
urlLoader.load(urlRequest);
```

In this example the HTTP URL path `http://localhost/wrox/ch8/data.txt` is supplied as a parameter in the constructor of the `URLRequest` object. Instead of passing the URL to the class constructor function, you can set the `URLRequest.url` property to reference the path:

```
urlRequest.url = "http://localhost/wrox/ch8/data.txt";
```

The `URLLoader.load()` method is what triggers the data load request. To handle the loading of data the `Event.COMPLETE` event should be handled on the `urlLoader` object.

 NOTE *You will need to set up a local host or use a remote server to run the initial examples in this section.*

Monitoring the URLRequest Object

When a network connection is available on a mobile device, the data retrieved by an application can be presented to a user. Should the network become unavailable, online data cannot be utilized by an application.

This poses potential problems for data-centric applications that rely on network connectivity, and so one of the roles of the `URLMonitor` class is to provide a solution that allows you to monitor a particular URL request and then notify the application if there are any changes in being able to execute that request.

The `URLMonitor` class is found in the `air.net` package and needs to be added to the import declarations, as shown in the following snippet:

```
import air.net.URLMonitor;
```

In the following snippet you see that the URLMonitor object, called urlMonitor, is initialized via the URLMonitor.start() method:

```
var urlRequest:URLRequest;
urlRequest = new URLRequest("http://localhost/wrox/ch8/data.txt");

var urlMonitor:URLMonitor = new URLMonitor(urlRequest);
urlMonitor.start();
```

The constructor for the new URLMonitor object takes a URLRequest object as a parameter, and in this example this is the same URLRequest object being used to reference the data file.

The StatusEvent Object

The StatusEvent class has a single event-type value called StatusEvent.STATUS, which should be used by the URLMonitor object to register an interest in status changes in network service availability. Whenever a change in network availability occurs in the mobile application, the StatusEvent object is dispatched.

Each StatusEvent object has a StatusEvent.code property that will return one of the following two values in an event handler that listens for the StatusEvent.STATUS event:

➤   "Service.available": This is the String value indicating that there is network availability.

➤   "Service.unavailable": This is the String value indicating that there is no network availability.

Both these values can therefore be used to determine whether an application should be *online* or *offline*.

To retrieve the code property, the URLMonitor object needs to register an interest in the StatusEvent.STATUS event using the URLMonitor.addEventListener() method, as shown in the following snippet:

```
var urlMonitor:URLMonitor = new URLMonitor(urlRequest);
urlMonitor.addEventListener(StatusEvent.STATUS, onStatus);
urlMonitor.start();
```

The event handler for the StatusEvent.STATUS event in this example is onStatus(), and this is where you should be able to handle the changes in network connectivity.

Next, try out displaying the change in status.

Creating the Maintaining Data App Example

You will need to set up a new Flex Mobile Project in Flash Builder.

Defining the Flex Mobile Project Settings

The following lists a few of the familiar settings that you will need to ensure are defined for the project:

➤   **Name:** Set the Name for the project to **MaintainingDataApp**.

➤   **Application ID:** Set the Application ID to **com.wrox.ch8.MaintainingDataApp**.

➤ **Application Template:** Set the Application Template to a View-Based Application, setting the initial view title to **MaintainingDataAppHome**.

Targeting Mobile Devices on Different Platforms

This example project can run on each of the mobile platforms supporting AIR, including Apple iOS, Google Android, and BlackBerry Tablet OS. No permissions need to be specified for either of the target platforms.

Creating Run and Debug Configurations

You can elect to run this project on the desktop or directly on your mobile device. For consistency, this chapter uses a Google Nexus One as the connected device.

TRY IT OUT Displaying the Change in Status of Network Availability

In the following steps, you'll begin to create Maintaining Data App, a Flex mobile project that will initially display the change in the network availability on a device. Later this application will be developed into an app that allows you to create data via the app, retrieve it, delete or update it — hence a "maintaining data" theme:

1. In the Package Explorer, navigate to the default package, open the `MaintainingDataApp.mxml` file, and then add a new style declaration for each of the `<s:View>` components in the project, setting the `backgroundColor` property to #999999 and the `color` property to #454545 (Listing 8-1).

Available for download on Wrox.com

LISTING 8-1: Setting style properties on the application's <s:View> components in MaintainingDataApp.mxml

```
<?xml version="1.0" encoding="utf-8"?>
<s:ViewNavigatorApplication xmlns:fx="http://ns.adobe.com/mxml/2009"
                            xmlns:s="library://ns.adobe.com/flex/spark"
                            firstView="views.MaintainingDataAppHome"
                            applicationDPI="160">

    <fx:Style>

        @namespace s "library://ns.adobe.com/flex/spark";

        s|View
        {
            backgroundColor:#999999;
            color:#454545;
        }

    </fx:Style>

</s:ViewNavigatorApplication>
```

2. In the Package Explorer, navigate to the Views package, open the `MaintainingDataAppHome.mxml` file, and replace the generated code with that shown in Listing 8-2.

LISTING 8-2: The initial starting point for MaintainingDataAppHome.mxml

```xml
<?xml version="1.0" encoding="utf-8"?>
<s:View xmlns:fx="http://ns.adobe.com/mxml/2009"
        xmlns:s="library://ns.adobe.com/flex/spark"
        title="Maintaining Data App"
        creationComplete="onCreationComplete">

    <fx:Script>
        <![CDATA[

            private function onCreationComplete():void {}

        ]]>
    </fx:Script>

    <s:layout>

        <s:VerticalLayout paddingLeft="20"
                          paddingRight="20"
                          paddingTop="20"
                          paddingBottom="20"/>

    </s:layout>

</s:View>
```

3. Note that the `<s:Label>` component with the id property is set to urlStatus; the width is set to 100%; the height is set to 30; the fontSize is set to 18; and the text is set to URL Status (Listing 8-3).

LISTING 8-3: Adding a `<s:Label>` component to the `<s:VGroup>` layout to display URL status in MaintainingDataAppHome.mxml

```xml
<s:layout>

    <s:VerticalLayout paddingLeft="20"
                      paddingRight="20"
                      paddingTop="20"
                      paddingBottom="20"/>

</s:layout>

<s:VGroup width="100%" height="150">

    <s:Label id="urlStatus"
             width="100%"
             height="30"
             paddingLeft="5"
             fontSize="18"
             text="URL Status"/>

</s:VGroup>
```

Here the `MaintainingDataAppHome.mxml` file contains a single label that is going to display the status of the network availability. The `text` property of the label should display the `StatusEvent.code` value.

4. Within the `<fx:Script>` declaration, import the `URLRequest` and `URLMonitor` classes (Listing 8-4).

LISTING 8-4: Importing the URLMonitor and URLRequest classes in MaintainingDataAppHome.mxml

```
<fx:Script>
    <![CDATA[

        import air.net.URLMonitor;
        import flash.net.URLRequest;

        private function onCreationComplete():void {}

    ]]>
</fx:Script>
```

5. Define two `URLMonitor` and `URLRequest` object variables called `urlMonitor` and `urlRequest`, respectively. Then in `onCreationComplete()` instantiate `urlMonitor` with the `URLRequest` object, which should be created from the data file `data.txt`, located on a local host (Listing 8-5).

LISTING 8-5: Creating urlRequest and urlMonitor in MaintainingDataAppHome.mxml

```
import air.net.URLMonitor;
import flash.net.URLRequest;

private var urlMonitor:URLMonitor;
private var urlRequest:URLRequest;

private function onCreationComplete():void
{
    urlRequest = new URLRequest("http://localhost/wrox/ch8/data.txt");
    urlMonitor = new URLMonitor(urlRequest);
}
```

6. Next, under `onCreationComplete()` add a new private function called `onStatus()`. Register the `StatusEvent.STATUS` event type and `onStatus()` with the `urlMonitor` via `addEventListener()`, then call `start()` to initialize the `URLMonitor` object. Finally, in `onStatus()` set the `text` property on the `urlStatus` label to the `e.code` value (Listing 8-6).

LISTING 8-6: Initializing urlMonitor and displaying the updated status code in MaintainingDataAppHome.mxml

```
private function onCreationComplete():void
{
    urlRequest = new URLRequest("http://localhost/wrox/ch8/data.txt");

    urlMonitor = new URLMonitor(urlRequest);
```

```
        urlMonitor.addEventListener(StatusEvent.STATUS, onStatus);
        urlMonitor.start();
}

private function onStatus(e:StatusEvent):void
{
        urlStatus.text = e.code;
}
```

The `data.txt` file contains a number of name-value pairs representing a number of teams and drivers from Formula 1, as shown in Listing 8-7.

LISTING 8-7: The contents of the data.txt file

```
t1=Mclaren&t2=Red Bull&d1=L. Hamilton&d2=J. Button&d3=S. Vettel&d4=M. Webber
```

7. Next run the example using a desktop run configuration for Google Nexus One. To demonstrate the change in network availability, turn your computer's Internet connection on and off. Figure 8-1 shows what is displayed when the service is unavailable.

At this point you can see that the application displays the status of the network service availability.

To utilize the network when the service is available you can use a conditional statement to invoke the `URLLoader` class and load the data. Follow the next steps to do just that:

8. Under the `urlStatus` `<s:Label>` component add a `<s:TextArea>` component with an `id` property set to `dataResult`, the `width` property set to `100%`, the `height` set to `66`, the `fontSize` set to `18` and `prompt` property set to `No data yet` (Listing 8-8).

FIGURE 8-1: Displaying the Service.unavailable message in Maintaining Data App running on the desktop

LISTING 8-8: Adding the dataResult Text Area component to display data returned in MaintainingDataAppHome.mxml

```
<s:VGroup width="100%" height="150">

        <s:Label id="urlStatus"
                width="100%"
                height="50"
                paddingLeft="5"
                fontSize="18"
```

continues

LISTING 8-8 *(continued)*

```
                    text="URL Status"/>

        <s:TextArea id="dataResult"
                    width="100%"
                    height="66"
                    fontSize="18"
                    prompt="No data yet."/>

    </s:VGroup>
```

9. Next import the URLLoader, adding another private variable called urlLoader of the same type. Then in onStatus() use the e.code value to load the urlRequest when the Service.available status is returned (Listing 8-9).

LISTING 8-9: Initializing urlLoader using the URLRequest object in MaintainingDataAppHome.mxml

```
import air.net.URLMonitor;
import flash.net.URLLoader;
import flash.net.URLRequest;

private var urlMonitor:URLMonitor;
private var urlLoader:URLLoader;
private var urlRequest:URLRequest;

private function onCreationComplete():void
{
        urlRequest = new URLRequest("http://localhost/wrox/ch8/data.txt");

        urlMonitor = new URLMonitor(urlRequest);
        urlMonitor.addEventListener(StatusEvent.STATUS, onStatus);
        urlMonitor.start();
}

private function onStatus(e:StatusEvent):void
{
        urlStatus.text = e.code;

        if(e.code == "Service.available")
        {
                urlLoader = new URLLoader();
                urlLoader.addEventListener(Event.COMPLETE, onLoadComplete);
                urlLoader.load(urlRequest);
        }
}

private function onLoadComplete(e:Event):void
{
        dataResult.text = urlLoader.data;
}
```

When the `data.txt` file is loaded via the `URLLoader` into the application, its contents are displayed (Figure 8-2).

The aim of the network connection is to retrieve data that the application can use directly when the request has been successful. This data could potentially be stored on the mobile device once loaded so the user can use it in an offline mode.

Of course, when the service is unavailable you get the "No data yet" message, as shown in Figure 8-3. If you recall, in Listing 8-8 this value is set on the `prompt` property of the `<s:TextInput>` component, and so is there by default when the application launches.

FIGURE 8-2: Displaying the contents of the data.txt file when the service is available in Maintaining Data App running on the desktop

FIGURE 8-3: Displaying the Service.unavailable message in Maintaining Data App running on the desktop

In the next section you'll take a look at one of the ways in which you can store data offline, using SQLite.

USING SQLITE FOR STORING DATA

AIR for mobile devices has the support for SQLite (`www.sqlite.org`), which is a database local to the mobile application. SQLite is a software library that implements a SQL (Structured Query Language) database engine, allowing you to store and use complex data as part of your Flash-based mobile applications. SQL is a language for accessing and manipulating databases, and with it you can perform a number of operations, including:

➤ Executing queries against a database

➤ Retrieving data from a database

➤ Inserting records into a database

➤ Updating records in a database

➤ Deleting records from a database

In the following subsections you'll take a look at each of these core operations and learn how to use SQLite, starting with creating a SQLite database.

Creating a SQLite Database

To create a database, you need to asynchronously resolve a file path pointing to a database file (.db file), and then open the file via a SQL connection using the SQLConnection class.

To create a database connection, you need to import the SQLConnection and the SQLEvent classes:

```
import flash.data.SQLConnection;
import flash.events.SQLEvent;
```

To handle errors that may arise in connecting to a database, you should also import the SQLErrorEvent class:

```
import flash.events.SQLErrorEvent;
```

To open a connection to the database:

1. Create a File object reference pointing to the database file (.db file) in the loadData() method.

2. Instantiate a new SQLConnection object.

3. Define a new private function called onOpen(). Then use addEventListener() to register the SQLEvent.OPEN event on the SQLConnection object and assign it onOpen() as the event handler.

4. Use the openAsync() method on the SQLConnection object, passing the File object reference as a parameter.

You'll take a more in-depth look at these steps in the next activity.

The SQLConnection object used to create and open the connection to the database is returned on the SQLEvent.target value in the event handler. You can use the SQLConnection.connected property on target to determine whether or not a successful connection to the database was made.

Database Tables

Tables are where data is created and stored in a database file. Tables are essentially made up of *rows* and *columns*, with each row representing a single data object entry and each column representing a property assigned to that data object. Then within the row itself a value is assigned to that column. In each table one column is designated as the *primary key*, a property of the data object that must have a unique value to distinguish it from all other data object entries in the table. This is typically an ID and is automatically generated when a new entry is added.

When you interact with a database to add new data or update existing data, you always reference the table name and a unique key value to reference a data object entity.

SQLite databases can hold any number of tables depending on file-size restrictions for the individual database. Tables can also be linked to other tables when a column or field in one table matches a column or field in the other.

To create a table and populate it with data, you need to use a sequence of SQL statements using the `flash.data.SQLStatement` class. A number of SQL statement operations will allow you to carry out various functions on the data contained within the database. The core ones are highlighted in Table 8-1.

TABLE 8-1: Core SQL Statement Operations

SQL STATEMENT	DESCRIPTION
CREATE	Creates a table in a database, using the following syntax: `CREATE TABLE tableName (column1 dataType, column2 dataType,...)`

INSERT	Inserts a new row in a table, using the following syntax:
	`INSERT INTO tableName (column1, column2, column3,...)`
	`VALUES (value1, value2, value3,...)`

SELECT	Selects data from a database, using the following syntax:
	`SELECT columnName(s)`
	`FROM tableName and SELECT * FROM tableName`

UPDATE	Updates existing records in a table, using the following syntax:
	`UPDATE tableName`
	`SET column1=value, column2=value2,...`
	`WHERE someColumn=someValue`

DELETE	Deletes rows from a table, using the following syntax:
	`DELETE FROM tableName`
	`WHERE columnName=someValue`

JOIN	Selects data matching in multiple tables, using the following syntax:
	`SELECT columnName(s)`
	`FROM someTable`
	`JOIN ON tableName1.columnName=tableName2.columnName`

The SQLStatement Object

To execute a SQL statement using ActionScript 3.0, the `SQLStatement` class needs to be imported:

```
import flash.data.SQLStatement;
```

The class has a number of properties and methods that you will need to use to interact with databases:

➤ `SQLStatement.sqlConnection`: A `SQLConnection` property representing the SQL connection assigned to the SQL statement

➤ `SQLStatement.text`: A string representing the SQL text

➤ `SQLStatement.parameters`: An array of strings, each string representing a parameter associated with a table column referenced in the SQL text

➤ `SQLStatement.execute()`: A method to run the SQL statement

Following the creation of a new `SQLConnection` object, the use of SQL statements essentially involves the following definitive steps:

1. Instantiate a new `SQLStatement` object.

2. Assign the `SQLConnection` object to the `SQLStatement.sqlConnection` property.

3. Define event handlers for `SQLEvent.RESULT` and `SQLError.Event.ERROR`.

4. Pass a SQL query to the `SQLStatement.text` property.

5. Call the `SQLStatement.execute()` method.

Over the next few sections you'll take a more in-depth look at Step 4, which involves using SQL statements and each of the commands outlined in Table 8-1.

Creating a SQLite Table

In the following snippet you see that the table `Teams` is created with two columns, the `ID` column and `TNAME` column:

```
var sqlText:String = "CREATE TABLE Teams("
                   + "ID INTEGER PRIMARY KEY, "
                   + "TNAME TEXT)";
```

Each value supplied in the parentheses for the `CREATE TABLE` SQL statement is in a particular order. Following the column name is the `ID` column. The next value is the column type, which is defined as an `INTEGER`; for `TNAME` the column type is `TEXT`. The `ID` is also defined as the `PRIMARY KEY`. Each new column defined for a table is separated by a comma (`,`).

Saving Data to Tables

Saving to a SQLite database involves inserting data into a table. To insert data into a table the `SQLStatement.parameters` property needs to be defined before executing the SQL statement.

For each value you want to insert you need to specify the table column it corresponds to, using the INSERT INTO query. You specify the table name followed by an opening bracket and the column names separated by commas after the closing bracket and a space; you then use the VALUES operator followed by the values you want to insert into the columns you've specified.

In the following snippet you see that the value Ferrari is supplied as a new team name for the TNAME column:

```
insertStatement = new SQLStatement();
insertStatement.text = "INSERT INTO Teams(TNAME) VALUES(Ferrari)";
insertStatement.execute();
```

Here this is done directly in the SQL text.

Using parameters that are defined on the SQLStatement.parameters property, you can dynamically insert data into tables using values from your mobile application.

```
var sqlText:String = "INSERT INTO Teams(TNAME) VALUES(:tname)";
insertStatement = new SQLStatement();
insertStatement.text = sqlText;
insertStatement.parameters[":tname"] = "Ferrari";
insertStatement.execute();
```

Notice here that the parameter for VALUES in the SQL text tname is preceded by a colon (:) in parentheses. This denotes that the text :tname is actually a parameter. To set a value for tname, the parameter's object references :tname.

Retrieving Data from a Table

To retrieve all the data entries in the table called Teams, you would use the SQL text highlighted in the following snippet:

```
var sqlText:String = "SELECT * FROM Teams";
```

The SELECT operation followed by an asterisk (*) denotes that all the data objects, that is, all rows, should be retrieved from the table.

To retrieve a single data row entry you need to reference the primary key and use the WHERE operator, as shown in the following snippet:

```
var sqlText:String = "SELECT * FROM Teams WHERE ID = 2";
```

Here the table row entry that has an ID value of 2 would be retrieved from the database.

 NOTE The SQLResult *class has a* data *property containing an array of objects returned from the SQL request. Each row returned via a SQL operation represents an index of the array, where* data[0] *is the first result to be returned.*

Instead of retrieving all data objects from a table, you can specify a table column property after the SELECT operator to retrieve a specific value from the table. The following snippet shows how you would retrieve the value of the property TNAME from the table row that has an ID value of 3:

```
var sqlText:String = "SELECT TNAME FROM Teams WHERE ID = 3";
```

The result of executing this SQL statement should return only one row from the database as long as the ID column was a primary key.

Updating Table Data

To update data already stored in the database, you need to use the UPDATE SQL statement. The UPDATE statement requires you to reference the primary key, along with values for each of the properties you want to update in a table.

The following code snippet shows how you would update the property TNAME in the Teams table, which corresponds to the row that has an ID value of 1:

```
var sqlText:String = "UPDATE Teams SET TNAME = McLaren WHERE ID = 1";
```

Notice that you need to define the name of the table you want to update; immediately after the table name the SET operator is used.

Deleting Data from Tables

To remove data from a table, you need to use the DELETE FROM SQL statement. The following snippet demonstrates how you would define the SQL to remove a team that has an ID value equal to 1:

```
var sqlText:String = "DELETE FROM Teams WHERE ID = 1";
```

With a well-structured table, you should need to supply the value only for your primary key to delete a single row.

You can also provide a number of values to remove from the database:

```
var sqlText:String = "DELETE FROM Teams WHERE ID = 1 OR 2";
```

Having covered the key SQL elements, you can now apply what you have learned in the next activity.

TRY IT OUT   Using SQLite to Create, Save, Update, and Delete Data

Begin by modifying the Maintaining Data App project to open a connection to a database. This file should have the onCreationComplete(), onStatus(), and onLoadComplete() methods covered previously. In this section you may assign a few functions that haven't been covered. Don't worry; these will be explained in due course.

1.   Add a <s:Label> and <s:TextArea> component to a <s:VGroup> container. Set the id property on the components to dbStatus and dbPath, respectively, the width property on both components to 100%, and the fontSize to 18. Then set the height of the label to 25, and text area to 80. Set the value of the text property on the label to Database Status, and the prompt property on the text area to Database Path (Listing 8-10).

LISTING 8-10: Adding a label and text area to display the native path and status of team.db in MaintainingDataAppHome.mxml

```
<s:layout>
        <s:VerticalLayout paddingLeft="20"
                          paddingRight="20"
                          paddingTop="20"
                          paddingBottom="20"/>
</s:layout>

<s:VGroup width="100%">

        <s:Label id="dbStatus"
                 width="100%"
                 height="25"
                 paddingLeft="5"
                 fontSize="18"
                 text="Database Status"/>

        <s:TextArea id="dbPath"
                    width="100%"
                    height="80"
                    fontSize="18"
                    prompt="Database Path"/>

</s:VGroup>
```

2. Within a `<s:HGroup>` container, add a `<s:Button>` component with the `label` property set to Open Database, the `height` property to 50, and its `click` property set to openDb(). Also set the `id` property to dbBtn (Listing 8-11).

LISTING 8-11: Adding a <s:Button> to open the database in MaintainingDataAppHome.mxml

```
<s:VGroup width="100%">

        <s:Label id="dbStatus"
                 width="100%"
                 height="25"
                 paddingLeft="5"
                 fontSize="18"
                 text="Database Status"/>

        <s:TextArea id="dbPath"
                    width="100%"
                    height="80"
                    fontSize="18"
                    prompt="Database Path"/>

        <s:HGroup width="100%"
                  height="65"
```

continues

LISTING 8-11 *(continued)*

```
                    verticalAlign="middle">

            <s:Button id="dbBtn"
                      label="Open Database"
                      height="50"
                      click="openDb()"/>

        </s:HGroup>

    </s:VGroup>
```

3. Under the first `<s:HGroup>` component add a second `<s:HGroup>` component that contains a single button with the `label` property set to `View Teams` and its `click` event set to the `viewTeams()` method, which you define later (Listing 8-12).

LISTING 8-12: Adding a <s:Button> to view teams in MaintainingDataAppHome.mxml

```
<s:HGroup width="100%"
          height="65"
          verticalAlign="middle">

    <s:Button id="dbBtn"
              label="Open Database"
              height="50"
              click="openDb()"/>

</s:HGroup>

<s:HGroup width="100%"
          height="50">

    <s:Button id="viewBtn"
              height="50"
              visible="false"
              label="View Teams"
              click="viewTeams()"/>

</s:HGroup>
```

With the View components and layout defined, let's take a look at the plumbing.

4. Import the `File` class and declare a `File` object variable called `db` in the project (Listing 8-13).

LISTING 8-13: Updating the import statements and declaring the database File object in MaintainingDataAppHome.mxml

```
import air.net.URLMonitor;

import flash.filesystem.File;
import flash.net.URLLoader;
import flash.net.URLRequest;

private var urlMonitor:URLMonitor;
```

```
private var urlLoader:URLLoader;
private var urlRequest:URLRequest;
private var db:File;
```

5. Next add a private method called `openDb()` within the `<fx:Script>` declaration. Ensure the `File` object reference `db` resolves to a database file in the application storage directory called `teams.db` in `openDB()` (Listing 8-14).

LISTING 8-14: Resolving a file path to the database via openDb() in MaintainingDataAppHome.mxml

```
private function onLoadComplete(e:Event):void
{
    dataResult.text = urlLoader.data;
}

private function openDb():void
{
    db = File.applicationStorageDirectory.resolvePath("teams.db");
}
```

6. Next create a new `SQLConnection` object called `sqlConnection` and use the `openAsync()` method to open the database file. Use `addEventListener()` to register an interest in the `SQLErrorEvent.ERROR` and `SQLEvent.OPEN` event types, assigning `onSQLError()` to the `ERROR` event, then use an `if` statement to determine whether the database file already exists to assign the `SQLEvent.OPEN` event. If the database doesn't exist, assign the event to `onCreateDb()`. If the database does exist, assign the `SQLEvent.OPEN` event to `onOpenDb()`, while also displaying the `nativePath` value in the `<s:TextField>` component `dbPath`. There should be three method stubs, one for each event. (Listing 8-15.)

LISTING 8-15: Opening a connection to the database in MaintainingDataAppHome.mxml

```
import flash.data.SQLConnection;
import flash.events.SQLErrorEvent;
import flash.events.SQLEvent;
import flash.filesystem.File;
import flash.net.URLLoader;
import flash.net.URLRequest;

private var urlMonitor:URLMonitor;
private var urlLoader:URLLoader;
private var urlRequest:URLRequest;
private var sqlConnection:SQLConnection;
private var db:File;

private function openDb():void
{
    db = File.applicationStorageDirectory.resolvePath("teams.db");

    sqlConnection = new SQLConnection();
```

continues

LISTING 8-15 *(continued)*

```
        sqlConnection.addEventListener(SQLErrorEvent.ERROR, onSQLError);

        if(db.exists)
        {
                sqlConnection.addEventListener(SQLEvent.OPEN, onOpenDb);
                dbPath.text = db.nativePath;

        } else {

                sqlConnection.addEventListener(SQLEvent.OPEN, onCreateDb);
        }

        sqlConnection.openAsync(db);
    }

    private function onCreateDb(event:SQLEvent):void {}

    private function onOpenDb(e:SQLEvent):void {}

    private function onSQLError(e:SQLErrorEvent):void {}
```

There isn't exactly a listener for creating a new database, so remember that you have to determine whether the database file exists. If the database doesn't exist, assign the SQLEvent.OPEN event to an onCreateDb() event handler, and if it does, assign the SQLEvent.OPEN event to an onOpenDb() event handler. Here when the openAsync() method is called on the database file, it will automatically create the database on a valid file path. In onCreateDb() you can then call the openAsync() to open the database. We'll take a look at this next.

7. Next modify onCreateDb() and onOpenDb() to update the database status text field dbStatus. When the database is opened, check to see whether the SQLConnection object returned is still connected via the SQLConnection.connection property; if it is, ensure the visible property on the viewBtn is set to true (Listing 8-16).

LISTING 8-16: Displaying the database creation, opening, and connection statuses in MaintainingDataAppHome.mxml

```
private function onCreateDb(e:SQLEvent):void
{
        dbStatus.text = "The database was created...";
        createTeamsTable();
}

private function onOpenDb(e:SQLEvent):void
{
        dbStatus.text = "The database was opened...";

        if(SQLConnection(e.target).connected)
```

```
        {
                viewBtn.visible = true;
        }

        dbBtn.enabled = false;
    }
```

8. Next update the onSQLError() method, using the SQLErrorEvent object returned, e, to display the errorID and the details values (Listing 8-17).

LISTING 8-17: Displaying the SQL error status in MaintainingDataAppHome.mxml

```
private function onSQLError(e:SQLErrorEvent):void
    {
        var err:String = "Error id:"
                        + e.error.errorID
                        + "\nDetails:"
                        + e.error.details;

        dbStatus.text = err + = "Error";

        dbBtn.enabled = false;

    }
```

Several errors can trigger the SQLErrorEvent.ERROR event type. For instance if you attempt to insert or update data into a table that hasn't been created yet, you are returned a SQLErrorEvent object with the errorID value set to 3115 and details property set to a No Such Table *TableName*, where *TableName* is the name of the table with the error.

9. Next complete the import statements by adding the SQLStatement class to the list of imports (Listing 8-18).

LISTING 8-18: Updating the import statements in MaintainingDataAppHome.mxml

```
import air.net.URLMonitor;

import flash.data.SQLConnection;
import flash.data.SQLResult;
import flash.data.SQLStatement;
import flash.events.SQLErrorEvent;
import flash.events.SQLEvent;
import flash.filesystem.File;
import flash.net.URLLoader;
import flash.net.URLRequest;
```

10. Underneath onSQLError(), define a new private function to create the Teams table in teams .db called createTeamsTable(). In createTeamsTable() execute the SQL statement to create the Teams table using sqlConnection as the SQLConnection object for the SQLStatement

object createTableSQL, defining the integer TEAM_ID as the primary key and the text TNAME as the second column of data. Assign the SQLEvent.RESULT event to a new event handler called onTeamsTable() (Listing 8-19).

LISTING 8-19: Executing the Create Table SQL statement for Teams in MaintainingDataAppHome.mxml

```
private function createTeamsTable():void
{
        var sqlText:String = "CREATE TABLE "
                            + "Teams(TEAM_ID INTEGER PRIMARY KEY, "
                            + "TNAME TEXT)";

        var createTableSQL:SQLStatement = new SQLStatement();
        createTableSQL.addEventListener(SQLEvent.RESULT, onTeamsTable);
        createTableSQL.addEventListener(SQLErrorEvent.ERROR, onSQLError);
        createTableSQL.sqlConnection = sqlConnection;
        createTableSQL.text = sqlText;
        createTableSQL.execute();
}

private function onTeamsTable(e:SQLEvent):void {}
```

11. In onTeamsTable(), update the text representing the database status. Then under onTeamsTable(), define a new private function to create the Drivers table in teams.db called createDriversTable(), making a call to the function in onTeamsTable(). In createDriversTable() execute the SQL statement to create the Drivers table using sqlConnection as the SQLConnection object for the SQLStatement object createTableSQL, defining the integer TEAM_ID as the primary key and the text TNAME as the second column of data. Assign the SQLEvent.RESULT event to a new event handler called onDriversTable() that updates the database status text notifying that the Drivers table was created (Listing 8-20).

LISTING 8-20: Executing the Create Table SQL statement for Drivers in MaintainingDataAppHome.mxml

```
private function onTeamsTable(e:SQLEvent):void
{
        dbStatus.text = "The Teams table was created";
        createDriversTable();
}

private function createDriversTable():void
{
        var sqlText:String = "CREATE TABLE "
                            + "Drivers(ID INTEGER PRIMARY KEY, "
                            + "DNAME TEXT, "
```

```
                              + "TEAM_ID INTEGER)";

        var createTableSQL:SQLStatement = new SQLStatement();
        createTableSQL.addEventListener(SQLEvent.RESULT, onDriversTable);
        createTableSQL.addEventListener(SQLErrorEvent.ERROR, onSQLError);
        createTableSQL.sqlConnection = sqlConnection;
        createTableSQL.text = sqlText;
        createTableSQL.execute();
    }

    private function onDriversTable(e:SQLEvent):void
    {
        dbStatus.text = "The Drivers table was created";
        dbBtn.setStyle('chromeColor','#51B22F');
    }
```

12. Now run the example, and you'll be able to see the mobile application as it is (Figure 8-4).

At this stage the View Teams button is still inactive. Its usage will simply navigate the user to another view in the application, the Teams View, which will display each of the teams in the database.

13. Next add the `viewTeams()` function, using `navigator.pushView()` to pass a new view, called `view.TeamsView`, as the first parameter, and `sqlConnection` as the second (Listing 8-21).

FIGURE 8-4: Displaying the MaintainingDataAppHome view in Maintaining Data App running on Android 2.3.4

Available for download on Wrox.com

LISTING 8-21: Navigating to the TeamsView via the viewTeams() function in MaintainingDataAppHome.mxml

```
private function viewTeams():void
{
        navigator.pushView(views.TeamsView, sqlConnection);
}
```

If the connection to the `teams.db` file is successful, passing the `sqlConnection` variable to the view will allow the application to execute additional SQL statements on the SQLConnection object.

Before you can interact with the database in the application, you will need to press the Open db button first, and then press the Create Teams Table button. Once the database and tables have been created, you press the View Teams button to move to the Teams View, which you'll create next.

Creating the Teams View

Next you'll follow how to create a working view for displaying each of the teams found in the SQLite database. The first milestone for the view looks like the one shown in Figure 8-5.

Here you see there are only a few View components: two labels, a list, and a single button. The title of the view is also set. The view will later be revisited to complete the Add Team, Delete Team, and Update Team functions. But for now start with getting this view implemented.

1. In Flash Builder, create a new View component called `TeamsView`, and add it to the `views` package.

2. In `TeamsView.mxml`, add a private function called `onViewActivate()` within the `<fx:Script>` block, then set the `viewActivate` property on the view to `onViewActivate()`. Also set the `title` property to `Teams View` (Listing 8-22).

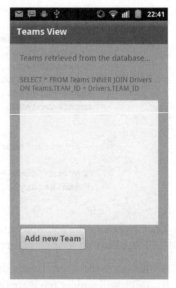

FIGURE 8-5: A preview of the Teams view in Maintaining Data App running on Android 2.3.4

LISTING 8-22: Assigning viewActivate to onViewActivate() and setting the title in TeamsView.mxml

```xml
<?xml version="1.0" encoding="utf-8"?>
<s:View xmlns:fx="http://ns.adobe.com/mxml/2009"
        xmlns:s="library://ns.adobe.com/flex/spark"
        title="Teams View"
        viewActivate="onViewActivate()">

    <fx:Script>
        <![CDATA[

            private function onViewActivate():void {}

        ]]>
    </fx:Script>

    <s:layout>
        <s:VerticalLayout paddingLeft="20"
                          paddingRight="20"
                          paddingTop="20"
                          paddingBottom="20"/>
    </s:layout>

</s:View>
```

3. Add two `<s:Label>` components, both with `width` properties set to `100%`, `height` set to `40`, and their `verticalAlign` properties set to `middle`. Both of these labels are for descriptive

purposes only — that is, they describe what the view is actually doing. For the first label, set the `color` property to #454545 and the `text` property to `Teams retrieved from the database...`; then for the second label, set the `text` property to `SELECT * FROM TEAMS INNER JOIN Drivers ON Teams.TEAM_ID = DRIVERS.Team_ID` (Listing 8-23).

LISTING 8-23: Adding descriptive labels in TeamsView.mxml

```
<s:layout>
        <s:VerticalLayout paddingLeft="20"
                          paddingRight="20"
                          paddingTop="20"
                          paddingBottom="20"/>
</s:layout>

<s:Label id="dbStatus"
         width="100%"
         height="40"
         color="#454545"
         text="Teams retrieved from the database..."
         verticalAlign="middle"/>

<s:Label width="100%"
         height="50"
         fontSize="14"
         text="SELECT * FROM Teams INNER JOIN Drivers ON Teams.TEAM_ID = Drivers.
TEAM_ID"
         verticalAlign="middle"/>
```

4. Add a `<s:List>` component. Set the `id` property to `teamsList`, with the `width` set to `100%`, the `height` set to `60%`, and its `enabled` property state set to `true`, and the `selectedIndex` property to `0` (Listing 8-24).

LISTING 8-24: Adding the List component teamsList in TeamsView.mxml

```
<s:layout>
        <s:VerticalLayout paddingLeft="20"
                          paddingRight="20"
                          paddingTop="20"
                          paddingBottom="20"/>
</s:layout>

<s:Label id="dbStatus"
         width="100%"
         height="40"
         color="#454545"
         text="Teams retrieved from the database..."
         verticalAlign="middle"/>

<s:Label width="100%"
         height="50"
```

continues

LISTING 8-24 *(continued)*

```
        fontSize="14"
        text="SELECT * FROM Teams INNER JOIN Drivers ON Teams.TEAM_ID = Drivers.
TEAM_ID"
        verticalAlign="middle"/>

<s:List id="teamsList"
        width="100%"
        height="60%"
        enabled="true"
        selectedIndex="0"/>
```

5. Add five new empty method stubs in the script section: selectTeams(), addTeam(), updateTeam(), deleteTeam(), and deleteDrivers(). Then in onViewActive(), make a call to the selectTeams() (Listing 8-25).

Available for download on Wrox.com

LISTING 8-25: Declaring the private functions selectTeams(), addTeam(), updateTeam(), deleteTeam(), and deleteDrivers() in TeamsView.mxml

```
<fx:Script>
        <![CDATA[

                private function onViewActive():void
                {
                        selectTeams();
                }

                private function selectTeams():void {}

                private function addTeam():void {}

                private function updateTeam():void {}

                private function deleteTeam():void {}

                private function deleteDrivers():void {}
        ]]>
</fx:Script>
```

6. Declare a SQLConnection object, and then in selectTeams(), cast the data object of the view as a SQLConnection object to the sqlConnection variable (Listing 8-26).

Available for download on Wrox.com

LISTING 8-26: Setting the SQL Connection object in TeamsView.mxml

```
private var sqlConnection:SQLConnection;

private function onViewActive():void
{
        selectTeams();
```

```
}

private function selectTeams():void
{
        sqlConnection = SQLConnection(data);
}
```

7. In `selectTeams()` define two variables, the first a string called `sqlText` with the value `SELECT * FROM Teams INNER JOIN Drivers ON Teams.TEAM_ID = Drivers.TEAM_ID`, and the second variable a `SQLStatement` object called `selectAllSQL`. Instantiate the `SQLStatement`, and then register the `SQLStatement` object's interest in the `SQLEvent .RESULT` and `SQLErrorEvent.ERROR` event. These events need to be handled by two new event handler methods, `onSQLError()` and `onSelectTeams()`. Assign `onSelectTeams()` to `SQLEvent.RESULT` and `onSQLError()` to the `SQLErrorEvent.ERROR` (Listing 8-27).

LISTING 8-27: Defining the Select teams SQL statement in TeamsView.mxml

```
private function selectTeams():void
{
        sqlConnection = SQLConnection(data);

        var sqlText:String = "SELECT * FROM Teams "
                            + "INNER JOIN Drivers "
                            + "ON Teams.TEAM_ID = Drivers.TEAM_ID";

        var selectAllSQL:SQLStatement = new SQLStatement();
        selectAllSQL.addEventListener(SQLEvent.RESULT, onSelectTeams);
        selectAllSQL.addEventListener(SQLErrorEvent.ERROR, onSQLError);
}

private function onSelectTeams(e:SQLEvent):void {}

private function onSQLError(e:SQLErrorEvent):void {}
```

8. Next assign the `selectAllSQL.sqlConnection` property and `sqlText` to the `selectAllSQL .text` property. Finally, call the `selectAllSQL.execute()` method (Listing 8-28).

LISTING 8-28: Executing the Select teams SQL statement in TeamsView.mxml

```
private function selectTeams():void
{
        sqlConnection = SQLConnection(data);

        var sqlText:String = "SELECT * FROM Teams";

        var selectAllSQL:SQLStatement = new SQLStatement();
        selectAllSQL.addEventListener(SQLEvent.RESULT, onSelectTeams);
        selectAllSQL.addEventListener(SQLErrorEvent.ERROR, onSQLError);
        selectAllSQL.sqlConnection = sqlConnection;
        selectAllSQL.text = sqlText;
        selectAllSQL.execute();
}
```

9. In `onSelectTeams()`, add two new variables, the first a `SQLStatement` called `selectTeamsSQL`, which needs to have the `SQLEvent.target` property assigned. Cast the `e.target` to `selectTeamsSQL`. The second variable is a `SQLResult` object called `result`. Use `selectTeamsSQL.getResult()` to assign the `SQLResult` object to `result` (Listing 8-29).

LISTING 8-29: Assigning the getResult() method to a SQLResult object in TeamsView.mxml

```
private function onSelectTeams(e:SQLEvent):void
{
    var selectTeamsSQL:SQLStatement = SQLStatement(e.target);
    var result:SQLResult = selectTeamsSQL.getResult();
}
```

10. Use `result.complete` and the `result.data.length` to determine whether data has been returned from the database. Then use an `if` statement to instantiate the `teamList.dataProvider`, which is an `ArrayCollection` object. Use a `for each` statement to iterate through the number of `team` objects found in `result.data`. Using the team objects found, create a new object `obj` with two properties, `teamName` and `teamId`. The value for `teamName` should be retrieved from the `team` object using `team["TNAME"]`, while the `teamId` should be retrieved from the `team` object using `team["TEAM_ID"]`. Also retrieve the driver names from `team["DNAME"]` and assign this to the `driver` property on `obj`. Finally, use the `ArrayCollection.addItem()` method on the `teamsList` object's `dataProvider` property to add the new object `obj` to the list (Listing 8-30).

LISTING 8-30: Adding the driver names to the list in TeamsView.mxml

```
private function onSelectTeams(e:SQLEvent):void
{
    var selectTeamsSQL:SQLStatement = SQLStatement(e.target);
    var result:SQLResult = selectTeamsSQL.getResult();

    if(result.complete)
    {
        if(result.data)
        {
            teamsList.dataProvider = new ArrayCollection();

            var tStr:String;
            var dStr:String;

            for each(var team:Object in result.data)
            {
                var obj:Object =
                {
                    teamName:team["TNAME"],
                    teamId:team["TEAM_ID"]
                };

                if(tStr == obj.teamName)
```

```
                                    {
                                            obj.drivers = dStr + ", " + team["DNAME"];
                                            teamsList.dataProvider.addItem(obj);

                                    } else {

                                            dStr = team["DNAME"];
                                            tStr = obj.teamName;
                                    }
                            }
                    }
            }
    }
```

11. Next complete the onSQLError() event handler. Simply update the dbStatus label to display the error code (Listing 8-31).

LISTING 8-31: Handling SQLErrorEvents via the onSQLError() method in TeamsView.mxml

```
private function onSQLError(e:SQLErrorEvent):void
{
        dbStatus.text = e.error.errorID.toString();
}
```

Up to now you've defined two of the six methods created for TeamsView.mxml, onViewActivate(), and selectTeams(), including their associated event handlers for the SQLEvent.RESULT event onSelectTeams() and SQLErrorEvent.ERROR event onSQLError().

Next take a look at creating an item renderer for the List component.

Creating an Item Renderer for the List Component

Creating an item renderer allows you to customize and control the default look and feel of a data item. In Chapter 7 the <s:List> component used for listing files simply consisted of a <s:Label> component. If you want to display the folder or file title as well as the creation date and file size, you should include other <s:Label> components.

In this section you'll take a look at how you can customize the <s:List> component to include subcomponents and dispatch the custom event types created.

1. In Flash Builder, create a new item renderer. Select File ➪ New ➪ Item Renderer (Figure 8-6).

2. In the pop-up that opens, set the Package field to views.components.renderers, set the Name field to TeamItemRenderer, and set the Select Template field to Icon item renderer for mobile list (MXML) (Figure 8-7).

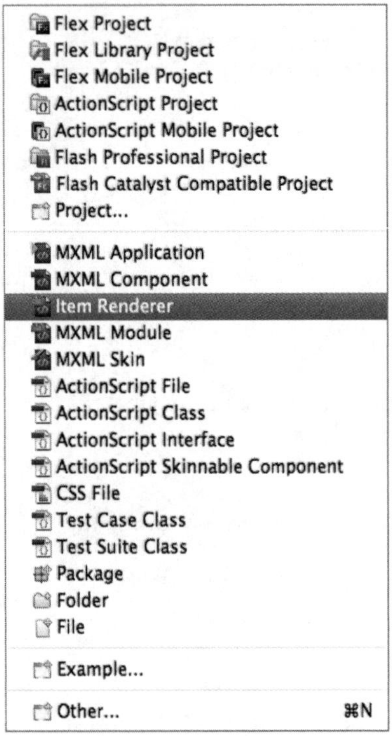

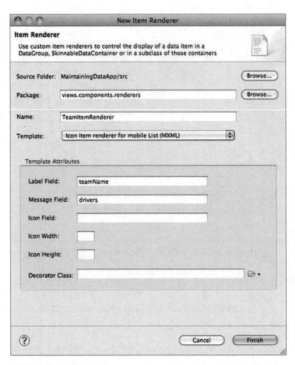

Flex Project
Flex Library Project
Flex Mobile Project
ActionScript Project
ActionScript Mobile Project
Flash Professional Project
Flash Catalyst Compatible Project
Project...
MXML Application
MXML Component
Item Renderer
MXML Module
MXML Skin
ActionScript File
ActionScript Class
ActionScript Interface
ActionScript Skinnable Component
CSS File
Test Case Class
Test Suite Class
Package
Folder
File
Example...
Other... ⌘N

FIGURE 8-6: Selecting MXML Item Renderer from the Flash Builder file menu

New Item Renderer
Item Renderer
Use custom item renderers to control the display of a data item in a DataGroup, SkinnableDataContainer or in a subclass of those containers
Source Folder: MaintainingDataApp/src
Browse...
Package: views.components.renderers
Browse...
Name: TeamItemRenderer
Template: Icon item renderer for mobile List (MXML)
Template Attributes
Label Field: teamName
Message Field: drivers
Icon Field:
Icon Width:
Icon Height:
Decorator Class:
Cancel
Finish

FIGURE 8-7: Creating a new Item Renderer in Maintaining Data App

Flash Builder automatically generates the default code for the new file in the `view.components.renderers` package (Listing 8-32).

LISTING 8-32: The code automatically generated for TeamItemRenderer.mxml

Available for download on Wrox.com

```
<?xml version="1.0" encoding="utf-8"?>
<s:IconItemRenderer xmlns:fx="http://ns.adobe.com/mxml/2009"
                    xmlns:s="library://ns.adobe.com/flex/spark"
                    labelField="teamName"
                    messageField ="drivers">

</s:IconItemRenderer>
```

Figure 8-8 shows the location of the new item renderer.

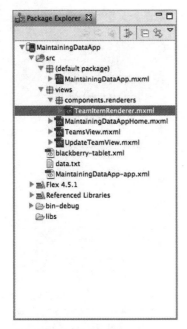

FIGURE 8-8: Highlighting the
TeamItemRenderer.mxml file
in the Package Explorer in
Maintaining Data App running on
Android 2.3.4

3. In `TeamItemRenderer.mxml`, set the selection color to `#68BAFA` and the row colors for the
List to alternate between `#CCCCC` and `#EEEEEE` (Listing 8-33).

**Available for
download on
Wrox.com**

> **LISTING 8-33:** Adding selection color and alternatingItemColor attributes for the <s:List>
> component in TeamItemRenderer.mxml

```
<?xml version="1.0" encoding="utf-8"?>
<s:IconItemRenderer xmlns:fx="http://ns.adobe.com/mxml/2009"
                    xmlns:s="library://ns.adobe.com/flex/spark"
                    labelField="teamName"
                    messageField="drivers"
                    alternatingItemColors="[#CCCCCC, #EEEEEE]"
                    selectionColor="#68BAFA">

</s:IconItemRenderer>
```

Completing the Teams View

Using the `TeamItemRenderer`, you will now complete the Teams view. The view will look something like that shown in Figure 8-9.

Here you update the view to include a view menu that allows the user to update or delete the selected item in the team list.

Next follow these steps:

1. Declare an integer `i` as the parameter for the `updateTeam()` method. In `updateTeam()`, create two new objects. The first is called `teamObj`, which references the selected item using the `getItemAt()` method on the `dataProvider` of `teamList`. The index is the value supplied to the method. The second object you need to create, called `dataObj`, should have four properties: `sqlConnection`, `teamId`, `teamName`, and `sqlType`. Assign the `sqlConnection` variable to `dataObj.sqlConnection`; then, using the `TeamsSQLEvent` object, assign `teamObj.teamId` to the `teamId` property and `teamObj.teamName` to `teamName`. The SQL query will be an update, so this should be set on `sqlType`. Finally, use the `navigator.pushView()` method to navigate to a new view you'll define shortly called `UpdateTeamsView.mxml`, passing the data object `dataObj` (Listing 8-34).

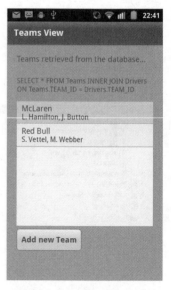

FIGURE 8-9: A preview of the Teams view in Maintaining Data App running on Android 2.3.4

Available for download on Wrox.com

LISTING 8-34: Defining a data object to pass to UpdateTeamView.mxml via the updateTeam() method in TeamsView.mxml

```
private function updateTeam(i:int):void
{
    var teamObj:Object = teamsList.dataProvider.getItemAt(i);

    var dataObj:Object =
    {
        sqlConnection:sqlConnection,
        teamId:teamObj.teamId,
        teamName:teamObj.teamName,
        sqlType:"UPDATE"
    };

    navigator.pushView(views.UpdateTeamView, dataObj);
}
```

2. Next declare an integer `i` as the parameter for the `deleteTeam()` method. In `deleteTeam()` define three new variables — the first, an object called `teamObj`; the second, a string called `sqlText`, with the value `"DELETE FROM Teams WHERE TEAM_ID = :teamId"`; then the third, a `SQLStatement` object called `deleteTeamSQL`. Using the `deleteTeamsSQL` object, register an interest in the `SQLEvent.Result` and `SQLErrorEvent.Error` events, assigning a new handler method called `onDeleteTeam()` to the `SQLEvent.Result` event and the `onSQLError()` method (as defined earlier) to the `SQLErrorEvent.ERROR` event (Listing 8-35).

LISTING 8-35: Defining the SQL to remove a team from the Teams table via the deleteTeam() method in TeamsView.mxml

```
private function deleteTeam(i:int):void
{
    var teamObj:Object = teamsList.dataProvider.getItemAt(i);

    var sqlText:String = "DELETE FROM Teams WHERE TEAM_ID = :teamId";

    var deleteTeamSQL:SQLStatement = new SQLStatement();
    deleteTeamSQL.addEventListener(SQLEvent.RESULT, onDeleteTeam);
    deleteTeamSQL.addEventListener(SQLErrorEvent.ERROR, onSQLError);
}

private function onDeleteTeam(e:SQLEvent):void {}
```

3. Complete the `deleteTeam()` method by assigning the `sqlConnection` object to the `deleteTeamsSQL.sqlConnection` property, and the `sqlText` string to the `deleteTeamSQL.text` property. Then set the `teamObj.teamId` value to the `deleteTeamsSQL.parameters` property, specifying `:teamId` as the key. Finally, call the `SQLStatement.execute()` method on the `deleteTeamSQL` object (Listing 8-36).

LISTING 8-36: Executing the SQL to remove a team from the Teams table via the deleteTeam() method in TeamsView.mxml

```
private function deleteTeam(i:int):void
{
    var teamObj:Object = teamsList.dataProvider.getItemAt(i);

    var sqlText:String = "DELETE FROM Teams WHERE TEAM_ID = :teamId";

    var deleteTeamSQL:SQLStatement = new SQLStatement();
    deleteTeamSQL.addEventListener(SQLEvent.RESULT, onDeleteTeam);
    deleteTeamSQL.addEventListener(SQLErrorEvent.ERROR, onSQLError);
    deleteTeamSQL.sqlConnection = sqlConnection;
    deleteTeamSQL.text = sqlText;
    deleteTeamSQL.parameters[":teamId"] = teamObj.teamId;
    deleteTeamSQL.execute();
}
```

4. In `onDeleteTeam()`, call the `deleteDrivers()` method, supplying the `teamId` property returned in the parameters on the `SQLEvent` object's `target` property (Listing 8-37).

LISTING 8-37: Handling the SQL to remove a team from the Teams table via the onDeleteTeam() method in TeamsView.mxml

```
private function onDeleteTeam(e:SQLEvent):void
{
    deleteDrivers(e.target.parameters[":teamId"]);
}
```

5. For `deleteDrivers()`, add two new variables, the first a string called `sqlText` with the value `DELETE FROM Driver WHERE TEAM_ID = :teamId`, then the second a `SQLStatement` object called `deleteDriverSQL`. Using the `deleteDriverSQL` object, register an interest in the `SQLEvent.Result` and `SQLErrorEvent.Error` events, assigning a new handler method called `onDeleteDrivers()` to the `SQLEvent.Result` event and the `onSQLError()` method (as defined earlier) to the `SQLErrorEvent.ERROR` event. In the `deleteDrivers()` method, assign the `sqlConnection` object to the `deleteDriversSQL.sqlConnection` property and the `sqlText` string to the `deleteDriversSQL.text` property. Then pass the `teamId` as a value to the `deleteDriversSQL.parameters` property, specifying `:teamId` as the key. Then call the `SQLStatement.execute()` method on the `deleteDriversSQL` object (Listing 8-38).

LISTING 8-38: Executing the SQL to delete a driver from teams.db in TeamsView.mxml

```
private function deleteDrivers(teamId:Number):void
{
    var sqlText:String = "DELETE FROM Driver WHERE TEAM_ID = :teamId";

    var deleteDriversSQL:SQLStatement = new SQLStatement();
    deleteDriversSQL.addEventListener(SQLEvent.RESULT, onDeleteDrivers);
    deleteDriversSQL.addEventListener(SQLErrorEvent.ERROR, onSQLError);
    deleteDriversSQL.sqlConnection = sqlConnection;
    deleteDriversSQL.text = sqlText;
    deleteDriversSQL.parameters[":teamId"] = teamId;
    deleteDriversSQL.execute();
}

private function onDeleteDrivers(e:SQLEvent):void {}
```

6. In `onDeleteDrivers()`, set the `text` property on `dbStatus` to `"The record was deleted successfully"`. Then call the `selectTeams()` method (Listing 8-39).

LISTING 8-39: Handling the SQL to remove a driver from the driver's table via the onDeleteDrivers() method in TeamsView.mxml

```
private function onDeleteDrivers(e:SQLEvent):void
{
    dbStatus.text = "The record was deleted successfully";
    selectTeams();
}
```

7. Returning to the MXML portion of the document, add a new button under the list component in a horizontal group with the `label` property set to `Add new Team` and the `click` event property set to `addTeam()` (Listing 8-40).

LISTING 8-40: Adding the Add Team button to the view in TeamsView.mxml

```
<s:List id="teamsList"
        width="100%"
        height="55%"
        enabled="true"
        selectedIndex="0"/>

<s:HGroup width="100%"
          height="50"
          gap="16">

    <s:Button click="addTeam()"
              height="50"
              label="Add new Team"/>

</s:HGroup>
```

8. Next, for the list component `teamsList`, set the `itemRenderer` property to the path to `TeamItemRenderer` (Listing 8-41).

LISTING 8-41: Setting the item renderer on the List component in TeamsView.mxml

```
<s:List id="teamsList"
        itemRenderer="views.components.renderers.TeamItemRenderer"
        width="100%"
        height="55%"
        enabled="true"
        selectedIndex="0"/>
```

9. In the `addTeam()` method, navigate to the `UpdateTeamsView.mxml` view passing a new `dataObj` variable as data for the view. Define two properties on the object `sqlConnection` and `sqlType`. Set the `sqlType` property to `INSERT` (Listing 8-42).

LISTING 8-42: Navigating to the UpdateTeamsView.mxml via addTeam() in TeamsView.mxml

```
private function addTeam():void
{
    var dataObj:Object =
    {
        sqlConnection:sqlConnection,
        sqlType:"INSERT"
    };

    navigator.pushView(views.UpdateTeamsView, dataObj);
}
```

10. Under `addTeam()`, add a new private function called `toggleMenu()` to the view, which takes the Boolean `toggle` as a parameter. This should be passed onto the `viewMenuOpen` property on the `FlexGlobals.topLevelApplication` object (Listing 8-43).

LISTING 8-43: in TeamsView.mxml

```
private function addTeam():void
{
        var dataObj:Object =
        {
                sqlConnection:sqlConnection,
                sqlType:"INSERT"
        };

        navigator.pushView(views.UpdateTeamView, dataObj);
}

private function toggleMenu(toggle:Boolean):void
{
        mx.core.FlexGlobals.topLevelApplication.viewMenuOpen = toggle;
}
```

11. Assign the `toggleMenu()` method to the `click` property on the `<s:List>`, passing the value `true` as an argument (Listing 8-44).

LISTING 8-44: in TeamsView.mxml

```
<s:List id="teamsList"
        itemRenderer="views.components.renderers.TeamItemRenderer"
        click="toggleMenu(true)"
        width="100%"
        height="55%"
        enabled="true"
        selectedIndex="0"/>
```

12. Finally, under the `<s:HGroup>` containing the Add new Team button, declare a set of three `<s:ViewMenuItem>` components, setting the `label` properties to `Update`, `Cancel`, and `Delete`, respectively. For the update menu item, set the `focusColor` property to `#51B22F`, and for the delete menu item, set the `focusColor` property to `#CB0909` (Listing 8-45).

LISTING 8-45: Defining the `<s:ViewMenuItem>` component for the view in TeamsView.mxml

```
<s:HGroup width="100%"
        height="50"
        gap="16">

    <s:Button click="addTeam()"
            height="50"
```

```
                        label="Add new Team"/>

    </s:HGroup>

    <s:viewMenuItems>

        <s:ViewMenuItem label="Update"
                        focusColor="#51B22F"
                        click="updateTeam(teamsList.selectedIndex)"/>

        <s:ViewMenuItem label="Cancel"
                        click="toggleMenu(false)"/>

        <s:ViewMenuItem label="Delete"
                        focusColor="#CB0909"
                        click="deleteTeam(teamsList.selectedIndex)"/>

    </s:viewMenuItems>
```

Creating the Insert and Update Views

To complete the application, in this section you'll take a look at creating the last view called
`UpdateTeamsView.mxml`. In `TeamView.mxml` are two methods, `addTeam()` and `updateTeam()`,
both of which will present the user with the update view. The update view will actually encompass
two views, Insert and Update. Both `addTeam()` and `updateTeam()` have been created to pass the
`sqlType` property as part of a data object for the view. Follow the next steps to learn how this is
utilized.

1. In Flash Builder, create a new View component called `UpdateTeamsView` in the views
package.

2. In `UpdateTeamsView.mxml`, modify the `<s:VerticalLayout>` attributes, setting the
padding properties `paddingLeft`, `paddingRight`, `paddingTop`, and `paddingBottom` to
20. Then underneath the `<s:layout>` declaration, add a `<s:Button>` component to the
`<s:navigationContent>` component with its `label` property set to `Back` and the `click`
property to `navigator.popView()` to navigate content (Listing 8-46).

LISTING 8-46: Setting the padding and back button navigation in UpdateTeamsView.mxml

```
<?xml version="1.0" encoding="utf-8"?>
<s:View xmlns:fx="http://ns.adobe.com/mxml/2009"
        xmlns:s="library://ns.adobe.com/flex/spark"
        xmlns:mx="library://ns.adobe.com/flex/mx"
        creationComplete="onCreationComplete()">

    <fx:Script>
        <![CDATA[
            private function onCreationComplete():void {}
        ]]>
```

continues

LISTING 8-46 *(continued)*

```
    </fx:Script>

    <s:layout>
        <s:VerticalLayout paddingLeft="20"
                          paddingRight="20"
                          paddingTop="20"
                          paddingBottom="20"/>
    </s:layout>

    <s:navigationContent>
        <s:Button label="Back"
                  click="navigator.popView()"/>
    </s:navigationContent>

</s:View>
```

3. Next declare two new objects to represent each driver, d1 and d2 (Listing 8-47).

LISTING 8-47: Declaring two new objects, d1 and d2, in UpdateTeamsView.mxml

```
<fx:Script>
    <![CDATA[

        private var d1:Object={};
        private var d2:Object={};

        private function onCreationComplete():void {}
    ]]>
</fx:Script>
```

4. Under onCreationComplete(), add a new function addTeam() to create the SQL statement addTeamSQL, which should insert a new team name to the database. Use a single parameter called teamName to set the team name, and assign onAddTeam() as the handler for the SQLEvent.RESULT event. Use the sqlConnection property on the view's data object to set the SQL connection on addTeamSQL. Then in onAddTeam() create an additional SQL statement called teamIdSQL that retrieves the TEAM_ID value from the team name. Finally, add a new stub called onTeamId() and assign it to the SQLEvent.RESULT event dispatched for teamIdSQL (Listing 8-48).

LISTING 8-48: Executing the SQL to insert a team into the Teams table via the addTeam() method in UpdateTeamView.mxml

```
private function onCreationComplete():void {}

private function addTeam(teamName:String):void
{
    var sqlText:String = "INSERT INTO Teams(TNAME) VALUES(:tname)";

    var addTeamSQL:SQLStatement = new SQLStatement();
```

```
        addTeamSQL.addEventListener(SQLEvent.RESULT, onAddTeam);
        addTeamSQL.addEventListener(SQLErrorEvent.ERROR, onSQLError);
        addTeamSQL.sqlConnection = data.sqlConnection;
        addTeamSQL.text = sqlText;
        addTeamSQL.parameters[":tname"] = teamName;
        addTeamSQL.execute();
}

private function onAddTeam(e:SQLEvent):void
{
        var addTeamSQL:SQLStatement = SQLStatement(e.target);
        addTeamSQL.removeEventListener(SQLEvent.RESULT, onAddTeam);
        addTeamSQL.removeEventListener(SQLErrorEvent.ERROR, onSQLError);

        if(addTeamSQL.getResult().lastInsertRowID != 0)
        {
                var sqlText:String = "SELECT TEAM_ID FROM Teams "
                                + "WHERE Teams.TNAME = (:tname)";

                var teamIdSQL:SQLStatement = new SQLStatement();
                teamIdSQL.addEventListener(SQLEvent.RESULT, onTeamId);
                teamIdSQL.addEventListener(SQLErrorEvent.ERROR, onSQLError);
                teamIdSQL.sqlConnection = data.sqlConnection;
                teamIdSQL.parameters[":tname"] = teamTxt.text;
                teamIdSQL.text = sqlText;
                teamIdSQL.execute();
        }
}

private function onTeamId(e:SQLEvent):void {}

private function onSQLError(e:SQLEvent):void {}
```

Notice in `onAddTeam()` that the last generated row identifier property, `lastInsertRowID`, is used to determine whether or not to execute the `SQLStatement` object `teamIdSQL` in an `if` statement. The value is retrieved by calling `getResult().lastInsertRowID` on the `SQLStatement` object, and returns 0 if the SQL executed is not an `INSERT` statement. The row identifier can be used to identify a row of a table within the database, uniquely.

5. Returning to the MXML, add a `<s:Label>` component to display a description for the view (Listing 8-49).

Available for download on Wrox.com

LISTING 8-49: Adding a descriptive label to the view in UpdateTeamsView.mxml

```
<s:layout>
        <s:VerticalLayout paddingLeft="20"
                          paddingRight="20"
                          paddingTop="20"
                          paddingBottom="20"/>
```

continues

LISTING 8-49 *(continued)*

```
</s:layout>

<s:navigationContent>
    <s:Button label="Back"
              click="navigator.popView()"/>
</s:navigationContent>

<s:Label id="description"
         width="100%"
         height="40"
         verticalAlign="middle"/>
```

6. Under the descriptive `<s:Label>` component, create three sets of `<s:HGroup>` containers vertically stacked in a single `<s:VGroup>` container, each containing a `<s:Label>` component and an associated `<s:TextInput>` component. Set the `width` property of `<s:VGroup>` to 100%, height to 212, paddingTop to 20, paddingLeft to 25, and paddingRight to 50. In the first `<s:HGroup>`, set the `id` property on the `<s:TextInput>` component to `teamTxt` and the `text` property on the `<s:Label>` component to `Team`. In the second `<s:HGroup>`, set the `id` property on the `<s:TextInput>` component to `driverOne`, and the `text` property of the `<s:Label>` component to `Driver No. 1`. Then in the third `<s:HGroup>` component, set the `text` property on the `<s:Label>` component to `Driver No. 2` and the `id` property on the `<s:TextInput>` component to `driverTwo`. Set each of the `height` properties on the components within the `<s:VGroup>` to 50, and for each of the `<s:HGroup>` components, additionally set the `width` to 100 and the horizontal align to `right`. For the `<s:TextInput>` components, set the `width` property to 50, and for the `<s:Label>` components, set the `verticalAlign` property to `middle` and `paddingRight` to 10 (Listing 8-50).

LISTING 8-50: Adding label and Text Input components for the Team, Driver 1, and Driver 2 in UpdateTeamsView.mxml

```
<s:Label id="description"
         width="100%"
         height="40"
         verticalAlign="middle"/>

<s:VGroup width="100%"
          height="212"
          paddingTop="20"
          paddingLeft="25"
          paddingRight="50">

    <s:HGroup width="100"
              height="50"
              horizontalAlign="right">

        <s:Label height="50"
```

```
                    text="Team"
                    verticalAlign="middle"
                    paddingRight="10"/>

        <s:TextInput id="teamTxt"
                     width="50"
                     height="50"/>

    </s:HGroup>

    <s:HGroup width="100"
              height="50"
              horizontalAlign="right">

        <s:Label height="50"
                 text="Driver No. 1"
                 verticalAlign="middle"
                 paddingRight="10"/>

        <s:TextInput id="driverOne"
                     width="50"
                     height="50"/>
    </s:HGroup>

    <s:HGroup width="100"
              height="50"
              horizontalAlign="right">

        <s:Label height="50"
                 text="Driver No. 2"
                 verticalAlign="middle"
                 paddingRight="10"/>

        <s:TextInput id="driverTwo"
                     width="50"
                     height="50"/>
    </s:HGroup>

</s:VGroup>
```

7. Under the `<s:VGroup>` block, add one more `<s:HGroup>` component that contains two button components, `button1` and `button2` (Listing 8-51).

LISTING 8-51: Adding button1 and button2 to UpdateTeamsView.mxml

```
<s:HGroup width="100"
          height="50"
          horizontalAlign="right">

    <s:Label height="50"
             text="Driver No. 2"
             verticalAlign="middle"
```

continues

LISTING 8-51 *(continued)*

```
                            paddingRight="10"/>

                <s:TextInput id="driverTwo"
                             width="50"
                             height="50"/>
        </s:HGroup>

    </s:VGroup>

    <s:HGroup width="100%"
              height="50"
              gap="16"
              horizontalAlign="center"
              verticalAlign="bottom">

        <s:Button id="button1"
                  height="50"/>

        <s:Button id="button2"
                  click="navigator.popView()"
                  height="50"
                  label="Cancel"/>

    </s:HGroup>
```

8. Next, in `onTeamId()`, retrieve the result of the SQL query and assign the `TEAM_ID` value to the variable `tID`. Then make two calls to a method called `addDriver()`, supplying two parameters, the value of the `text` property on the `<s:TextInput>` component for each driver, and `tId` (Listing 8-52).

LISTING 8-52: Assigning the team ID to addDriver() via the onTeamId() method in UpdateTeamView.mxml

```
private function onTeamId(e:SQLEvent):void
{
    var teamIdSQL:SQLStatement = SQLStatement(e.target);
    var result:SQLResult = teamIdSQL.getResult();

    var tId:Number = result.data[0]["TEAM_ID"];

    addDriver(driverOne.text, tId);
    addDriver(driverTwo.text, tId);
}

private function addDriver(driverName:String, teamId:Number):void {}

private function onSQLError(e:SQLEvent):void {}
```

9. In `addDriver()`, create the SQL statement to insert a new driver. Use two parameters that identify the driver, a string called `driverName` and a number called `teamId`. Assign `onAddDriver()` as the handler for the `SQLEvent.RESULT` event. In `onAddDriver()`, update the `description.text` to let the user know the record was inserted successfully (Listing 8-53).

> **LISTING 8-53:** Executing the SQL to insert a driver via the addDriver() method in UpdateTeamView.mxml

```
private function addDriver(driverName:String, teamId:Number):void
{
    var sqlText:String = "INSERT INTO Drivers(DNAME, TEAM_ID) "
                       + "VALUES(:dname, :teamId)";

    var addDriverSQL:SQLStatement = new SQLStatement();
    addDriverSQL.addEventListener(SQLEvent.RESULT, onAddDriver);
    addDriverSQL.addEventListener(SQLErrorEvent.ERROR, onSQLError);
    addDriverSQL.sqlConnection = data.sqlConnection;
    addDriverSQL.text = sqlText;
    addDriverSQL.parameters[":dname"] = driverName;
    addDriverSQL.parameters[":teamId"] = teamId;
    addDriverSQL.execute();
}

private function onAddDriver(e:SQLEvent):void
{
    var sqlStatement:SQLStatement = SQLStatement(e.target);
    sqlStatement.removeEventListener(SQLEvent.RESULT, onAddDriver);
    sqlStatement.removeEventListener(SQLErrorEvent.ERROR, onSQLError);

    if(sqlStatement.getResult().lastInsertRowID != 0)
    {
        description.text = "The record was inserted successfully";
    }
}

private function onSQLError(e:SQLEvent):void {}
```

As the view changes from `TeamsView.mxml` to `EditTeamView.mxml`, the `teamName` will be forwarded, but the drivers' names will not. To update the drivers, the user needs to be presented with the drivers from the associated team. So these need to be retrieved from the database.

10. Above `onSQLError()`, add two new stubs, `selectDrivers()` and `onSelectDrivers()` (Listing 8-54).

> **LISTING 8-54:** Declaring selectDrivers() and onSelectDrivers() in UpdateTeamsView.mxml

```
private function selectDrivers():void {}

private function onSelectDrivers(e:SQLEvent):void {}
```

11. In `selectDrivers()`, create the SQL statement to select all the drivers from the database with a specific `teamId` called `selectDriversSQL`. Assign `onSelectDrivers()` as the handler for the `SQLEvent.RESULT` event. Then in `onSelectDrivers()`, set the properties of the driver objects `d1` and `d2`, and finally update the `text` properties on each of the driver `<s:TextInput>` components (Listing 8-55).

LISTING 8-55: Executing the SQL statement to select a driver in UpdateTeamsView.mxml

```
private function selectDrivers():void
{
        var sqlText:String = "SELECT * FROM Drivers "
                           + "WHERE TEAM_ID = (:teamId)";

        var selectDriversSQL:SQLStatement = new SQLStatement();
        selectDriversSQL.addEventListener(SQLEvent.RESULT, onSelectDrivers);
        selectDriversSQL.addEventListener(SQLErrorEvent.ERROR, onSQLError);
        selectDriversSQL.sqlConnection = data.sqlConnection;
        selectDriversSQL.text = sqlText;
        selectDriversSQL.parameters[":teamId"] = Number(data.teamId);
        selectDriversSQL.execute();
}

private function onSelectDrivers(e:SQLEvent):void
{
        var result:SQLResult = SQLStatement(e.target).getResult();

        d1.name = result.data[0]["DNAME"];
        d1.id = result.data[0]["ID"];
        d1.teamId = result.data[0]["TEAM_ID"];

        d2.name = result.data[1]["DNAME"];
        d2.id = result.data[1]["ID"];
        d2.teamId = result.data[1]["TEAM_ID"];

        driverOne.text = d1.name;
        driverTwo.text = d2.name;
}
```

12. Above the `onSQLError()` event handler, add four new method stubs: `updateTeam()`, `onUpdateTeam()`, `updateDriver()`, and `onUpdateDriver()`. The `updateDriver()` method should take two arguments: `driverName` and `driverId`, while `onUpdateTeam()` and `onUpdateDriver()` should have `SQLEvent` objects defined (Listing 8-56).

LISTING 8-56: Declaring the updateTeam(), onUpdateTeam(), updateDriver(), and onUpdateDriver() methods in UpdateTeamsView.mxml

```
private function updateTeam():void {}

private function onUpdateTeam(e:SQLEvent):void {}
```

```
    private function updateDriver(driverName:String, driverId:Number):void {}

    private function onUpdateDriver(e:SQLEvent):void {}

    private function onSQLError(e:SQLErrorEvent):void {}
```

13.   In `updateTeam()`, create the SQL statement that updates the TNAME based on the `teamId` set on the view (Listing 8-57).

LISTING 8-57: Executing the SQL statement to update a team in UpdateTeamsView.mxml

```
private function updateTeam():void
{
        var sqlText:String = "UPDATE Teams SET TNAME = (:tname) "
                            + "WHERE TEAM_ID = (:teamId)";

        var updateTeamSQL:SQLStatement = new SQLStatement();
        updateTeamSQL.addEventListener(SQLEvent.RESULT, onUpdateTeam);
        updateTeamSQL.addEventListener(SQLErrorEvent.ERROR, onSQLError);
        updateTeamSQL.sqlConnection = data.sqlConnection;
        updateTeamSQL.text = sqlText;
        updateTeamSQL.parameters[":tname"] = teamTxt.text;
        updateTeamSQL.parameters[":teamId"] = Number(data.teamId);
        updateTeamSQL.execute();
}
```

14.   In `onUpdateTeam()`, make two calls to `updateDriver()`. The first call should supply the `driverOne.text` property value as the first parameter, then `d1.id` as the second parameter. The second call should supply `driverTwo.text` and `d2.id`. After the second `updateDriver()` call, remove the view from the application by calling `navigator.popview()`. In `updateDriver()`, create the SQL statement that updates the driver name with the assigned `driverId` (Listing 8-58).

LISTING 8-58: Executing the SQL statement to update a driver via the updateDriver() method in UpdateTeamsView.mxml

```
private function onUpdateTeam(e:SQLEvent):void
{
        updateDriver(driverOne.text, d1.id);
        updateDriver(driverTwo.text, d2.id);

        navigator.popView();
}

private function updateDriver(driverName:String, driverId:Number):void
{
        var sqlText:String = "UPDATE Drivers SET DNAME = (:driverName) "
                            + "WHERE ID = (:driverId)";

        var updateTeamSQL:SQLStatement = new SQLStatement();
```

continues

LISTING 8-58 *(continued)*

```
        updateTeamSQL.addEventListener(SQLEvent.RESULT, onUpdateDriver);
        updateTeamSQL.addEventListener(SQLErrorEvent.ERROR, onSQLError);
        updateTeamSQL.sqlConnection = data.sqlConnection;
        updateTeamSQL.text = sqlText;
        updateTeamSQL.parameters[":driverName"] = driverName;
        updateTeamSQL.parameters[":driverId"] = driverId;
        updateTeamSQL.execute();
}

private function onUpdateDriver(e:SQLEvent):void {}
```

15. In `onUpdateDrivers()`, set the `text` property on `description` to `"The record was updated successfully"` (Listing 8-59).

LISTING 8-59: Displaying the record update status via the onUpdateDriver() method in UpdateTeamView.mxml

```
private function onUpdateDriver(e:SQLEvent):void
{
        description.text = "The record was updated successfully";
}
```

16. Next update the `onSQLError()` method, setting the `text` property on `description` to `"Unable to execute SQL command."` (Listing 8-60).

LISTING 8-60: Displaying the SQL error status in UpdateTeamView.mxml

```
private function onSQLError(e:SQLEvent):void
{
        description.text = "Unable to execute SQL command.";
}
```

17. Modify the `onCreationComplete()` method to determine what to set on the view's `title` property, as well as the `text` property on the `<s:Label>` component for the description, and the `label` property for `button1`. Use the `sqlType` property on the view's `data` object to distinguish between UPDATE and INSERT, setting the visibility on `button2` to `false` for INSERT and `true` for UPDATE (Listing 8-61).

LISTING 8-61: Initializing the view via onCreationComplete() in UpdateTeamsView.mxml

```
private function onCreationComplete():void
{
        if(data.sqlType == "UPDATE")
        {
                title = "Update Team View";
```

```
            description.text = "Make changes to the team...";

            teamTxt.text = data.teamName;

            button1.label = "Save changes";
            button2.visible = true;

            selectDrivers();

    } else if (data.sqlType == "INSERT")
    {
            title = "Add Team View";
            description.text = "Add a new team to the database...";

            button1.label = "Insert Team";
            button2.visible = true;
    }
}
```

18. Add the `onBtnOne()` method to call `updateTeam()` when the view is in Update mode, and call `addTeam()` when the view is in Insert mode, supplying the team name set on the `text` property of `teamTxt` (Listing 8-62).

LISTING 8-62: Creating the button1 click handler in UpdateTeamsView.mxml

```
private function onBtnOne():void
{
        if(data.sqlType == "UPDATE")
        {
                updateTeam();

        } else {

                addTeam(teamTxt.text);

        }
}
```

19. Lastly, assign the `onBtnOne()` method to the `click` property on `button1` (Listing 8-63).

LISTING 8-63: Assigning the onBtnOne() method to the button1 click property in UpdateTeamsView.mxml

```
<s:HGroup width="100%"
          height="50"
          gap="16"
          horizontalAlign="center"
```

continues

LISTING 8-63 *(continued)*

```
        verticalAlign="bottom">

    <s:Button id="button1"
              click="onBtnOne()"
              height="50"/>

    <s:Button id="button2"
              click="navigator.popView()"
              height="50"
              label="Cancel"/>

</s:HGroup>
```

20. Now it's time to run the application. Use either the desktop or device profile.

21. Navigate to the Add Team view. As well as the clearly set title Add New Team, you should also be able to see the three labels alongside their corresponding input fields (Figure 8-10).

Start entering data in each field. In the first field, set the team to **McLaren**; for Driver 1 set the driver to **L. Hamilton**; and for Driver 2 set the driver to **J. Button** (Figure 8-11).

FIGURE 8-10: Displaying the Add Team view in Maintaining Data App running on Android 2.3.4

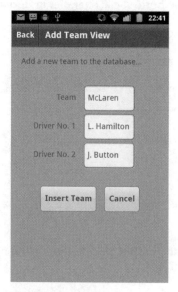

FIGURE 8-11: Adding the McLaren team and drivers to the database via the Add Team view in Maintaining Data App running on Android 2.3.4

22. Click Insert Team. This should bring you back to the Teams view. Add another team to the database, this time just setting the team name to **Red Bull** (Figure 8-12).

23. Next return to the Teams view where you should see both teams McLaren and Red Bull. If you close the application both teams will be displayed without having to re-enter their information (Figure 8-13).

FIGURE 8-12: Adding the Red Bull team name to the database via the Add Team view in Maintaining Data App running on Android 2.3.4

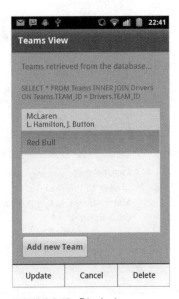

FIGURE 8-13: Displaying the team names from the database via the Teams View in Maintaining Data App running on Android 2.3.4

24. Next click the Update button for Red Bull. This should take you to the Update view. When the view is initialized, notice that the database doesn't return the values for Driver 1 or Driver 2. This is because these fields were left blank when the original insertion for the team was made (Figure 8-14).

25. Next enter the drivers for Red Bull. For Driver 1, set the text field to **S. Vettel**. Then for Driver 2, set the text field to **M. Webber** (Figure 8-15).

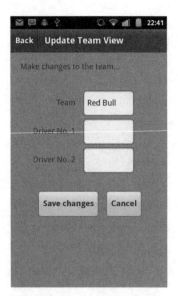

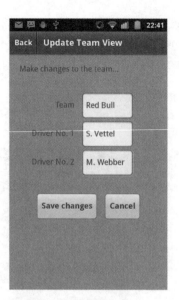

FIGURE 8-14: Displaying the Update Team view for Red Bull in Maintaining Data App running on Android 2.3.4

FIGURE 8-15: Adding new drivers to the Red Bull team in Maintaining Data App running on Android 2.3.4

26. If you click Save Changes and then return to update the Red Bull team, you will see that all the details are correctly saved.

SUMMARY

With a simple concept this chapter demonstrated many of the features of SQLite, and highlighted how effective SQLite can be to store data in a database that mobile applications can rely on, using AIR.

When compared with ActionScript, SQL is an entirely different language, but its fundamental structure and operations are relatively easy to grasp. It helps if you learn the different operators used in SQL to leverage the interaction between the client-facing view and underlying services.

In the next chapter you will learn more about using video and audio in mobile applications, where you will create an example media player linked to a series of media items.

Before moving onto the next chapter, take a look at the following exercises, aimed at building on your working knowledge of utilizing data in applications.

EXERCISES

1. Display a country flag next to each driver, which represents the driver's nationality in the Update Teams view (`views.UpdateTeamsView.mxml`).

    Hint: Create a new table of nationalities that stores the nationality name and a path to the image file.

2. Implement a data synchronizing solution that updates the information in both the Teams and Drivers tables from server-side data.

    Hint: Add a new column in the Teams table that references the last modified date for each of the teams held server-side. Team and driver data should be updated only if the last modified date on the server side is more recent than that stored for the teams.

▶ WHAT YOU LEARNED IN THIS CHAPTER

TOPIC	KEY CONCEPT
Working with data offline	The `ServiceMonitor` and `URLMonitor` can be used to establish whether an application needs to work offline.
	Use the `StatusEvent.STATUS` to determine network availability.
Creating a SQLite database	Use the `File` and `SQLCOnnection` classes to initialize the creation of a new database.
Creating a database table	Use the `CREATE` SQL statement to create a new table in a database, specifying the table name, data properties columns, and a unique identifier known as the primary key.
Saving data to a table	Use the `INSERT` SQL statement to add new data to a table, specifying the name of the table you want to insert data into, accompanied by the associated column names and data values.
Retrieving data from a table	Use the `SELECT` SQL statement to retrieve existing data from a table, specifying the table name and any properties you want to retrieve.
	The asterisk * represents retrieving all data.
	Use the `WHERE` SQL statement to pass any number of query arguments to the database to isolate values you want to retrieve.
Updating data in a table	Use the `UPDATE` SQL statement to update data in a table, specifying the table name and the properties and values you want to update.
	Use the `WHERE` SQL statement to pass any number of query arguments to the database to isolate values you want to update.
Deleting data from a table	Use the `DELETE` SQL statement to remove data from a table.
	Use the `WHERE` SQL statement to pass any number of query arguments to the database to isolate values you want to delete.

9

Working with Audio and Video

WHAT YOU WILL LEARN IN THIS CHAPTER:

- ➤ Introduction to the Open Source Media Framework

- ➤ Creating media resources and elements

- ➤ Accessing media traits

- ➤ Handling media trait events

- ➤ Using Media Player classes to play media

- ➤ Utilizing the Video Player component to play video

This chapter introduces you to aspects of the Open Source Media Framework (OSMF, www.osmf.org) and explores the core classes found in the framework that are used to work with audio and video.

You'll also build a media player example demonstrating the capabilities of OSMF, and using the Flex `<s:VideoPlayer>` component to examine how you can use video within your mobile applications.

INTRODUCING THE OPEN SOURCE MEDIA FRAMEWORK

The Open Source Media Framework is an open source development framework for Flash-based media players, aimed at simplifying the build of media based applications, in particular utilizing audio and video.

Figure 9-1 shows the OSMF logo.

The open nature of OSMF and its pluggable architecture facilitates a collaborative development effort in the Flash community, with

FIGURE 9-1: The OSMF logo

Adobe and many third parties developing plug-ins that can swap in and out of media players. In addition, the core OSMF source code is updated at periodic intervals.

However, you should note that at the time of writing the *release* version of OSMF is version 1.5, while the latest working version is *sprint* 1.6.

You will need to download a copy of the OSMF source code to include as part of your mobile projects. Download the release version from the Source Forge website at `http://sourceforge.net/projects/osmf.adobe/files/`.

Over the next few sections you take a look at the fundamentals of OSMF, including:

➤ Using media resources

➤ Working with media elements

➤ Handling media traits

➤ Utilizing the media player

Many of the OSMF core concepts are explained purely from an AS3 perspective. Using the Flex framework, you find that the features are wrapped in a single video component `<s:VideoPlayer>`, which is covered later.

Creating a URLResource Object

In OSMF *media resources* are essentially used to reference the physical path of a media object. They are used by *media elements* to process the media.

The `URLResource` class is one type of media resource that holds a reference to a `URL` property. To create a `URLResource` object you first need to import the class, which is found in the `org.osmf.media` package:

```
import org.osmf.media.URLResource;
```

In the following snippet you see the creation of a new `URLResource` object:

```
var urlResource:URLResource;
urlResource = new URLResource("http://localhost/wrox/ch9/sound.mp3");
```

Here the URL path to the .mp3 file `sound.mp3` is supplied as an argument to the constructor of the `URLResource` class, generating a resource that can be utilized by the framework.

In addition to `URLResource`, a number of different types of media resources can be created, including:

➤ `DynamicStreamingResource`: To create a media resource that references multiple representations of a single item, allowing a media player to dynamically switch from one representation to another, for instance different bit rates

➤ `MulticastResource`: To create a media resource that is able of carrying multicast streaming information

➤ `StreamingURLResource`: To create a media resource that can be streamed

After creating a media resource, it needs to be assigned to a media element; the next section takes a look at creating media elements and the generic `MediaElement` class.

Creating a MediaElement Object

OSMF includes a number of media element types, each representing a specific type of media object to be interpreted by the framework:

➤ `AudioElement`: This is used for streaming and progressive audio playback of MP3 and AAC files. It also supports audio-only streams from Flash Media Server.

➤ `DurationElement`: This is used for wrapping a media object to give it temporal (time-based) capabilities.

➤ `F4MElement`: This is used for loading media from XML documents that adhere to the Flash Media Manifest format via F4M files.

➤ `ImageElement`: This is used for loading and presenting any PNG, GIF, or JPG image.

➤ `LightWeightVideoElement`: This is used for simple RTMP streaming and progressive video playback.

➤ `ParallelElement`: This is used for concurrently presenting a number of media elements in a single media composition.

➤ `ProxyElement`: This is used for controlling access to a wrapped media element.

➤ `SerialElement`: This is used for sequentially presenting a number of media elements in a single media composition.

➤ `VideoElement`: This is used for streaming and progressive video playback of Flash Video (FLV) and MP4 files, and it also supports streaming from Flash Media Server.

These media elements represent a particular media implementation. The `ParallelElement` and `SerialElement` objects both represent media compositions, while the `AudioElement` and `VideoElement` are representations of elements of specific media types.

Each implementation is derived from the generic `MediaElement` class, a generic media element that can represent any particular type of simplified or complex media entity.

To create a `MediaElement` object, you need to import the class, which is found in the `org.osmf.media` package:

```
import org.osmf.media.MediaElement;
```

You then assign a resource to the resource property on the `MediaElement` object:

```
var mediaElement:MediaElement = new MediaElement();
mediaElement.resource = urlResource;
```

The following sections take a look at the creation of `AudioElement` and `VideoElement` objects.

Creating an AudioElement Object

An `AudioElement` is a media element specifically created for audio playback, supporting streaming and progressive formats.

When using OSMF to play audio, you will need to import the `AudioElement` class found in the `org.osmf.elements` package:

```
import org.osmf.elements.AudioElement;
```

To create an `AudioElement`, you first need to create a new `URLResource` object that references an audio file or stream, and then assign that `URLResource` object to the `resource` property in the `AudioElement` object, as shown in the following snippet:

```
var urlResource:URLResource;
urlResource = new URLResource("http://localhost/wrox/ch9/sound.mp3");

var audioElement:AudioElement = new AudioElement();
audioElement.resource = urlResource;
```

Creating a VideoElement Object

The `VideoElement` is another media element type; this is specifically used for video playback, supporting all streaming and progressive formats.

When using OSMF to play video, you need to import the `VideoElement` class, found in the `org.osmf.elements` package:

```
import org.osmf.elements.VideoElement;
```

You then create a `URLResource` object to a video and assign it to the resource property on the `VideoElement` object:

```
var urlResource:URLResource;
urlResource = new URLResource("http://localhost/wrox/ch9/video.mp4");

var videoElement:VideoElement = new VideoElement();
videoElement.resource = urlResource;
```

To actually play audio using an `AudioElement` or video using the `VideoElement`, it needs to be assigned to a `MediaPlayer` object; this will be covered shortly.

The next section covers another concept in OSMF that all media elements can expose, *media traits*.

Media Traits

Media traits essentially define a media element's characteristics and are dynamic in nature, so depending on the resource assigned to a media element the framework will effectively generate a trait for the media element, if it is possible to do so.

Consider an audio file, a video file, and a still image resource, and when they are loaded into an application. You would probably expect to be able play the audio and video files, but not the still image, because an image is not playable. You would also expect to be able to alter the volume of the audio and video files, but again not the image, because, of course, an image doesn't have a sound track.

In OSMF, *audible* and *playable* characteristics, like the ones described, are two of a number of characteristics that provide features and define how you can interact with different media types. These characteristics are known as *traits*.

A *trait* is a particular characteristic that defines a capability exhibited by a media element type.

In some scenarios you will need to access the traits of media elements to determine whether certain tasks can be carried out on the media. For instance, does a `VideoElement` have a playable characteristic so that it can be played?

OSMF has a number of traits, some of which are listed here:

➤ `AudioTrait`: A trait that exposes properties that indicate the left-to-right panning of sound, whether sound is muted, and also the volume level of the sound

➤ `TimeTrait`: A trait that exposes properties that indicate the duration and current time properties of a media type in seconds

➤ `PlayTrait`: A trait that exposes properties that indicate whether media playback can be stopped and started

➤ `SeekTrait`: A trait that exposes properties that indicate whether the media is currently seeking, and exposes the `canSeekTo()` and `seek()` methods

One of the tricks to using traits is learning what properties and features you want or need to use in your applications, then refer to each of the trait classes to see which ones are appropriate. Another useful class is the `MediaTraitType` class, which is used primarily to identify traits.

Using the MediaTraitType Class to Identify Traits

Up to now you've learned how you create media resource objects and assign them to media elements. During the playback of those media elements you may want to be able to seek a position of an audio file, or simply display the full duration of a video.

Furthermore, in the previous section you saw how each trait type had particular properties, but how do you know whether a media element has a particular trait? You can determine whether a media element type has a particular trait by using the `MediaTraitType` class found in the `org.osmf.traits` package.

This class has a number of static properties that define particular traits, including:

➤ `MediaTraitType.AUDIO`: To identify and reference `AudioTrait` instances

➤ `MediaTraitType.BUFFER`: To identify and reference `BufferTrait` instances

➤ `MediaTraitType.DISPLAY_OBJECT`: To identify and reference `DisplayObjectTrait` instances

➤ `MediaTraitType.LOAD`: To identify and reference `LoadTrait` instances

➤ `MediaTraitType.PLAY`: To identify and reference `PlayTrait` instances

➤ `MediaTraitType.SEEK`: To identify and reference `SeekTrait` instances

➤ `MediaTraitType.TIME`: To identify and reference `TimeTrait` instances

To determine whether a `MediaElement` object has a particular trait, you can use the `hasTrait()` method, supplying the name of the trait via one of the static constants on the `MediaTraitType` class.

The following snippet shows how to determine whether a `MediaElement` object has the `AudioTrait`, using the `MediaTraitType.AUDIO` constant as the argument for `hasTrait()`:

```
var mediaElement:MediaElement = new MediaElement();

if(mediaElement.hasTrait(MediaTraitType.AUDIO))
{
    // Media has the audio trait
}
```

Retrieving a trait allows you to access the properties and invoke the methods on `MediaElement` objects.

To actually retrieve and use a trait, again you use the `MediaTraitType` class, this time supplying one of the static constants to the `getTrait()` property on the `MediaElement` object:

```
var mediaElement:MediaElement = new MediaElement();

if(mediaElement.hasTrait(MediaTraitType.AUDIO))
{
    var audioTrait:AudioTrait;
    audioTrait = mediaElement.getTrait(MediaTraitType.AUDIO);
}
```

In the following example you see that once the `AudioTrait` object has been retrieved, you can use it to set the `volume` property to 5 on the `MediaElement` object:

```
var mediaElement:MediaElement = new MediaElement();

if(mediaElement.hasTrait(MediaTraitType.AUDIO))
{
    var audioTrait:AudioTrait;
    audioTrait = mediaElement.getTrait(MediaTraitType.AUDIO);
    audioTrait.volume = 5;
}
```

This is just one example of how to utilize media traits in the framework.

Using the MediaPlayer to Play Media Elements

The `MediaPlayer` class is essentially a controller that can be used to play any of the media element types that are supported in OSMF.

So, for example, if you supply a `MediaPlayer` object an `ImageElement`, it can generate an image, and if you pass a `MediaPlayer` object a `VideoElement`, it can render a video.

The following lists each of the public properties exposed by a `MediaPlayer` object:

➤ `audioPan`: A number representing the pan property of the media

➤ `autoDynamicStreamSwitch`: A Boolean indicating whether the media will automatically switch between dynamic streams

➤ `autoPlay`: A Boolean defining whether the media starts playing as soon as its load operation has successfully completed

➤ `autoRewind`: A Boolean defining whether the media is returned to the beginning of playback after playback of the media completes

➤ `buffering`: A Boolean indicating whether the media is currently buffering

➤ `bufferLength`: A number returning the length, measured in seconds, of the content currently in the media's buffer

➤ `bufferTime`: A number that indicates the desired length of the media's buffer, in seconds

➤ `bytesLoaded`: A number that returns the bytes of the media that have been loaded

➤ `bytesLoadedUpdateInterval`: A number representing the interval between the dispatch of change events for the `bytesLoaded` property

➤ `bytesTotal`: A number representing the total number of bytes of the media that will be loaded

➤ `canBuffer`: A Boolean to indicate whether the media can buffer

➤ `canLoad`: A Boolean to indicate whether the media can be loaded

➤ `canPause`: A Boolean to indicate whether the media can be paused

➤ `canPlay`: A Boolean to indicate whether the media can be played

➤ `canSeek`: A Boolean to indicate whether the media is seekable

➤ `currentDynamicStreamIndex`: An integer representing the index of the dynamic stream currently rendering

➤ `currentTime`: A number returning the current time of the playhead in seconds

➤ `currentTimeUpdateInterval`: A number to define the interval between the dispatch of change events for the current time in milliseconds

➤ `displayObject`: The `DisplayObject` for the media

➤ `drmEndDate`: A date representing the end date for the playback window

➤ `drmPeriod`: A number returning the length of the playback window, in seconds

➤ `drmStartDate`: A date representing the start date for the playback window

➤ `drmState`: A string indicating the current state of the DRM for this media

➤ `duration`: A number representing the duration of the media's playback, in seconds

➤ `dynamicStreamSwitching`: A Boolean to indicate whether a dynamic stream switch is currently in progress

➤ `hasAudio`: A Boolean to indicate whether the media has audio

➤ `hasDRM`: A Boolean to indicate whether the media element has the `DRMTrait`

➤ `isDVRRecording`: A Boolean to indicate whether the media is DVR-enabled and currently recording

➤ `isDynamicStream`: A Boolean to indicate whether the media consists of a dynamic stream

➤ `loop`: A Boolean to indicate whether the media should play again after playback has completed

➤ `maxAllowedDynamicStreamIndex`: An integer representing the maximum allowed dynamic stream index

➤ `media`: A `MediaElement` defining the source media element being controlled by the media player

➤ `mediaHeight`: A number defining the height of the media, in pixels

➤ `mediaWidth`: A number defining the width of the media, in pixels

➤ `muted`: A Boolean to indicate whether the media is currently muted

➤ `numDynamicStreams`: An integer representing the total number of dynamic stream indices

➤ `paused`: A Boolean to indicate whether the media is currently paused

➤ `playing`: A Boolean to indicate whether the media is currently playing

➤ `seeking`: A Boolean to indicate whether the media is currently seeking

➤ `state`: A string representing the current state of the media

➤ `temporal`: A Boolean to indicate whether the media is temporal

➤ `volume`: A number representing the volume of the media

The `MediaPlayer` class also provides many convenient functions to control media, including:

➤ `authenticate(username:String = null, password:String = null)`: To authenticate the media

➤ `authenticateWithToken(token:Object)`: To authenticate the media using an object that serves as a token

➤ `canSeekTo(seconds:Number)`: To determine whether the media is capable of seeking to the specified time, measured in seconds

➤ `getBitrateForDynamicStreamIndex(index:int)`: To retrieve the bit rate in kilobytes for a specified dynamic stream index

➤ `pause()`: To pause the media, if it is not already paused

➤ `play()`: To play the media, if it is not already playing

➤ `seek(time:Number)`: To jump to the specified time in the media file

➤ `stop()`: To stop playback and return to the beginning of the media file

➤ `switchDynamicStreamIndex(index:int)`: To switch to a specific dynamic stream index

For your OSMF project you will need to import the `MediaPlayer` class; this can be found in the `org.osmf.media` package:

```
import org.osmf.media.MediaPlayer;
```

To utilize an AudioElement object, you need to create a MediaPlayer object, and then assign the AudioElement object to the MediaPlayer object's media property:

```
var urlResource:URLResource;
urlResource = new URLResource("http://localhost/wrox/ch9/sound.mp3");

var audioElement:AudioElement = new AudioElement();
audioElement.resource = urlResource;

var mediaPlayer:MediaPlayer = new MediaPlayer();
mediaPlayer.media = audioElement;
```

To play audio, you simply call the MediaPlayer object's play() method:

```
var mediaPlayer:MediaPlayer = new MediaPlayer();
mediaPlayer.media = audioElement;
mediaPlayer.play();
```

Using the MediaPlayerSprite Class to Play Media Resources

The MediaPlayerSprite class allows you to assign a resource object to the resource property on a MediaPlayerSprite object. The MediaPlayerSprite extends MediaPlayer, but also contains instances of the MediaContainer and MediaFactory classes, which allow you to set the scale mode of the media and automatically generate the appropriate MediaElement object, which will be passed to the MediaPlayer.

To use the MediaPlayerSprite class in your projects, you need to use the following import statement:

```
import org.osmf.media.MediaPlayerSprite;
```

The following snippet demonstrates how to use a MediaPlayerSprite object and play an audio file:

```
var urlResource:URLResource;
urlResource = new URLResource("http://localhost/wrox/ch9/sound.mp3");

var mediaPlayerSprite:MediaPlayerSprite = new MediaPlayerSprite();

addChild(mediaPlayerSprite);

mediaPlayerSprite.resource = urlResource;
```

Alternatively, you could assign a media element type to the media property on the MediaPlayerSprite object. For example, in the following snippet an AudioElement object is created from a path to the sound.mp3 file. This is then assigned to a MediaPlayerSprite object's media property. Here's how you would assign an AudioElement:

```
var urlResource:URLResource;
urlResource = new URLResource("http://localhost/wrox/ch9/sound.mp3");

var audioElement:AudioElement = new AudioElement();
```

```
audioElement.resource = urlResource;

var mediaPlayerSprite:MediaPlayerSprite = new MediaPlayerSprite();

addChild(mediaPlayerSprite);
mediaPlayerSprite.media = audioElement;
```

Handling Trait Events

Let's say you wanted to display a visual message to the user in your application when a video needs to "buffer" content, or when a sound clip has been "paused" rather than "stopped." There are *trait events* that are intrinsic to OSMF, which help to present a particular response for media elements, like the ones just highlighted.

The `TraitEventDispatcher` class, which we'll cover shortly, is able to monitor a media element to check when a trait has been added, and is subsequently able to handle dispatched trait events. But before you look at how to use the dispatcher, you'll need to know a little more about the events you want to handle.

In this section you'll take a brief look at the `AudioEvent`, `PlayEvent`, and `TimeEvent` objects.

Using an AudioEvent Object

An `AudioEvent` object is dispatched when the properties of an audio trait have changed for a media element; hence, a derived `MediaElement` object needs to have an `AudioTrait` object.

The `AudioEvent` class can be found in the `org.osmf.events` package:

```
import org.osmf.events.AudioEvent;
```

The class itself has three static event-type properties:

➤ `AudioEvent.MUTED_CHANGE`: A string `"mutedChange"`, dispatched when the muted property of the media has changed

➤ `AudioEvent.PAN_CHANGE`: A string `"panChange"`, dispatched when the pan property of the media has changed

➤ `AudioEvent.VOLUME_CHANGE`: A string `"volumeChange"`, dispatched when the volume property of the media has changed

Three read-only public properties for the `AudioEvent` object also can be accessed via an event handler for each of the event types:

➤ `muted`: A Boolean indicating whether the audio for the media element is muted

➤ `pan`: A number representing the pan

➤ `volume`: A number representing the volume level of the audio for the media element

The audio of a `MediaElement` object that has an `AudioTrait` can be changed through a `volume` property, which should trigger an `AudioEvent.VOLUME_CHANGE` event to be dispatched.

Using the PlayEvent and PlayState Objects

A `PlayEvent` object is an OSMF event that is dispatched when the properties of a play trait have changed for a media element. A derived `MediaElement` object needs to have a `PlayTrait` object in order for `PlayEvent` objects to be dispatched.

When a `PlayEvent` is triggered, you can detect changes to the play state of a media element, or detect whether a media element can be paused.

You have to import the `PlayEvent`, which can be found in the `org.osmf.events` package:

```
import org.osmf.events.PlayEvent;
```

This class has two static event-type properties:

➤ `PlayEvent.CAN_PAUSE_CHANGE`: A string `"canPauseChange"`, dispatched when the `canPause` property has changed

➤ `PlayEvent.PLAY_STATE_CHANGE`: A string `"playStateChange"`, dispatched when the playing or paused property of the media has changed

A `PlayEvent` object also exposes two public properties:

➤ `canPause`: A Boolean indicating whether the `PlayTrait` can be paused

➤ `playState`: A string defining the current `PlayState` of the media element

The `playState` property returned on the `PlayEvent` object is actually tied to a static constant held by the `org.osmf.traits.PlayState` class. This has three static constants:

➤ `PlayState.PAUSED`: A string defining the play state as paused

➤ `PlayState.PLAYING`: A string defining the play state as playing

➤ `PlayState.STOPPED`: A string defining the play state as stopped

Using a TimeEvent Object

A `TimeEvent` object is dispatched when there is a change in the properties of a media element object that has a time/temporal trait:

```
import org.osmf.events.TimeEvent;
```

The class itself has three static event types:

➤ `TimeEvent.COMPLETE`: A string `"complete"`, dispatched when the media has completed playback

➤ `TimeEvent.CURRENT_TIME_CHANGE`: A string `"currentTimeChange"`, dispatched when the time property of the media has changed

➤ `TimeEvent.DURATION_CHANGE`: A string `"durationChange"`, dispatched when the duration property of the media has changed

A `TimeEvent` object exposes a public `time` property, which holds the value represented by the change in the media's `TimeTrait`.

Using the TraitEventDispatcher Class

A `TraitEventDispatcher` object allows you to receive trait events from a `MediaElement` object, and thus utilize updates and changes to media properties. In addition to dispatching the trait events of a `MediaElement` object, the `TraitEventDispatcher` has an added bonus with its ability to monitor a `MediaElement` object to tell when traits have been added or removed.

To utilize this functionality, you need to import the `TraitEventDispatcher` class found in the `org.osmf.traits` package:

```
import org.osmf.traits.TraitEventDispatcher;
```

The `TraitEventDispatcher` object is one way in which you can listen for OSMF events. First you need to create a `TraitEventDispatcher` object, and then assign each of the events you want to listen to via the `addEventListener()` method to the `TraitEventDispatcher` object. You then need to assign a media element to the media property on the `TraitEventDispatcher` object.

The following snippet shows how an `AudioElement` object is added to a `TraitEventDispatcher` object called `traitDispatcher`, where the `AudioEvent.VOLUME_CHANGE` and `TimeEvent.COMPLETE` events are listened for and handled by the `onVolumeChange()`, `onPlayStateChange()`, and `onComplete()` event handlers, respectively:

```
var traitDispatcher:TraitEventDispatcher = new TraitEventDispatcher();
traitDispatcher.media = audioElement;

traitDispatcher.addEventListener(AudioEvent.VOLUME_CHANGE, onVolumeChange);
traitDispatcher.addEventListener(TimeEvent.COMPLETE, onComplete);
```

Another way in which you can listen for OSMF events is by using a `MediaPlayer` object, as shown in the following snippet, which shows how the `TimeEvent.COMPLETE` event type is registered with a `MediaPlayer` object:

```
mediaPlayer.addEventListener(TimeEvent.COMPLETE, onComplete);
```

USING THE FLEX OSMF WRAPPER

In addition to the OSMF classes that can be utilized to render video, two components can be used to accomplish video playback, the `<s:VideoDisplay>` and `<s:VideoPlayer>` components. Both are Flex wrappers for OSMF-based AS3 classes.

The `<s:VideoDisplay>` component is a basic renderer for video playback, without media controls to interact with the video. Here you'll explore how to use the `<s:VideoPlayer>` component, allowing you to render videos in your mobile applications and control playback.

Using the VideoPlayer Component

This section takes you through some of the properties and methods of the `<s:VideoPlayer>` component, a skinnable component that also exposes some familiar properties of OSMF, covered earlier.

In total, 14 public properties are exposed with the `<s:VideoPlayer>` component:

➤ `autoDisplayFirstFrame`: A Boolean used to define whether to display the first frame of a video

➤ `autoPlay`: A Boolean used to define whether a video automatically plays when it first loads

➤ `autoRewind`: A Boolean to define whether a video automatically rewinds when it reaches its end

➤ `bytesLoaded`: A number representing the bytes of data that have been loaded

➤ `bytesTotal`: A number representing the total bytes of data that will be loaded

➤ `currentTime`: A number indicating the current position of the video

➤ `duration`: A number representing the full running time of the video

➤ `loop`: A Boolean to define whether a video restarts once it has ended

➤ `mediaPlayerState`: A static string indicating the current state of the video player; the values include UNINITIALIZED, READY, PLAYING, PAUSED, BUFFERING, and PLAYBACK_ERROR

➤ `muted`: A Boolean indicating whether the video player's volume is set to zero

➤ `pauseWhenHidden`: A Boolean to pause the video when it is hidden

➤ `playing`: A Boolean indicating whether the video is currently playing

➤ `scaleMode`: A string defining how to size the video content; the values "none," "stretched," "letterbox," or "zoom" can be assigned

➤ `source`: A string that defines the path to the video content

In addition to these properties are four public methods that are associated with the `<s:VideoPlayer>` component:

➤ `pause()`: To pause a video

➤ `play()`: To play a video

➤ `seek(seconds:Number)`: To seek to a specified time in a video

➤ `stop()`: To stop a video

These methods are exactly the same ones exposed by the `MediaPlayer` and `MediaPlayerSprite` classes, covered earlier.

Creating a MediaPlayer Example

You will now need to set up a new Flex Mobile Project in Flash Builder.

Defining the Flex Mobile Project Settings

The following lists a few of the familiar settings you will need to ensure are defined for the project:

➤ **Name:** Set the Name for the project as **MediaPlayerApp**.

➤ **Application ID:** Set the Application ID as **com.wrox.ch9.MediaPlayerApp**.

➤ **Application Template:** Set the Application Template to a View-Based Application, setting the initial view title to **MediaPlayerAppHome**.

Targeting Mobile Devices on Different Platforms

This example project can run on each of the mobile platforms supporting AIR, including Apple iOS, Google Android, and BlackBerry Tablet OS. No permissions need to be specified for any of the target platforms.

Creating Run and Debug Configurations

You can elect to run this project on the desktop or directly on your mobile device. This chapter focuses on running the app on the desktop; however, both approaches can be employed.

Building the Media Player App

The following steps will take you through the build of a media player app targeted for mobile using a combination of Flex and ActionScript classes:

1. In the MediaPlayerApp project, create a new ActionScript class named MediaItemVO in a new package called model.vo.

2. In MediaItemVO, add four public variables of string type: title, description, url, and duration (Listing 9-1).

LISTING 9-1: Creating MediaItemVO.as

```
package model.vo
{
    public class MediaItemVO
    {
        public var title:String;
        public var description:String;

        [Bindable]
        public var url:String;
        public var duration:String;

        public function MediaItemVO()
        {

        }
    }
}
```

3. Create a new MXML item renderer called MediaItemRenderer.

4. In MediaItemRenderer add a <s:VerticalLayout> declaration to the <s:layout>, setting the gap property to 5, the paddingLeft property to 10, the paddingTop property to 20, and paddingBottom property to 5. Next update the text property on the item renderer's default <s:Label> component. The value supplied to this property should be the data.title and data.duration properties. Also set the fontSize property to 18. Add another <s:Label> component that sets the data.description property on the text property, and also the fontSize to 16 (Listing 9-2).

LISTING 9-2: Assigning the layout and data object properties in MedialtemRenderer.xml

```xml
<?xml version="1.0" encoding="utf-8"?>
<s:ItemRenderer xmlns:fx="http://ns.adobe.com/mxml/2009"
                xmlns:s="library://ns.adobe.com/flex/spark"
                autoDrawBackground="true">

    <s:layout>
        <s:VerticalLayout gap="5"
                          paddingLeft="10"
                          paddingTop="20"
                          paddingBottom="5"/>
    </s:layout>

    <s:Label text="{data.title} ({data.duration})"
             fontSize="18"/>

    <s:Label text="{data.description}"
             fontSize="16"/>

</s:ItemRenderer>
```

5. In `MediaPlayerAppHome.mxml` add the namespace declaration `xmlns:vo` to the view, specifying the `model.vo.*` package. Also set the `title` property for the view to `Media Player App`. Ensure that the `<fx:Declarations>` and `<fx:Script>` tags are present (Listing 9-3).

LISTING 9-3: Setting the title and xmlns:vo namespace properties in MediaPlayerAppHome.mxml

```xml
<?xml version="1.0" encoding="utf-8"?>
<s:View xmlns:fx="http://ns.adobe.com/mxml/2009"
        xmlns:s="library://ns.adobe.com/flex/spark"
        xmlns:vo="model.vo.*"
        title="Media Player App">

    <fx:Script>
        <![CDATA[ ]]>
    </fx:Script>

    <fx:Declarations>

    </fx:Declarations>

</s:View>
```

6. Within the `<fx:Script>` block, define a new bindable string called `basePath` to hold a reference to a local server path, in which the videos will be stored (Listing 9-4).

LISTING 9-4: Setting the basePath for the videos in MediaPlayerAppHome.mxml

```
<fx:Script>
    <![CDATA[

        [Bindable]
        private var basePath:String = "http://localhost/video/";
    ]]>
</fx:Script>
```

Setting the `basePath` to `"http://localhost/video/"` presumes you have a web server running on you machine with the `video` folder at the root. The content used in the example can be found in the `bin-debug` folder for the project. So, when you run this example, you can also set the `basePath` to `""`, removing the reference to the local web server.

7. In the `<fx:Declarations>` tag, define a new `<s:ArrayList>` called `arrList`. Define three `<vo:MediaItemVO>` objects. On the first `MediaItemVO` object, set the `id` property to `mediaItem1`, then set the `title` property to `Sintel`, the `description` property to `The search for a baby dragon.`, the `url` property to `sintel_trailer.flv`, and the `duration` property to `0:52`. For the second `MediaItemVO` object, set the `id` to `mediaItem2`, set the `title` to `Big Buck Bunny`, and the `description` to `Meet three bullying rodents..` Set the `url` to `big_buck_bunny_trailer.flv` and the `duration` to `0:33`. Then for the third `MediaItemVO` object, set the `id` to `mediaItem3`, set the `title` to `Elephants Dream`, and the `description` to `Emo is introduced to the machine.` Then set the `url` to `elephants_dream_trailer.flv` and the `duration` to `1:15` (Listing 9-5).

LISTING 9-5: Declaring an <s:ArrayList> of MediaItemVO objects in MediaPlayerAppHome.mxml

```
<fx:Declarations>

    <s:ArrayList id="arrList">

        <vo:MediaItemVO id="mediaItem1"
                        title="Sintel"
                        description="The search for a baby dragon."
                        url="sintel_trailer.flv"
                        duration="0:52"/>

        <vo:MediaItemVO id="mediaItem2"
                        title="Big Buck Bunny"
                        description="Meet three bullying rodents."
                        url="big_buck_bunny_trailer.flv"
                        duration="0:33"/>

        <vo:MediaItemVO id="mediaItem3"
                        title="Elephants Dream"
                        description="Emo is introduced to the machine."
```

```
                                    url="elephants_dream.flv"
                                    duration="1:15"/>

            </s:ArrayList>

    </fx:Declarations>
```

You can package the video files used in this example project for testing on a mobile device. First you need to ensure that the videos are included in the packaging. Select File ⇨ Properties ⇨ Flex Build Packaging, and then enable your target platform. Then select the files you want to include. You will need to set the basePath to "", and this will then allow you to reference each of the videos *relative* to the installation folder.

8. Next define two states, portrait and landscape (Listing 9-6).

LISTING 9-6: Declaring the portrait and landscape states in MediaPlayerAppHome.mxml

```
<fx:Declarations>

        <s:State name="portrait"/>
        <s:State name="landscape"/>

        <s:ArrayList id="arrList">

                <vo:MediaItemVO id="mediaItem1"
                                title="Sintel"
                                description="The search for a baby dragon."
                                url="sintel_trailer.flv"
                                duration="0:52"/>

                <vo:MediaItemVO id="mediaItem2"
                                title="Big Buck Bunny"
                                description="Meet three bullying rodents."
                                url="big_buck_bunny_trailer.flv"
                                duration="0:33"/>

                <vo:MediaItemVO id="mediaItem3"
                                title="Elephants Dream"
                                description="Emo is introduced to the machine."
                                url="elephants_dream.flv"
                                duration="1:15"/>

        </s:ArrayList>

    </fx:Declarations>
```

9. Under the closing <fx:Declarations> tag, add a <s:Group> container, setting its width property to 100%. For the container, add two <s:layout> definitions, <s:layout.portrait> and <s:layout.landscape>, adding the <s:VerticalLayout> declaration to the portrait state and a <s:HorizontalLayout> declaration for the landscape layout. Set the gap, paddingBottom, paddingLeft, paddingRight, and paddingTop properties to 0 for both states (Listing 9-7).

LISTING 9-7: Defining the layout properties for the <s:Group> container for portrait and landscape states in MediaPlayerAppHome.mxml

```
</fx:Declarations>

<s:Group width="100%">

    <s:layout.portrait>
        <s:VerticalLayout gap="0"
                          paddingBottom="0"
                          paddingLeft="0"
                          paddingRight="0"
                          paddingTop="0"/>
    </s:layout.portrait>

    <s:layout.landscape>
        <s:HorizontalLayout gap="0"
                            paddingBottom="0"
                            paddingLeft="0"
                            paddingRight="0"
                            paddingTop="0"/>
    </s:layout.landscape>

</s:Group>
```

10. Next add a <s:VideoPlayer> component to the <s:Group> container. Set the id property on the component to mediaPlayer. Then set the autoPlay property to false and the autoDisplayFirstFrame and autoRewind properties to true. Also set the fontSize to 16 and fontWeight to normal. Set the scaleMode property to letterbox and the interactionMode to touch. Lastly set the source property of the video to use the basePath property and the first video in arrList, via the mediaItem1.url property (Listing 9-8).

LISTING 9-8: Adding the <s:VideoPlayer> to the <s:Group> container in MediaPlayerAppHome.mxml

```
</fx:Declarations>

<s:Group width="100%">

    <s:layout.portrait>
        <s:VerticalLayout gap="0"
                          paddingBottom="0"
                          paddingLeft="0"
                          paddingRight="0"
                          paddingTop="0"/>
    </s:layout.portrait>

    <s:layout.landscape>
        <s:HorizontalLayout gap="0"
                            paddingBottom="0"
```

```
                                    paddingLeft="0"
                                    paddingRight="0"
                                    paddingTop="0"/>
        </s:layout.landscape>

        <s:VideoPlayer id="mediaPlayer"
                        autoDisplayFirstFrame="true"
                        autoPlay="false"
                        autoRewind="true"
                        fontSize="16"
                        fontWeight="normal"
                        interactionMode="touch"
                        scaleMode="letterbox"
                        source="{basePath}{mediaItem1.url}"
                        volume="5"/>

    </s:Group>
```

11. After the `<s:VideoPlayer>` component, add a `<s:List>` component, setting the id property to mediaPlaylist. Assign the MediaItemRenderer to the itemRenderer property. Then set the dataProvider property to the ArrayList object, arrList. Set both the width and height properties to 100%. Then finally, set the click property on the `<s:List>` component to a new event handler called onClick(). You'll take a look at that function shortly (Listing 9-9).

> **LISTING 9-9:** Adding the `<s:List>` to the `<s:Group>` container in MediaPlayerAppHome.mxml

```
<s:VideoPlayer id="mediaPlayer"
                autoDisplayFirstFrame="true"
                autoPlay="false"
                autoRewind="true"
                fontSize="16"
                fontWeight="normal"
                interactionMode="touch"
                scaleMode="letterbox"
                source="{basePath}{mediaItem1.url}"
                volume="5"/>

    <s:List id="mediaPlaylist"
            itemRenderer="views.renderers.MediaItemRenderer"
            width="100%"
            height.landscape="100%"
            dataProvider="{arrList}"
            click="onClick(event)"/>
```

12. In the `<fx:Script>` block, add a protected function called onClick() with a single parameter e, an Event object. In the function, use the selectedIndex property on the `<s:List>` component mediaPlaylist to retrieve a MediaItemVO object. Use the url property on the MediaItemVO object to build a full path to a video, combined with the basePath. Assign this to the mediaPlayer.source (Listing 9-10).

LISTING 9-10: Defining the onClick() method in MediaPlayerAppHome.mxml

```
[Bindable]
private var basePath:String = "http://localhost/video/";

protected function onClick(e:Event):void
{
    var mediaItem:MediaItemVO;
    mediaItem = arrList.source[mediaPlaylist.selectedIndex];

    mediaPlayer.source = basePath + mediaItem.url;
}
```

13. Above the onClick() method, add a protected function called onComplete() with a single parameter e, a TimeEvent object, which should be imported above the private basePath variable. In onComplete(), use the selected index on the <s:List> component to determine which item to play once the current item has completed (Listing 9-11).

LISTING 9-11: Defining the onComplete() method in MediaPlayerAppHome.mxml

```
import org.osmf.events.TimeEvent;

[Bindable]
private var basePath:String = "http://localhost/videos/";

protected function onComplete(e:TimeEvent):void
{
    var index:int = mediaPlaylist.selectedIndex;
    index++;

    if(index < arrList.source.length)
    {
        mediaPlaylist.selectedIndex = index;

        mediaPlayer.source = basePath + arrList.source[index].url;

        mediaPlayer.play();
    }
}

protected function onClick(e:Event):void
{
    var mediaItem:MediaItemVO;
    mediaItem = arrList[mediaPlaylist.selectedIndex];

    mediaPlayer.source = basePath + mediaItem.url;
}
```

14. Update the <s:VideoPlayer> component so that it references the onComplete() event handler (Listing 9-12).

LISTING 9-12: Assigning the complete method in MediaPlayerAppHome.mxml

```
<s:VideoPlayer id="mediaPlayer"
               complete="onComplete(event)"
               autoDisplayFirstFrame="true"
               autoPlay="false"
               autoRewind="true"
               fontSize="16"
               fontWeight="normal"
               interactionMode="touch"
               scaleMode="letterbox"
               source="{basePath}{mediaItem1.url}"
               volume="5"/>
```

15. Under the `basePath` declaration, add four new protected functions: `onCreationComplete()`, `onAddedToStage()`, `onOrientationChange()`, and `updateLayout()`. Assign the `onCreationComplete()` method to the view's `creationComplete` attribute (Listing 9-13).

LISTING 9-13: Declaring the onCreationComplete(), onAddedToStage(), onOrientationChange() and updateLayout() methods in MediaPlayerAppHome.mxml

```
<s:View xmlns:fx="http://ns.adobe.com/mxml/2009"
        xmlns:s="library://ns.adobe.com/flex/spark"
        xmlns:vo="model.vo.*"
        title="Media Player App"
        creationComplete="onCreationComplete()">

    <fx:Script>
        <![CDATA[

            import org.osmf.events.TimeEvent;

            [Bindable]
            private var basePath:String = "http://localhost/videos/";

            protected function onCreationComplete():void {}

            protected function onAddedToStage():void {}

            protected function onOrientationChange():void {}

            protected function updateLayout():void {}
```

16. In `updateLayout()`, define two integers for width and height: `w` and `h`, respectively. Add a `switch` statement that uses the `currentState` property of the view to distinguish between the portrait and landscape layouts. When the view is in a portrait layout, set the `actionBarVisible` property of the view to `true`, and then use the `systemManager.screen.width` property to assign the full width of the device's screen to the `w` variable. Use the 4:3 screen ratio and `width` to calculate the height for variable `h`. For the landscape layout, set the `actionBarVisible` property to `false`, and then use the `systemManager.screen.width` and `systemManager.screen.height` properties to assign values to `w` and `h`, respectively. Following the `switch` statement, assign the `w` and `h` variables to the `width` and `height` properties, respectively, on `mediaPlayer` (Listing 9-14).

LISTING 9-14: Defining the width and height of media player via the updateLayout() method in MediaPlayerAppHome.mxml

```
protected function updateLayout():void
{
        var w:int;
        var h:int;

        switch(currentState)
        {
                case "portrait":
                {
                        actionBarVisible = true;
                        w = systemManager.screen.width;
                        h = w / (4/3);
                }
                break;
                case "landscape":
                {
                        actionBarVisible = false;
                        w = systemManager.screen.width;
                        h = systemManager.screen.height;
                }
                break;
        }

        mediaPlayer.width = w;
        mediaPlayer.height = h;
}
```

17. In `onCreationComplete()`, register the `Event.ADDED_TO_STAGE` event property with the view, assigning the `onAddedToStage()` function as the event handler and at the same time defining a single `Event` object parameter for the method, `e`. Then in `onAddedToStage()`, register the `StageOrientationEvent.ORIENTATION_CHANGE` event with the stage via the `e.target.stage` property, assigning `onOrientationChange()` as the event handler. For `onOrientationChange()`, add a single `StageOrientationEvent` object, `e`, as a parameter. Lastly, call the `updateLayout()` method in both `onOrientationChange()` and `onAddedToStage()` (Listing 9-15).

LISTING 9-15: Completing the onCreationComplete(), onAddedToStage(), and onOrientationChange() methods in MediaPlayerAppHome.mxml

```
protected function onCreationComplete():void
{
        this.addEventListener(Event.ADDED_TO_STAGE, onAddedToStage);
}

protected function onAddedToStage(e:Event):void
```

```
    {
        e.target.stage.addEventListener( StageOrientationEvent.ORIENTATION_CHANGE,
                                         onOrientationChange );
        updateLayout();
    }

protected function onOrientationChange(e:StageOrientationEvent):void
    {
        updateLayout();
    }
```

18. Finally, update the MediaPlayerApp.mxml file to include styles for the application. Replace the <fx:Declarations> with an <fx:Style> declaration. Inside the <fx:Style> declaration, specify s as the spark namespace. Then define three style declarations that will be used in the application: one for the View component, one for the List component, and one for the Video Player component. For the <s:View> components, define the backgroundColor property as #3F3F3F, and the color property as #393839. Then for the <s:List> component, define the alternatingItemColors property as #3F3F3F, #3F3F3F, the contentBackgroundColor property as #3F3F3F, the selectionColor property as #B2B2B2, the fontSize property as 18, and the color property as #393839. Then for the <s:VideoPlayer> component, set the chromeColor property to #3F3F3F and the color property to #FFFFFF (Listing 9-16).

LISTING 9-16: Setting the styles via the <fx:Style> declaration in MediaPlayerApp.mxml

```xml
<?xml version="1.0" encoding="utf-8"?>
<s:ViewNavigatorApplication xmlns:fx="http://ns.adobe.com/mxml/2009"
                            xmlns:s="library://ns.adobe.com/flex/spark"
                            firstView="views.MediaPlayerAppHome">
    <fx:Style>

        @namespace s "library://ns.adobe.com/flex/spark";

        s|View
        {
            backgroundColor:#3F3F3F;
            color:#393839;
        }

        s|List
        {
            fontSize:18;
            color:#FFFFFF;
            alternatingItemColors:#3F3F3F, #3F3F3F;
            selectionColor:#B2B2B2;
            contentBackgroundColor:#3F3F3F;
        }

        s|VideoPlayer
```

continues

LISTING 9-16 *(continued)*

```
        {
                chromeColor:#3F3F3F;
                color:#FFFFFF;
        }

    </fx:Style>

</s:ViewNavigatorApplication>
```

19. Now run the example using a desktop run configuration. When the Media Player application launches in the portrait view, underneath the Media Player App title for the app you'll see the video player and playlist component populated with the media items.

You can now click Play on the video player's controls to start video playback (Figure 9-2).

When you rotate the device to landscape view, you'll see that the player occupies the full screen and the playlist is no longer visible on screen (Figure 9-3).

FIGURE 9-2: Playing the first item in the Media Player App

FIGURE 9-3: Rotating the device to change the layout of the components in Media Player App

When you rotate the device back to the portrait view, clicking a new item in the list will change the current video being played (Figure 9-4).

SUMMARY

Over the course of this chapter you have explored the key concepts of OSMF, learning from the core how to create resources and media elements, how to handle media trait events, and how to distinguish between different media trait characteristics.

You also took a look at creating a rather simple media player application that used the <s:VideoPlayer> component.

In the next chapter you take a look at using some of the device features available to AIR mobile applications. You'll take a look at how to utilize the device's camera, microphone, web browser, and geo-location instruments.

FIGURE 9-4: Playing the second item in the Media Player App

EXERCISES

1. Add a Settings view to the Media Player application that allows the user to change some of the default settings on the <s:VideoPlayer> component — for example, auto play and continuous play.

2. Include a still image of each video in the playlist.

3. Update the playlist to include audio and image items.

4. Package the Media Player application, selecting one of the target platforms and including associated video items.

▶ **WHAT YOU LEARNED IN THIS CHAPTER**

TOPIC	KEY CONCEPT
Creating media resources	Use `URLResource` to create a media resource to a media item that uses an HTTP location reference.
Creating media elements	Reference the `MediaElement` class to create a generic media object.
	Reference the `AudioElement` class to create an element specifically for audio playback.
	Reference the `VideoElement` class to create an element specifically for video playback.
Using media traits	Traits represent the characteristics of a media object.
	The `AudioTrait` represents audible characteristics of media and exposes properties like `AudioTrait.volume`.
	The `PlayTrait` represents playable characteristics of media and exposes properties like `PlayTrait`.
	The `BufferTrait` represents bufferable characteristics of media and exposes properties like the `BufferTrait`.
	The `TimeTrait` represents temporal characteristics of media and exposes properties like the `TimeTrait`.
Handling media trait events	Reference the `AudioEvent` to handle events dispatched from an `AudioTrait` — for example, `AudioEvent.VOLUME_CHANGE`.
	Reference the `PlayEvent` to handle events dispatched from a media objects `PlayTrait` — for example, `PlayEvent.PAUSED`.
	Reference the `TimeEvent` to handle events dispatched from a media objects `TimeTrait` — for example, `TimeEvent.COMPLETE`.
Using the MediaPlayer class	Assign a `MediaElement` object to the `MediaPlayer.media` property to reference media.
	Use the `MediaPlayer.play()` method to start playback.
Using the MediaPlayerSprite class	Assign a `URLResource` object to the `MediaPlayerSprite.resource` property, or a `MediaElement` object to the `MediaPlayerSprite.media` property to reference media.
Using the Video Player component	Use the `<s:VideoPlayer>` Flex component.
	Use a URL path to assign media to the component using the `VideoPlayer.source`.
Controlling media using the Video Player component	Use `<s:VideoPlayer>.play()` to play content.
	Use `<s:VideoPlayer>.pause()` to pause content.
	Use `<s:VideoPlayer>.stop()` to stop content.

10

Utilizing Device Features

WHAT YOU WILL LEARN IN THIS CHAPTER:

➤ Launching the device's native camera application

➤ Using an image taken with the camera

➤ Capturing audio with the device's microphone

➤ Playing audio captured from the microphone

➤ Displaying dynamic HTML content and web pages

➤ Utilizing the device's geolocation sensor

In this chapter you'll take an in-depth look at some of the cool features of Adobe AIR that allow you to use the functionality that is integral to most mobile devices.

First you'll take a look at the `CameraUI` class, examining how you can take photos using the device's camera and include the images in your AIR mobile application. You'll explore the Microphone API, taking a close look at how you can record and play back audio streams using the device's microphone. You then turn your attention to integrating a device's web control and presenting web pages into your mobile applications using the `StageWebView` class. Finally, you take a look at using the device's Geolocation sensor to retrieve and incorporate GPS location data.

For each of the four sections, you'll build an example demonstrating the capabilities of the core feature.

USING THE DEVICE'S CAMERA

One of the many features of all mobile devices is the camera, and unless you've been living in a cave for the past decade you can use mobile devices to take still photos and video. Although AIR for desktop has been able to use the camera for a while, the AIR 2.5 release gave developers their first opportunity to create mobile applications incorporating the camera.

In this section you'll examine how to use the `CameraUI` class to utilize photos taken with the native camera in Flash mobile applications.

Using the CameraUI Class

Using the `flash.media.CameraUI` class, you can use the device camera to load an image into an application. As you can imagine this provides many possibilities for mobile applications and a user's personal imagery.

For AS3-based mobile projects you will need to import the `CameraUI` class found in the `flash .media` package:

```
import flash.media.CameraUI;
```

This class has only two API features that can be used to gain access to the native camera app on the host device:

➤ `CameraUI.isSupported`: To determine whether the native camera application can be launched

➤ `CameraUI.launch()`: To launch the camera app

> **NOTE** *While native camera functionality via the* `CameraUI` *class is supported on Apple iOS and BlackBerry Tablet OS, not all devices running Google Android support the API. You should consider implementing non-camera activity for those devices.*

In the following section you'll take a closer look at the `CameraUI` class and build an example.

Creating a Camera App Example

You will need to set up a new Flex Mobile Project in Flash Builder.

Defining the Flex Mobile Project Settings

The following lists a few of the familiar settings you will need to ensure are defined for the project:

➤ **Name:** Set the Name for the project to **CameraApp**.

➤ **Application ID:** Set the Application ID to **com.wrox.ch10.CameraApp**.

➤ **Application Template:** Set the Application Template to a View-Based Application, setting the initial view title to **CameraAppHome**.

Targeting Mobile Devices on Different Platforms

This example project can run on each of the mobile platforms supporting AIR, including Apple iOS, Google Android, and BlackBerry Tablet OS. For Google Android and BlackBerry Tablet OS, a number of permissions need to be set to allow the application to use the device's camera. For Apple iOS, no permissions need to be defined specifically.

Defining Google Android Permissions

In the AIR application descriptor file generated with the project in Flash Builder, ensure the `android.permission.CAMERA` permission is included as a manifest addition for the Android OS, as shown in the following code snippet:

```
<android>
    <manifestAdditions>
        <![CDATA[
            <manifest>
                <uses-permission android:name="android.permission.CAMERA"/>
            </manifest>
        ]]>
    </manifestAdditions>
</android>
```

Defining BlackBerry Tablet OS Permissions

For BlackBerry Tablet OS applications, you need to specify both the `use_camera` and `access_shared` permissions, to allow the application to launch the native camera app and to allow the application to use the image file written to the device, respectively. Ensure these values are set in the `blackberry-tablet.xml` file, as shown in the following code snippet:

```
<?xml version="1.0" encoding="UTF-8"?>
<qnx>
    <author>jganderson</author>
    <authorId>gYAAgFbt6rihu</authorId>
    <buildId>101</buildId>
    <platformVersion>1.0.6.2390</platformVersion>
    <permission>use_camera</permission>
    <permission>access_shared</permission>
</qnx>
```

Defining Apple iOS Settings

Because the application will need to use the device's camera, you can prevent the application from being installed on an iOS device that doesn't have a camera by specifying the `UIRequiredDeviceCapabilities` key in the AIR application descriptor file via the `<InfoAdditions>`, and setting the value to an array containing the `still-camera` string, as shown in the following snippet:

```
<iPhone>
    <InfoAdditions>
        <![CDATA[
            <key>UIDeviceFamily</key>
            <array>
                <string>1</string>
                <string>1</string>
            </array>
            <key>UIStatusBarStyle</key>
            <string>UIStatusBarStyleBlackTranslucent</string>
            <key>UIRequiredDeviceCapabilities</key>
            <array>
                <string>still-camera</string>
```

```
            </array>
        ]]>
    </InfoAdditions>
</iPhone>
```

Building the Camera App

In Listing 10-1 you will see the early stages of the CameraAppHome.mxml file.

LISTING 10-1: The initial starting point for CameraAppHome.mxml

```xml
<?xml version="1.0" encoding="utf-8"?>
<s:View xmlns:fx="http://ns.adobe.com/mxml/2009"
        xmlns:s="library://ns.adobe.com/flex/spark"
        creationComplete="onCreationComplete()"
        title="Camera App">

    <fx:Script>
        <![CDATA[

            private function onCreationComplete():void {}

            private function launch():void {}

        ]]>
    </fx:Script>

    <s:layout>

        <s:VerticalLayout paddingLeft="20"
                          paddingRight="20"
                          paddingBottom="20"
                          paddingTop="20"/>
    </s:layout>

</s:View>
```

1. Under the `<s:layout>` block, add a `<s:VGroup>` layout container that contains three components: a `<s:Label>`, a `<s:Image>`, and a `<s:Button>`. Set the text property on the `<s:Label>` component to `Take a picture and view it below...`, set the width to 100%, and the height to 25. For the `<s:Image>`, set the id property to `capturedImage`, and the `backgroundColor` to `#000000`. Finally, set the label property on the `<s:Button>` component to `Launch Camera`, set the click event property to the `launch()` method, and then the width to 100% and the height to 75 (Listing 10-2).

LISTING 10-2: Adding the <s:Label>, <s:Image>, and <s:Button> components in CameraAppHome.mxml

```xml
<s:layout>
    <s:VerticalLayout paddingLeft="20"
                      paddingRight="20"
```

```
                        paddingBottom="20"
                        paddingTop="20"/>
    </s:layout>

    <s:VGroup horizontalAlign="center"
            width="100%">

        <s:Label text="Take a picture and view it below..."
                width="100%"
                height="25"/>

        <s:Image id="capturedImage"
                backgroundColor="#000000"/>
        <s:Button click="launch()"
                label="Launch Camera"
                width="100%"
                height="75"/>

    </s:VGroup>
```

2. Next add a new private variable cameraUI, which is a CameraUI object. In onCreationComplete() check that the CameraUI is supported before instantiating a new CameraUI object. Then assign the MediaEvent.COMPLETE event on the CameraUI object to a new event handler called onComplete() (Listing 10-3).

LISTING 10-3: Declaring the CameraUI object and assigning the MediaEvent.COMPLETE event in CameraAppHome.mxml

```
private var cameraUI:CameraUI;

private function onCreationComplete():void
{
    if(CameraUI.isSupported)
    {
        cameraUI = new CameraUI();

        cameraUI.addEventListener(MediaEvent.COMPLETE, onComplete);
    }
}

private function onComplete(e:MediaEvent):void {}
```

3. In launch(), check that the CameraUI is supported before calling the CameraUI.launch() method, supplying MediaType.IMAGE as a parameter (Listing 10-4).

LISTING 10-4: Launching the native camera application via the launch() function in CameraAppHome.mxml

```
private function onCreationComplete():void
{
    if(CameraUI.isSupported)
```

continues

LISTING 10-4 *(continued)*

```
            {
                    cameraUI = new CameraUI();

                    cameraUI.addEventListener(MediaEvent.COMPLETE, onComplete);
            }
    }

    private function launch():void
    {
            if(CameraUI.isSupported)
            {
                    cameraUI.launch(MediaType.IMAGE);
            }
    }
```

4. In onComplete() use the MediaEvent object e to display the image captured in the application. Cast the e.data object as a MediaPromise to mediaPromise, then assign the mediaPromise.file.url property to the image component capturedImage (Listing 10-5).

LISTING 10-5: Using the MediaPromise object on the MediaEvent to set the source of image component in CameraAppHome.mxml

```
private function onComplete(e:MediaEvent):void
{
        var mediaPromise:MediaPromise = e.data as MediaPromise;

        capturedImage.source = mediaPromise.file.url;
}
```

5. Under onComplete() create a new private method called onImageLoadComplete(), to handle when an image has loaded. Define an Event object e as a parameter for the method, casting the e.currentTarget property as an Image object to a new variable img. Set the width property on the object to the full width of the view, subtracting 10 pixels. Then set the height of the image object to half the view, subtracting 10 pixels thereafter also (Listing 10-6). This will allow you to manipulate an Image object representing the captured image taken with the native camera, and then resize it in the application.

LISTING 10-6: Setting the width and height of the captured image via the onImageLoadComplete() method in CameraAppHome.mxml

```
private function onComplete(e:MediaEvent):void
{
        var mediaPromise:MediaPromise = e.data as MediaPromise;

        capturedImage.source = mediaPromise.file.url;
}

private function onImageLoadComplete(e:Event):void
{
```

```
        var img:Image = e.currentTarget as Image;
        img.width = this.width - 10;
        img.height = this.height/2 - 10;
    }
```

6. Define the `complete` attribute in the `<s:Image>` component. Assign the
    `onImageLoadComplete()` method, passing the default `event` object as the argument
    (Listing 10-7).

LISTING 10-7: Defining the complete event attribute of the <s:Image> in CameraAppHome.mxml

```
<s:Image id="capturedImage"
         backgroundColor="#000000"
         complete="onImageLoadComplete(event)"/>
```

7. Update the `CameraApp.mxml` file to include styles for the application. Replace the
    `<fx:Declarations>` tag with an `<fx:Style>` declaration. Inside `<fx:Style>`, specify s as
    the spark namespace. For the `<s:View>` components, define the `backgroundColor` property
    as `#3F3F3F`, and the `color` property as `#393839`. Then for the `<s:Label>` component,
    define the `fontSize` property as 22 (Listing 10-8).

LISTING 10-8: Setting the styles via the <fx:Style> declaration in CameraAppHome.mxml

```
<?xml version="1.0" encoding="utf-8"?>
<s:ViewNavigatorApplication xmlns:fx="http://ns.adobe.com/mxml/2009"
                            xmlns:s="library://ns.adobe.com/flex/spark"
                            firstView="views.CameraAppHome">
    <fx:Style>

        @namespace s "library://ns.adobe.com/flex/spark";

        s|View
        {
            backgroundColor:#3F3F3F;
            color:#393839;
        }

        s|Label
        {
            fontSize:18;
        }

    </fx:Style>

</s:ViewNavigatorApplication>
```

8. Run the application using a device profile. You should see the screen shown in Figure 10-1.

9. Click the Launch Camera button, and this should run the device's native camera
    application, as shown in Figure 10-2.

FIGURE 10-1: The Camera App project running on Android 2.3.4

FIGURE 10-2: The native camera running on Android 2.3.4

10. Take a picture. Click the OK button to confirm you're happy with the image (Figure 10-3). This should return you the camera view, with the image loaded (Figure 10-4).

FIGURE 10-3: The native camera presenting Cancel, Retake, and OK options, running on Android 2.3.4

FIGURE 10-4: The image taken with the native camera app displayed in the Camera App project running on Android 2.3.4

CAPTURING SOUND USING THE DEVICE'S MICROPHONE

The microphone is another core feature of the mobile device. A mobile's sound capture device is commonly used in memo applications, which allow users to record a voice message and play it back later.

In this section you'll explore how to use the `Microphone` class to record audio streams, using the device's microphone.

Using the Microphone Class

For AS3-based mobile projects, you need to import the `Microphone` class, found in the `flash.media` package:

```
import flash.media.Microphone;
```

In total, 11 properties are associated with `Microphone`:

➤ `Microphone.activityLevel`: Returns a number representing the amount of sound the microphone is detecting

➤ `Microphone.gain`: A number representing the amount by which the microphone should multiply the signal before transmitting it

➤ `Microphone.index`: Returns the index of the microphone, represented by the array returned by `Microphone.names`

➤ `Microphone.muted`: Returns a Boolean indicating whether the user has denied access to the microphone

➤ `Microphone.name`: Returns a string representing the name of the current sound capture device

➤ `Microphone.names`: A static property that returns an array of strings containing the names of all the available sound capture devices

➤ `Microphone.rate`: An integer representing the rate at which the microphone captures sound, in kHz

➤ `Microphone.silenceLevel`: Returns a number representing the amount of sound required to activate the microphone and dispatch the activity event

➤ `Microphone.silenceTimeout`: Returns an integer representing the number of milliseconds between the time the microphone stops detecting sound and the time the activity event is dispatched

➤ `Microphone.soundTransform`: A `SoundTransform` object that controls the sound of this microphone object when it is in loopback mode

➤ `Microphone.useEchoSuppression`: Returns a Boolean indicating whether echo suppression is enabled

In addition to these properties, four methods are associated with the `Microphone` class:

➤ `Microphone.getMicrophone(index:int = -1)`: To return a reference to a `Microphone` object for capturing audio

➤ `Microphone.setLoopBack(state:Boolean = true)`: To route the audio captured by the microphone to local speakers

➤ `Microphone.setSilenceLevel(silenceLevel:Number, timeout:int = -1)`: To set the minimum input level that should be considered for sound and the amount of silent time signifying that silence has actually begun

➤ `Microphone.setUseEchoSuppression(useEchoSuppression:Boolean)`: To specify whether to use the echo suppression feature of the audio codec

You can use the `Microphone` features only as long as sound capture capabilities exist on the mobile device. Using the `Microphone.names` property you get a list of all the available sound capture devices that are supported by the Microphone API. You can then use the array to determine which microphone to use to record from by calling `Microphone.getMicrophone()`.

In the following snippet, the `Microphone` object is determined through determining the number of microphones available, and it then gets the first microphone from a list using `getMicrophone(0)`:

```
if(Microphone.names.length > 0)
{
    var microphone:Microphone = Microphone.getMicrophone(0);
}
```

Here you see that when there is at least one microphone returned, the first one in the list, 0, is passed to `getMicrophone()`, representing the `Microphone.index` property that can also be retrieved from a `Microphone` instance.

Using the SampleDataEvent Class

For AS3-based mobile projects you need to import the `SampleDataEvent` class, found in the `flash.events` package:

```
import flash.events.SampleDataEvent;
```

The `SampleDataEvent` is dispatched when a `Microphone` object has new audio data to provide. It is also dispatched when a `Sound` object makes a request for new audio data, when the `Sound` object hasn't loaded an MP3 file. As you will see later, using a combination of both `Sound` and `Microphone` objects, you can play back recorded audio using `SampleDataEvent` objects.

The `SampleDataEvent` class has two public properties:

➤ `SampleDataEvent.data`: A `ByteArray` object representing the data in an audio stream

➤ `SampleDataEvent.position`: A number representing the position of the data in an audio stream

The event has one event type, a public constant called `SampleDataEvent.SAMPLE_DATA`.

Capturing the Audio from a Microphone

To capture audio from the microphone on the device, you need to add an event listener for the `SampleDataEvent.SAMPLE_DATA` event type and assign it an event handler, as shown in the following snippet:

```
if(Microphone.names.length > 0)
{
        var microphone:Microphone = Microphone.getMicrophone(0);
        microphone.addEventListener(SampleDataEvent.SAMPLE_DATA, onSample);
}
```

Once an application is running and after the microphone instance has been initialized, each time a user speaks into the microphone the `onSample()` event handler defined will be invoked. The `SampleDataEvent` object returned in `onSample()` contains the audio stream recorded on the `data` property. To play back an audio stream, this data needs to be written to a `flash.utils.ByteArray` object. In the following snippet, you see a new `ByteArray` instance being created, and the `data` property on the `SampleDataEvent` object being used to transfer the byte array to the new instance. Two methods of the `ByteArray` object, `ByteArray.readFloat()` and `ByteArray.writeFloat()`, are used to read data and write it, respectively.

```
private var soundByteArray:ByteArray;

private function onSample(e:SampleDataEvent):void
{
        soundByteArray = new ByteArray();

        while(e.data.bytesAvailable)
        {
                var audioSample:Number = e.data.readFloat();
                soundByteArray.writeFloat(audioSample);
        }
}
```

Playing the Audio from a ByteArray

Once you have recorded audio stream data in a `ByteArray` object, you can create a new `Sound` object to play back that data:

```
private var soundObj:Sound = new Sound();
```

As with the `Microphone` object, you also need to listen for the `SampleDataEvent.SAMPLE_DATA` event type as an event for the `Sound` object. In the following snippet the `SAMPLE_DATA` event handler on the `Sound` object instance `soundObj` is assigned the function `playSound()`. Following the event listener assignment, the `play()` method on `soundObj` is called, as shown in the following snippet:

```
soundObj.addEventListener(SampleDataEvent.SAMPLE_DATA, playSound);
soundObj.play();
```

In `playSound()` the aim is to effectively broadcast the sample audio data to the `Sound` object, which is waiting to receive an audio stream after its `play()` method has been called. The following snippet shows how this is done:

```
private function playSound(e:SampleDataEvent):void
{
        if (!soundByteArray.bytesAvailable > 0)
        {
                return;

        } else {

                for (var i:int=0; i < 8192; i++)
                {
                        var audioSample:Number = 0;

                        if (soundByteArray.bytesAvailable > 0)
                        {
                                audioSample = soundByteArray.readFloat();
                        }

                        e.data.writeFloat(audioSample);
                        e.data.writeFloat(audioSample);
                }
        }
}
```

In this snippet, notice that the `BytesArray.bytesAvailable` property is used to determine whether there is actually an audio stream of data. There is a `for` loop used to check that there are bytes available on `soundByteArray`, and if bytes are available, that data is read and then written to the `SampleDataEvent` object's `data` property.

It is recommended that between 2,048 and 8,192 data samples be provided for better playback quality. The `writeFloat()` method is called twice so that the audio data sample hits both the left and right audio channels.

In the next section you take a closer look at the features of the Microphone API and build a working mobile example.

Creating a Microphone App Example

You will need to set up a new Flex Mobile Project in Flash Builder.

Defining the Flex Mobile Project Settings

The following lists a few of the familiar settings you will need to ensure are defined for the project:

➤ **Name:** Set the Name for the project to **MicrophoneApp**.

➤ **Application ID:** Set the Application ID to **com.wrox.ch10.MicrophoneApp**.

➤ **Application Template:** Set the Application Template to a View-Based Application, setting the initial view title to **MicrophoneAppHome**.

Targeting Devices on Different Platforms

This example project can run on each of the mobile platforms supporting AIR, including Apple iOS, Google Android, and BlackBerry Tablet OS. For Google Android and BlackBerry Tablet OS, a number of permissions need to be set to allow the application to record audio. For Apple iOS, no permissions need to be defined specifically.

Defining Google Android Permissions

In the AIR application descriptor file generated with the project in Flash Builder, ensure the `android.permission.RECORD_AUDIO` permission is included as a manifest addition for the Android OS, as shown in the following code snippet:

```
<android>
   <manifestAdditions>
      <![CDATA[
         <manifest>
            <uses-permission android:name="android.permission.RECORD_AUDIO"/>
         </manifest>
      ]]>
   </manifestAdditions>
</android>
```

Defining BlackBerry Tablet OS Permissions

For BlackBerry Tablet OS applications, you need to specify both the `record_audio` and `play_audio` permissions to allow the application to record and play audio, respectively. Ensure these values are set in the `blackberry-tablet.xml` file, as shown in the following code snippet:

```
<?xml version="1.0" encoding="UTF-8"?>
<qnx>
   <author>jganderson</author>
   <authorId>gYAAgFbt6rihu</authorId>
   <buildId>101</buildId>
   <platformVersion>1.0.6.2390</platformVersion>
   <permission>record_audio</permission>
   <permission>play_audio</permission>
</qnx>
```

Defining Apple iOS Settings

Because the application will need to use the device's microphone, you can prevent the application from being installed on a device that doesn't have audio recording capabilities by specifying the `UIRequiredDeviceCapabilities` key in the AIR application descriptor file via the `<InfoAdditions>`, and setting the value to an array containing the `microphone` string, as shown in the following snippet:

```
<iPhone>
   <InfoAdditions>
      <![CDATA[
         <key>UIDeviceFamily</key>
         <array>
            <string>1</string>
```

```
            <string>1</string>
        </array>
        <key>UIStatusBarStyle</key>
        <string>UIStatusBarStyleBlackTranslucent</string>
        <key>UIRequiredDeviceCapabilities</key>
        <array>
                <string>microphone</string>
        </array>
    ]]>
    </InfoAdditions>
</iPhone>
```

Building the Microphone App

In Listing 10-9 you will see the early stages of the `MicrophoneAppHome.mxml` file. In addition to the `onCreationComplete()` function, you'll see three accompanying functions: `startRecording()`, `stopRecording()`, and `playRecording()`.

LISTING 10-9: The initial starting point for MicrophoneAppHome.mxml

```
<?xml version="1.0" encoding="utf-8"?>
<s:View xmlns:fx="http://ns.adobe.com/mxml/2009"
        xmlns:s="library://ns.adobe.com/flex/spark"
        creationComplete="onCreationComplete()"
        title="Microphone App">

    <fx:Script>
        <![CDATA[

            private function onCreationComplete():void {}

            private function startRecording():void {}

            private function stopRecording():void {}

            private function playRecording():void {}

        ]]>
    </fx:Script>

    <s:layout>

        <s:VerticalLayout paddingLeft="20"
                          paddingRight="20"
                          paddingBottom="20"
                          paddingTop="20"/>

    </s:layout>

</s:View>
```

1. Under the `<s:layout>` declaration add each of the components for the view. In a `<s:VGroup>` container add a `<s:Label>`, a `<s:ComboBox>`, and `<s:HGroup>` containing three `<s:Button>` components. For the `<s:Label>` set the id property to description and height to 30. For the `<s:ComboBox>` set the id to microphones, textAlign to center, focusEnabled to false, the width to 397, and height to 55. The three buttons in the `<s:HGroup>` should be labeled Record, Stop, and Playback, in that order, with their respective id properties set to startBtn, stopBtn, and playBtn. Assign the startRecording() method to the click property on startBtn and the chromeColor to #51B22F, assign the stopRecording() method to the click property on stopButton, the chromeColor to #CB0909, and assign the playRecording() method to the playBtn. For both stopBtn and playBtn set the enabled states to false (Listing 10-10).

LISTING 10-10: Adding the `<s:Label>`, `<s:ComboBox>`, and `<s:Button>` components to the view in MicrophoneAppHome.mxml

```
<s:layout>

        <s:VerticalLayout paddingLeft="20"
                          paddingRight="20"
                          paddingBottom="20"
                          paddingTop="20"/>

</s:layout>

<s:VGroup width="437"
          gap="20"
          horizontalAlign="center">

    <s:Label id="description"
             text="Select microphone then start recording..."
             height="30"/>

    <s:ComboBox id="soundCaptureDevices"
                width="397"
                height="55"
                textAlign="center"
                focusEnabled="false"/>

    <s:HGroup width="437"
              gap="20"
              horizontalAlign="center">

    <s:Button id="startBtn"
              label="Record"
              chromeColor="#51B22F"
              click="startRecording()"/>

    <s:Button id="stopBtn"
              label="Stop"
              chromeColor="#CB0909"
              click="stopRecording()"
```

continues

LISTING 10-10 *(continued)*

```
                        enabled="false"/>

        <s:Button id="playBtn"
                  label="Playback"
                  click="playRecording()"
                  enabled="false"/>

        </s:HGroup>

    </s:VGroup>
```

2. Above `onCreationComplete()` import the `SampleDataEvent`, `Microphone`, `Sound`, `ByteArray`, and `ArrayCollection` classes into `MicrophoneAppHome.mxml` (Listing 10-11).

LISTING 10-11: Importing SampleDataEvent, Microphone, Sound, ByteArray, and ArrayCollection classes into MicrophoneAppHome.mxml

```
<fx:Script>
    <![CDATA[

        import flash.events.SampleDataEvent;
        import flash.media.Microphone;
        import flash.media.Sound;
        import flash.utils.ByteArray;
        import mx.collections.ArrayCollection;

        private function onCreationComplete():void {}
```

3. Next declare three private variables: `microphone`, `soundByteArray`, and `soundObj` (Listing 10-12).

LISTING 10-12: Declaring the private variables microphone, soundByteArray, and soundObj in MicrophoneAppHome.mxml

```
import flash.events.SampleDataEvent;
import flash.media.Microphone;
import flash.media.Sound;
import flash.utils.ByteArray;
import mx.collections.ArrayCollection;

private var microphone:Microphone;
private var soundByteArray:ByteArray;
private var soundObj:Sound;

private function onCreationComplete():void {}
```

4. In `onCreationComplete()` retrieve the microphones available and assign them to the `dataProvider` on the `ComboBox` component microphones. Then set the `selectedIndex` property on microphones to 0 (Listing 10-13).

LISTING 10-13: Assigning the microphones available on the device to the `<s:ComboBox>` component in MicrophoneAppHome.mxml

```
private function onCreationComplete():void
{
        microphones.dataProvider = new ArrayCollection(Microphone.names);
        microphones.selectedIndex = 0;
}
```

5. In `startRecording()`, set the `enabled` states for the three `<s:Button>` components. For `playBtn` and `startBtn`, set the `enabled` property to `false`, and for `stopBtn` set the `enabled` property to `true`. This ensures that the play and start buttons can't be initialized while a recording is in progress. Then instantiate the new `ByteArray` object, `soundByteArray`, to allow for new sound data to be written (Listing 10-14).

LISTING 10-14: Setting the states for playBtn, startBtn, and stopBtn, and instantiating soundByteArray in MicrophoneAppHome.mxml

```
private function startRecording():void
{
        playBtn.enabled = false;
        startBtn.enabled = false;
        stopBtn.enabled = true;

        soundByteArray = new ByteArray();
}
```

6. Next assign the microphone selected in the `<s:ComboBox>` to the `Microphone` instance `microphone`. Assign the `SampleDataEvent.SAMPLE_DATA` event type to a new event handler called `onSampleData()`. Use `setSilenceLevel()` to set the silence level to `0`, and the associated timeout to `1000` milliseconds. (Listing 10-15). Also set the `rate` property to `44`.

LISTING 10-15: Setting the microphone properties via the startRecording() method in MicrophoneAppHome.mxml

```
private function startRecording():void
{
        playBtn.enabled = false;
        startBtn.enabled = false;
        stopBtn.enabled = true;

        soundByteArray = new ByteArray();

        var index:int = soundCaptureDevices.selectedIndex;
        microphone = Microphone.getMicrophone(index);
        microphone.addEventListener(SampleDataEvent.SAMPLE_DATA, onSampleData);
        microphone.rate = 44;
        microphone.setSilenceLevel(0, 1000);
}

private function onSampleData(e:SampleDataEvent):void {}
```

7. In `stopRecording()`, also set the `enabled` states for the three `<s:Button>` components. For `playBtn` and `startBtn`, set the `enabled` property to `true`, and for `stopBtn` set the `enabled` property to `false`. This ensures that a new recording can be started once Stop has been pressed. Then remove the `SampleDataEvent.SAMPLE_DATA` event from `microphone` to prevent further data being written to `soundByteArray` through `onSample()` (Listing 10-16).

LISTING 10-16: Setting the microphone properties via the onCreationComplete() method in MicrophoneAppHome.mxml

```
private function stopRecording():void
{
    playBtn.enabled = true;
    startBtn.enabled = true;
    stopBtn.enabled = false;

    microphone.removeEventListener(SampleDataEvent.SAMPLE_DATA, onSampleData);
}
```

8. In `onSample()`, write the data returned in the `SampleDataEvent` object e to the `ByteArray` object (Listing 10-17).

LISTING 10-17: Writing audio stream data to soundByteArray via onSampleData() in MicrophoneAppHome.mxml

```
private function onSampleData(e:micData:SampleDataEvent):void
{
    soundByteArray.writeBytes(micData.data);
}
```

9. Underneath `playRecording()`, add a private function called `playSound()`. In `playRecording()` set the `ByteArray` object's position property to `0`, then instantiate the `Sound` object, assigning the `SampleDataEvent.SAMPLE_DATA` event to `playSound()` and calling the `play()` method (Listing 10-18).

LISTING 10-18: Instantiating the Sound object and initializing play via playRecording() in MicrophoneAppHome.mxml

```
private function playRecording():void
{
    var trans:SoundTransform = new SoundTransform(1, -1);

    soundByteArray.position = 0;

    soundObj = new Sound();
    soundObj.addEventListener(SampleDataEvent.SAMPLE_DATA, playSound);
    soundObj.play(0, 1, trans);
}

private function playSound(e:SampleDataEvent):void {}
```

10. In `playSound()`, check that the `soundByteArray` has had data written to it using the `bytesAvailable` property, then use the `readFloat()` and `writeFloat()` methods (Listing 10-19).

LISTING 10-19: Reading the audio stream on soundByteArray and writing it to the Sound object in MicrophoneAppHome.mxml

```
private function playSound(e:SampleDataEvent):void
{
        if(!soundByteArray.bytesAvailable > 0)
        {
                return;

        } else {

                for (var i:int = 0; i < 8192; i++)
                {
                        var audioSample:Number = 0;

                        if(soundByteArray.bytesAvailable > 0)
                        {
                                audioSample = soundByteArray.readFloat();
                        }

                        e.data.writeFloat(audioSample);
                        e.data.writeFloat(audioSample);
                }
        }
}
```

11. Update the `MicrophoneApp.mxml` file to include styles for the application. Replace the `<fx:Declarations>` tag with an `<fx:Style>` declaration. Inside `<fx:Style>`, specify s as the spark namespace. For the `<s:View>` components, define the `backgroundColor` property as #999999, and the `color` property as #393839. Then for the `<s:Label>` component, define the `fontSize` property as 22 (Listing 10-20).

LISTING 10-20: Setting the styles via the <fx:Style> declaration in MicrophoneAppHome.mxml

```
<?xml version="1.0" encoding="utf-8"?>
<s:ViewNavigatorApplication xmlns:fx="http://ns.adobe.com/mxml/2009"
                            xmlns:s="library://ns.adobe.com/flex/spark"
                            firstView="views.MicrophoneAppHome">
        <fx:Style>

                @namespace s "library://ns.adobe.com/flex/spark";

                s|View
                {
                        backgroundColor:#999999;
```

continues

LISTING 10-20 *(continued)*

```
                color:#393839;
        }

        s|Label
        {
                fontSize:18;
        }

    </fx:Style>

</s:ViewNavigatorApplication>
```

12. Run the example using a device configuration. When the Microphone application launches, underneath the title for the app you'll see the description `<s:Label>`, `<s:ComboBox>`, and the three collective control `<s:Button>` components vertically aligned (Figure 10-5).

For Android the `<s:ComboBox>` component is simply populated with the text AndroidMicrophone, as the `Microphone.names` property returns only one microphone (Figure 10-6). Also notice that the Stop and Playback buttons are both disabled, while the Record button is enabled.

FIGURE 10-5: Displaying the microphones available on the device in the Microphone App running on Android 2.3.4

FIGURE 10-6: Selecting the microphone in the Microphone App running on Android 2.3.4

On Apple iOS 4, the name of the Microphone on the iPhone 4 is iOSMicrophone. For the BlackBerry OS on the PlayBook, the Microphone is QNX Microphone.

13. Next press the Record button to use the microphone selected in the `<s:ComboBox>` component and start recording with your voice. Record a message, saying something like "Hello, My name is Earl." You should notice that the Record button component `startBtn` will become disabled, while `stopBtn` will become enabled, and the `playBtn` will remain disabled (Figure 10-7).

14. To stop the recording in progress, press the Stop button. Notice that both the Record and Playback buttons become enabled, whereas `stopBtn` is disabled again (Figure 10-8).

15. Finally, to play the recording you've just made, press the Playback button and you should hear the recording you made (Figure 10-9).

FIGURE 10-7: Recording audio using the device microphone in the Microphone App running on Android 2.3.4

FIGURE 10-8: Enabling the Record and Playback buttons after a recording has ended in the Microphone App running on Android 2.3.4

FIGURE 10-9: Disabling the Record button during playback in the Microphone App running on Android 2.3.4

UTILIZING THE DEVICE'S WEB CONTROLLER

The `flash.media.StageWebView` class can be used to display HTML content within a Flash-based AIR for mobile application and is an alternative to the `HTMLLoader` class, which isn't supported on mobile devices.

Using the StageWebView Class

This section looks at the `StageWebView` object. The `StageWebView` class utilizes the mobile operating system's web control to render HTML; so, depending on what device an app is using `StageWebView`, the features experienced could vary.

For AS mobile projects you need to import the `StageWebView` class found in the `flash.media` package:

```
import flash.media.StageWebView;
```

Seven properties are associated with `StageWebView`:

➤ `StageWebView.isHistoryBackEnabled`: Returns a Boolean indicating whether there is a previous page in the web control's browsing history

➤ `StageWebView.isHistoryForwardEnabled`: Returns a Boolean indicating whether there is a next page in the web control's browsing history

➤ `StageWebView.isSupported`: A static property that returns a Boolean, indicating whether the `StageWebView` class is supported on the current device

➤ `StageWebView.location`: Returns a string representing a URL of the current location

➤ `StageWebView.stage`: Returns a Stage reference on which the `StageWebView` object is displayed

➤ `StageWebView.title`: Returns a string defining the `HTML title` property of the web page

➤ `StageWebView.viewPort`: Returns a `Rectangle` object representing the area where the `StageWebView` object is displayed

To use the `StageWebView` object, you attach it directly to a stage using the `StageWebView.stage` property, as shown in the following code snippet:

```
var webView:StageWebView = new StageWebView();
webView.stage = stage;
```

Using the `StageWebView.isSupported` property, you can determine whether the feature is supported:

```
if(StageWebView.isSupported)
{
        var webView:StageWebView = new StageWebView();
        webView.stage = stage;
}
```

When the StageWebView object is attached to the stage, it is displayed on top of all Flash display objects, so you will have to take care in sizing and positioning the rendering area via a Rectangle instance defined for the viewPort property. The following snippet creates a new Rectangle for the viewPort property:

```
if(StageWebView.isSupported)
{
        var webView:StageWebView = new StageWebView();
        webView.stage = this.stage;
        webView.viewPort = new Rectangle(0, 0, 240, 380);
}
```

Here viewPort is defined by a rectangle whose x and y positions are both set to 0, with the width set to 240 and the height to 380. Before taking a look at how to load a web page in the StageWebView instance, have a look at the remaining methods and features of the StageWebView class:

➤ StageWebView.assignFocus(direction:String = "none"): To assign the focus of the app to the content within the StageWebView object

➤ StageWebView.dispose(): To dispose of the StageWebView instance from the stage

➤ StageWebView.drawViewPortToBitmapData(bitmap:BitmapData): To draw what is currently visible in the viewPort to a bitmap

➤ StageWebView.historyBack(): To navigate to the previous page in the web view's browsing history

➤ StageWebView.historyForward(): To navigate to the next page in the web view's browsing history

➤ StageWebView.loadString(text:String, mimeType:String = "text/html"): To load and display a specified HTML string

➤ StageWebView.loadURL(url:String): To load and display the page at the specified URL

➤ StageWebView.reload(): To reload the current page

➤ StageWebView.stop(): To halt the current Load operation

In total, nine methods are associated with the StageWebView class. In the following snippet, you see the StageWebView.loadString() method being used to load HTML directly into the StageWebView instance:

```
if(StageWebView.isSupported)
{
        var webView:StageWebView = new StageWebView();
        webView.stage = this.stage;
        webView.viewPort = new Rectangle(0, 0, 240, 380);

        var html:String = "<html><head><title>Doc Title</title></head>"
                        + "<body>Hello, world</body></html>";

        webView.loadString(html);
}
```

The `StageWebView.loadURL()` method is what is used to load specific URLs directly into the `StageWebView` instance, as shown in the following snippet:

```
if(StageWebView.isSupported)
{
        var webView:StageWebView = new StageWebView();
        webView.stage = this.stage;
        webView.viewPort = new Rectangle(0, 0, 240, 380);

        webView.loadURL("http://www.google.com");
}
```

 NOTE *The HTTP protocol string* `http://` *has to be specified in the string when you want to load a URL via the* `StageWebView.loadURL()` *call.*

Next you'll take a closer look at utilizing some of the methods and features of `StageWebView` in the Browser App example.

Creating a Browser App Example

You will need to set up a new Flex Mobile Project in Flash Builder.

Defining the Flex Mobile Project Settings

The following lists a few of the familiar settings you will need to ensure are defined for the project:

➤   **Name:** Set the Name for the project to **BrowserApp**.

➤   **Application ID:** Set the Application ID to **com.wrox.ch10.BrowserApp**.

➤   **Application Template:** Set the Application Template to a View-Based Application, setting the initial view title to **BrowserApp**Home.

Targeting Devices on Different Platforms

This example project can run on each of the mobile platforms supporting AIR, including Apple iOS, Google Android, and BlackBerry Tablet OS.

Defining Google Android Permissions

In the AIR application descriptor file generated with the project in Flash Builder, ensure the `android.permission.INTERNET` permission is included as a manifest addition for the Android OS, as shown in the following code snippet:

```
<android>
    <manifestAdditions>
        <![CDATA[
            <manifest>
                <uses-permission android:name="android.permission.INTERNET"/>
```

```
          </manifest>
        ]]>
      </manifestAdditions>
   </android>
```

This will grant the application's access to the use of the Internet on the device.

Defining BlackBerry Tablet OS Permissions

For BlackBerry Tablet OS applications, you need to specify the `access_internet` permission, to allow the application to use the Internet. Ensure this value is set in the `blackberry-tablet.xml` file, as shown in the following code snippet:

```
<?xml version="1.0" encoding="UTF-8"?>
<qnx>
   <author>jganderson</author>
   <authorId>gYAAgFbt6rihu</authorId>
   <buildId>101</buildId>
   <platformVersion>1.0.6.2390</platformVersion>
   <permission>access_internet</permission>
</qnx>
```

Defining Apple iOS Settings

Because the application will need to use an Internet connection, you can prevent the application from being installed on a device that doesn't have WIFI capability, by specifying the `UIRequiredDeviceCapabilities` key in the AIR application descriptor file via the `<InfoAdditions>` and setting the value to an array containing the `wifi` string, as shown in the following snippet:

```
<iPhone>
   <InfoAdditions>
      <![CDATA[
         <key>UIDeviceFamily</key>
         <array>
            <string>1</string>
            <string>1</string>
         </array>
         <key>UIStatusBarStyle</key>
         <string>UIStatusBarStyleBlackTranslucent</string>
         <key>UIRequiredDeviceCapabilities</key>
         <array>
                <string>wifi</string>
         </array>
      ]]>
   </InfoAdditions>
</iPhone>
```

Building the Browser App

In Listing 10-21 you'll see the early stages of the `BrowserAppHome.mxml` file. In addition to the `onCreationComplete()` function, you'll see three accompanying private functions: `back()`, `forward()`, and `go()`.

LISTING 10-21: The initial starting point for BrowserAppHome.mxml

```xml
<?xml version="1.0" encoding="utf-8"?>
<s:View xmlns:fx="http://ns.adobe.com/mxml/2009"
        xmlns:s="library://ns.adobe.com/flex/spark"
        creationComplete="onCreationComplete()"
        title="Browser App">

    <fx:Script>
        <![CDATA[

            private function onCreationComplete():void {}

            private function back():void {}

            private function forward():void {}

            private function go():void {}

        ]]>
    </fx:Script>

    <s:layout>

        <s:VerticalLayout paddingLeft="20"
                          paddingRight="20"
                          paddingBottom="20"
                          paddingTop="20"/>

    </s:layout>

</s:View>
```

1. Under the `<s:layout>` declaration, add two `<s:Button>` components to the view's
    `<s:NavigationContent>` declaration. For the first button set the `label` property to `back`,
    the `id` property to `backBtn`, and the `click` property to `back()`. For the second button
    set the `label` property to `forward`, the `id` property to `forwardBtn`, and the `click` property
    to `forward()`. Set the `enabled` property on both buttons to `false` (Listing 10-22).

LISTING 10-22: Adding navigational <s:Button> components for the web view in
BrowserAppHome.mxml

```xml
<s:layout>

    <s:VerticalLayout paddingLeft="20"
                      paddingRight="20"
                      paddingBottom="20"
                      paddingTop="20"/>

</s:layout>

<s:navigationContent>

    <s:Button id="backBtn"
              label="back"
              enabled="false"
```

```
                       click="back()"/>

        <s:Button id="forwardBtn"
                  label="forward"
                  enabled="false"
                  click="forward()"/>

    </s:navigationContent>
```

2. Under the `<s:navigationContent>` declaration, add a `<s:VGroup>` containing `<s:Label>`, `<s:TextInput>`, and `<s:Button>` components arranged horizontally in an `<s:HGroup>`. For the `<s:Label>` component, set the `id` property to `pageTitle`, the `paddingLeft` property to 5, the `fontSize` property to 16, the `width` property to 100%, the `height` property to 20, and the `text` property to `pageTitle`. For the `<s:TextInput>` component, set the `id` to `pageAddress`, the `width` property to 100%, the `height` property to 50, the `fontSize` property to 18, and the `text` property to `page address`. And for the `<s:Button>`, set the `id` property to `goBtn`, the `label` property to `Go`, the `height` property to 50, and the `click` property to `go()` (Listing 10-23).

LISTING 10-23: Adding the `<s:Label>`, `<s:TextInput>`, and `<s:Button>` components to the view in BrowserAppHome.mxml

```
<s:navigationContent>

        <s:Button id="backBtn"
                  enabled="false"
                  click="back()"/>

        <s:Button id="forwardBtn"
                  enabled="false"
                  click="forward()"/>

</s:navigationContent>

<s:VGroup width="100%"
          height="95">

        <s:Label id="pageTitle"
                 paddingLeft="5"
                 fontSize="16"
                 width="100%"
                 height="20"
                 text="pageTitle"/>

        <s:HGroup width="100%"
                  height="70"
                  y="200">

                <s:TextInput id="pageAddress"
                             width="100%"
                             height="50"
                             fontSize="18"
                             text="page address"/>

                <s:Button id="goBtn"
```

continues

LISTING 10-23 *(continued)*

```
                        label="Go"
                        height="50"
                        click="go()"/>

            </s:HGroup>

    </s:VGroup>
```

3. In `onCreationComplete()`, define a new `Rectangle` object for the web view called `rectangle`. Set the x property to 0 and y to 185. Set the `width` on `rectangle` to `Stage.stageWidth` property and `height` to `Stage.stageHeight` minus the 185, subtracted for the y positioning. Then create the `StageWebView` object `webView`, assigning the `Event.COMPLETE` event type to a new private function called `onComplete()`. Assign the `stage` property of the view to the `StageWebView` object's `stage` property, `webView.stage`. Then finally assign the `rectangle` to the `StageWebView` object's `viewPort` property, before calling the `loadURL()` method to load the URL `http://www.bbc.co.uk` (Listing 10-24).

LISTING 10-24: Defining the StageWebView instance webView via the onCreationComplete() method in BrowserAppHome.mxml

```
private var webView:StageWebView;

private function onCreationComplete():void
{
        var rectangle:Rectangle = new Rectangle();
        rectangle.x = 0;
        rectangle.y = 185;
        rectangle.width = stage.stageWidth;
        rectangle.height = (stage.stageHeight - 185);

        webView = new StageWebView();
        webView.addEventListener(Event.COMPLETE, onComplete);
        webView.stage = stage;
        webView.viewPort = rectangle;
        webView.loadURL("http://www.bbc.co.uk");
}

private function onComplete(e:Event):void {}
```

4. Add a black dividing line that separates `webView` from the other components in the view. Create a `Sprite` object called `divider`, setting the `graphics` property to define the object. Assign the `divider` to the `webView.stage` property (Listing 10-25).

LISTING 10-25: Adding a horizontal dividing line to the stage in BrowserAppHome.mxml

```
private function onCreationComplete():void
{
        var rectangle:Rectangle = new Rectangle();
        rectangle.x = 0;
```

```
        rectangle.y = 185;
        rectangle.width = stage.stageWidth;
        rectangle.height = (stage.stageHeight - 185);

        webView = new StageWebView();
        webView.addEventListener(Event.COMPLETE, onComplete);
        webView.stage = stage;
        webView.viewPort = rectangle;
        webView.loadURL("http://www.bbc.co.uk");

        var divider:Sprite = new Sprite();
        divider.graphics.beginFill(0x000000);
        divider.graphics.drawRect(0, 180, stage.stageWidth, 5);
        divider.graphics.endFill();

        webView.stage.addChild(divider);
    }
```

5. Next complete the event handler for the `Event.COMPLETE` method. In `onComplete()` set the `text` property on `pageTitle` to `webView.title`, and the `text` property on `pageAddress` to `webView.location`. Then use the `StageWebView.isHistoryForwardEnabled` and `StageWebView.isHistoryBackEnabled` to determine whether the two navigational buttons `backBtn` and `forwardBtn` should be disabled or enabled (Listing 10-26).

LISTING 10-26: Setting the pageTitle, pageAddress, and the button states for backBtn and forwardBtn in BrowserApp.mxml

```
private function onComplete(e:Event):void
{
    pageTitle.text = webView.title;
    pageAddress.text = webView.location;

    backBtn.enabled = webView.isHistoryBackEnabled;
    forwardBtn.enabled = webView.isHistoryForwardEnabled;
}
```

6. In `back()`, use `StageWebView.isHistoryBackEnabled`, this time invoking the `webView.historyBack()` method to go to the last visited page. Similarly, in `forward()`, use the `StageWebView.isHistoryForwardEnabled` property to check whether the `historyForward()` method can be called (Listing 10-27).

LISTING 10-27: Completing the back() and forward() methods in BrowserAppHome.mxml

```
private function back():void
{
    if(webView.isHistoryBackEnabled)
    {
        webView.historyBack();
    }
```

continues

LISTING 10-27 *(continued)*

```
}

private function forward():void
{
        if(webView.isHistoryForwardEnabled)
        {
                webView.historyForward();
        }
}
```

7. Call the `loadURL()` method on `webView` in `go()`, supplying `pageAddress.text` as the parameter (Listing 10-28).

LISTING 10-28: Completing the go() method in BrowserAppHome.mxml

```
private function go():void
{
        webView.loadURL(pageAddress.text);
}
```

8. Run the project, using either a *device* or *desktop* configuration profile. When the view is created the web page should load in the `StageWebView` object. The title of the web page is displayed, along with the URL (Figure 10-10).

FIGURE 10-10: Title of web page and URL are displayed in the Browser App running on Android 2.3.4.

Using the `StageWebView` object, you can interact with the web page using multitouch and gestures.

 NOTE *For a recap on multitouch and gestures, please visit Chapter 4.*

If you make a "pinch" gesture on the `StageWebView` object, you can manipulate the view by zooming in or out of the web page. If you make the "swiping" gesture you can also scroll through the web page (Figure 10-11).

9.   Next enter a new URL in the Address field and click the Go button. You will see that the `StageWebView` object is updated with the new URL and the "back" button's enabled state is set to `true`. The title of the web page is also updated (Figure 10-12).

FIGURE 10-11: Scroll enabled StageWebView in the Browser App running on Android 2.3.4

FIGURE 10-12: The back button is now enabled in the Browser App running on Android 2.3.4

10.   Click the "back" button, and you should see that the `StageWebView` object returned to the previous web page. Now the "forward" button's enabled state is set to `true` while the "back" button is disabled (Figure 10-13).

If you run the project on an Android device without a network connection, then of course the web page will not load into the `StageWebView` object. In this situation you should be presented with a user-friendly message, "Web page not available" (Figure 10-14).

FIGURE 10-13: The forward button is now enabled in the Browser App running on Android 2.3.4

FIGURE 10-14: The Web Page Not Available message displaying in the Browser App running on Android 2.3.4

Using the `flash.net.URLMonitor` class you could implement a way to detect that the page was unreachable due to the lack of Internet connection and provide the user with an alternative message.

 NOTE *You can learn more about the* `URLMonitor` *class in Chapter 8.*

UTILIZING THE DEVICE'S GEOLOCATION SENSOR

In this section you'll examine how to use the `Geolocation` and `GeolocationEvent` classes to retrieve the location of a mobile device using AIR.

Using the Geolocation Class

Using the `flash.sensors.Geolocation` class, you can utilize the GPS information retrieved by a device. This allows an application to pinpoint, with a degree of accuracy, the longitude, latitude, and altitude coordinates.

For AS3-based mobile projects you will need to import the `Geolocation` class found in the `flash.sensors` package:

```
import flash.sensors.Geolocation;
```

This class has only three API features that can be used to gain access to the native camera app on the host device:

➤ `Geolocation.isSupported`: A static property of Boolean type that indicates whether the device actually supports Geolocation and retrieving GPS data

➤ `Geolocation.setRequestedUpdateInterval(interval:Number)`: A method to set a timer to retrieve an update from the GPS

➤ `Geolocation.muted`: A property of Boolean type that indicates whether the use of GPS is enabled on the device

Both the `isSupported` and `muted` properties should be used in combination to retrieve GPS data, as you will see shortly.

Using the GeolocationEvent Class

The `flash.events.GeolocationEvent` class provides the properties that actually deliver the GPS information through updates to the device.

For AS3-based mobile projects you will need to import the `GeolocationEvent` class found in the `flash.events` package:

```
import flash.sensors.Geolocation;
```

Each `GeolocationEvent` object has the following geolocation based properties:

➤ `Geolocation.altitude`: A number defining the altitude in meters

➤ `Geolocation.heading`: A number defining the direction of movement in degrees

➤ `Geolocation.horizontalAccuracy`: A number defining the horizontal accuracy in meters

➤ `Geolocation.latitude`: A number defining the latitude in degrees

➤ `Geolocation.longitude`: A number defining the longitude in degrees

➤ `Geolocation.speed`: A number defining the speed in meters per second

➤ `Geolocation.timestamp`: A number representing the number of seconds since the `Geolocation` object was initialized at run time

➤ `Geolocation.verticalAccuracy`: A number defining the vertical accuracy in meters

In order to use the geolocation sensor and retrieve a `GeolocationEvent` object, you need to add an event listener on a `Geolocation` object for the `GeolocationEvent.UPDATE` event type, assigning it to an event handler:

```
if(Geolocation.isSupported && !geolocation.muted)
{
    var geolocation:Geolocation = new Geolocation();
    geolocation.addEventListener(GeolocationEvent.UPDATE, onUpdate);
}
```

Creating a Geolocation App Example

You will need to set up a new Flex Mobile Project in Flash Builder.

Defining the Flex Mobile Project Settings

The following lists a few of the familiar settings you will need to ensure are defined for the project:

➤ **Name:** Set the Name for the project to **GeolocationApp**.

➤ **Application ID:** Set the Application ID to **com.wrox.ch10.GeolocationApp**.

➤ **Application Template:** Set the Application Template to a View-Based Application, setting the initial view title to **GeolocationAppHome**.

Targeting Devices on Different Platforms

This example project can run on each of the mobile platforms supporting AIR, including Apple iOS, Google Android, and BlackBerry Tablet OS. For Google Android and BlackBerry Tablet OS, a number of permissions need to be set to allow geolocation capabilities. For Apple iOS, no permissions need to be defined specifically.

Defining Google Android Permissions

In the AIR application descriptor file generated with the project in Flash Builder, ensure you include the `android.permission.ACCESS_FINE_LOCATION` and the `android.permission.INTERNET` permission as a manifest addition for the Android OS, as shown in the following code snippet:

```
<android>
   <manifestAdditions>
      <![CDATA[
         <manifest>
            <uses-permission
               android:name="android.permission.ACCESS_FINE_LOCATION"/>

            <uses-permission
               android:name="android.permission.INTERNET"/>
         </manifest>
      ]]>
   </manifestAdditions>
</android>
```

The `ACCESS_FINE_LOCATION` permission will grant the application access to the device's GPS, allowing you to retrieve longitude and latitude coordinates. The `INTERNET` permission will grant the application access to utilize a Google Maps API.

Defining BlackBerry Tablet OS Permissions

Similarly, for BlackBerry Tablet OS applications, you need to specify the `read_geolocation` and `access_internet` permissions, to allow the application to use the GPS and to access the Internet, respectively.

Ensure these values are set in the `blackberry-tablet.xml` file, as shown in the following code snippet:

```xml
<?xml version="1.0" encoding="UTF-8"?>
<qnx>
    <author>jganderson</author>
    <authorId>gYAAgFbt6rihu</authorId>
    <buildId>101</buildId>
    <platformVersion>1.0.6.2390</platformVersion>
    <permission>read_geolocation</permission>
    <permission>access_internet</permission>
</qnx>
```

Defining Apple iOS Settings

Because the application will need to utilize the GPS, you can prevent the application from being installed on a device that doesn't have GPS capability by specifying the `UIRequiredDeviceCapabilities` key in the AIR application descriptor file via the `<InfoAdditions>`, and setting the value to an array containing the `gps` string, as shown in the following snippet:

```xml
<iPhone>
    <InfoAdditions>
        <![CDATA[
            <key>UIDeviceFamily</key>
            <array>
                <string>1</string>
                <string>1</string>
            </array>
            <key>UIStatusBarStyle</key>
            <string>UIStatusBarStyleBlackTranslucent</string>
            <key>UIRequiredDeviceCapabilities</key>
            <array>
                    <string>gps</string>
            </array>
        ]]>
    </InfoAdditions>
</iPhone>
```

Utilizing the Google Static Maps API

In the latter part of coding the Geolocation App, you use the Google Static Maps API to load an image map representing the longitude and latitude coordinates.

In the following snippet, you'll see that the `center` is defined as `London, UK`; this basically sets the location to be returned by the API:

```
http://maps.google.com/maps/api/staticmap?center=London,UK&zoom=15&size=200
x200&sensor=true&maptype=road
```

Alternatively, you can use the longitude and latitude values to set the location via the `center` property, which you will cover when building the Geolocation App shortly.

In the URL you also see the `zoom` property set to `15`, which represents the level at which the map should be zoomed in. The `size` property, here set at 200×200, determines the width and height of the image returned from the server. The `maptype` is set to `road`, indicating that only the road map type should be returned. Lastly, the `sensor` value is set to `true`, which relates to whether the request is made via a GPS call. Figure 10-15 shows the resulting API call.

The scope of this chapter doesn't extend to covering the full features of the Google Static Maps API, but if you want to learn more take a look at the Static Maps API V2 Developer Guide found at `http://code.google.com/apis/maps/documentation/staticmaps/`.

FIGURE 10-15: A Google static image displaying a 200×200 road view of London

Building the Geolocation App

In Listing 10-29 you'll see the early stages of the `GeolocationAppHome.mxml` file.

LISTING 10-29: The initial stages of GeolocationAppHome.mxml

```
<?xml version="1.0" encoding="utf-8"?>
<s:View xmlns:fx="http://ns.adobe.com/mxml/2009"
        xmlns:s="library://ns.adobe.com/flex/spark"
        creationComplete="onCreationComplete()"
        title="Geolocation App">

    <fx:Script>
        <![CDATA[

            private function onCreationComplete():void {}

            private function exit():void
            {
                NativeApplication.nativeApplication.exit();
            }

        ]]>
    </fx:Script>

    <s:navigationContent>

        <s:Button label="Quit"
                click="exit()"/>

    </s:navigationContent>

    <s:layout>

    <s:VerticalLayout paddingLeft="20"
```

```
                            paddingRight="20"
                            paddingBottom="20"
                            paddingTop="20"/>
            </s:layout>

    </s:View>
```

1. Above the `onCreationComplete()` method, import the `Geolocation` class and define a `Geolocation` object (Listing 10-30).

LISTING 10-30: Defining a Geolocation object in GeolocationAppHome.mxml

```
<fx:Script>
        <![CDATA[

                import flash.sensors.Geolocation;

                private var geolocation:Geolocation;

                private function onCreationComplete():void {}

                private function exit():void
                {
                        NativeApplication.nativeApplication.exit();
                }

        ]]>
</fx:Script>
```

2. In `onCreationComplete()` instantiate the Geolocation object if geolocation is supported on the device (Listing 10-31)

LISTING 10-31: Determining whether Geolocation is supported and creating a new Geolocation object in GeolocationAppHome.mxml

```
private function onCreationComplete():void
{
        if(Geolocation.isSupported)
        {
                geolocation = new Geolocation();
        }
}
```

3. After the `Geolocation` object has been created, detect whether retrieving GPS data is disabled via the `muted` property. If the `muted` returns `false`, set the

requested update interval on the Geolocation object to 5000 milliseconds using setRequestedUpdateInterval(). Then assign the GeolocationEvent.UPDATE on the Geolocation object to a new event handler called onUpdate() (Listing 10-32).

LISTING 10-32: Setting the update interval and assigning the update event on the Geolocation object in GeolocationAppHome.mxml

```
private function onCreationComplete():void
{
        if(Geolocation.isSupported)
        {
                geolocation = new Geolocation();

                if(!geolocation.muted)
                {
                        geolocation.setRequestedUpdateInterval(5000);
                        geolocation.addEventListener(GeolocationEvent.UPDATE,
                                                     onUpdate);
                }
        }
}

private function onUpdate(e:GeolocationEvent):void {}
```

4. Under the <s:layout> declaration, add a <s:Label> component and set the text property to Geolocation data...; also add a <s:TextArea> component setting the id property to geolocationTxt and the height property to 300 and paddingBottom to 10 (Listing 10-33).

LISTING 10-33: Adding the <s:Label> and <s:TextArea> components to the view in GeolocationAppHome.mxml

```
<s:layout>
        <s:VerticalLayout paddingLeft="20"
                          paddingRight="20"
                          paddingBottom="20"
                          paddingTop="20"/>
</s:layout>

<s:Label text="Geolocation data..."/>

<s:TextArea id="geolocationTxt"
            height="300"
            paddingBottom="10"/>
```

5. In onUpdate(), use the GeolocationEvent object e to assign each of the Geolocation object properties longitude, latitude, altitude, horitontalAccuracy, verticalAccuracy, speed and timestamp to the text property on the <s:TextArea> component, geolocationTxt (Listing 10-34).

LISTING 10-34: Assigning the geolocation details to the text property on the <s:TextArea> component in GeolocationAppHome.mxml

```
private function onUpdate(e:GeolocationEvent):void
{
        geolocationTxt.text = "longitude: " + e.longitude
                        + "\n"
                        + "latitude: " + e.latitude
                        + "\n"
                        + "altitude: " + e.altitude
                        + "\n"
                        + "horizontalAccuracy: " + e.horizontalAccuracy
                        + "\n"
                        + "verticalAccuracy: " + e.verticalAccuracy
                        + "\n"
                        + "speed: " + e.speed
                        + "\n"
                        + "timestamp: " + e.timestamp;
}
```

6. Update the GeolocationApp.mxml file to include styles for the application. Replace the <fx:Declarations> tag with an <fx:Style> declaration. Inside <fx:Style>, specify s as the spark namespace. For the <s:View> components, define the backgroundColor property as #CCCCCC, and the color property as #393839. Then for the <s:Label> component, define the fontSize property as 24 (Listing 10-35).

LISTING 10-35: Setting the styles via the <fx:Style> declaration in GeolocationApp.mxml

```
<?xml version="1.0" encoding="utf-8"?>
<s:ViewNavigatorApplication xmlns:fx="http://ns.adobe.com/mxml/2009"
                            xmlns:s="library://ns.adobe.com/flex/spark"
                            firstView="views.GeolocationAppHome">
        <fx:Style>

                @namespace s "library://ns.adobe.com/flex/spark";

                s|View
                {
                        backgroundColor:#CCCCCC;
                        color:#393839;
                }

                s|Label
                {
```

continues

LISTING 10-35 *(continued)*

```
        fontSize:24;
    }

    </fx:Style>

</s:ViewNavigatorApplication>
```

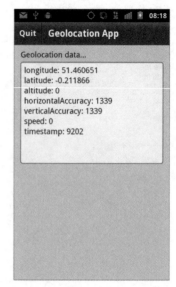

7. Run the project using a *device* configuration profile. Ensure the GPS settings on the device are enabled. When the view is first created, the GeolocationEvent object should return location data, which is then displayed in the <s:TextArea> (Figure 10-16).

8. Under the <s:TextArea> component, add a <s:Label> and <s:Image>. Set the text property on the <s:Label> component to Google maps image..., and set the id property on the <s:Image> component to googleImage (Listing 10-36).

FIGURE 10-16: Geolocation data returned in the Geolocation App running on Android 2.3.4

Available for download on Wrox.com

LISTING 10-36: Adding the <s:Label> and <s:Image> components in GeolocationAppHome.mxml

```
<s:Label text="Geolocation data..."/>

<s:TextArea id="geolocationTxt"
            height="300"
            paddingBottom="15"/>

<s:Label text="Google maps image..."/>

<s:Image id="googleImage"/>
```

9. Assign the longitude and latitude returned in the GeolocationEvent object e to the center property on the Google image maps API URL. Also set the zoom property to 15, the size property to 435×200, and sensor to true (Listing 10-37).

Available for download on Wrox.com

LISTING 10-37: Assigning a google image map location to the source property of the <s:Image> component in GeolocationAppHome.mxml

```
private function onUpdate(e:GeolocationEvent):void
{
    geolocationTxt.text = "longitude: " + e.longitude
```

```
                        + "\n"
                        + "latitude: " + e.latitude
                        + "\n"
                        + "altitude: " + e.altitude
                        + "\n"
                        + "horizontalAccuracy: " + e.horizontalAccuracy
                        + "\n"
                        + "verticalAccuracy: " + e.verticalAccuracy
                        + "\n"
                        + "speed: " + e.speed
                        + "\n"
                        + "timestamp: " + e.timestamp;

        googleImage.source = "http://maps.google.com/maps/api/staticmap?"
                        + "center=" + e.latitude + "," + e.longitude
                        + "&zoom=15"
                        + "&size=435x200"
                        + "&sensor=true";
    }
```

10. Run the project once again using a device configuration profile. This time when the view is created the `GeolocationEvent` object should return data and the image from Google (Figure 10-17).

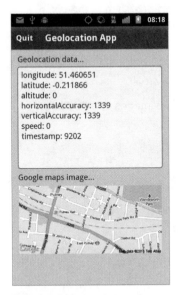

FIGURE 10-17: Displaying the Google static image map in the Geolocation App running on Android 2.3.4

SUMMARY

Over the course of this chapter you have explored three of the key features available in AIR for mobile devices.

First you learned how to utilize the device's camera app to take an image using the handset and to load it into the AIR application.

You then learned how to use the device's microphone to record and play back audio streams.

Using the device's web control you also learned how to include support for displaying web pages within an AIR application.

Finally, you learned how to use the device's Geolocation sensor, allowing you to use GPS data.

In the next chapter, you take a look at updating the AIR mobile applications installed on the device, whether it would be to enhance an existing feature, add a new one, or fix a bug.

EXERCISES

1. Extend the Camera App example by allowing the user to add a filter, rendering the captured image in black and white.

2. For the Microphone App example, allow the user to store and reference each of the voice messages saved.

3. With the Browser App example, provide an option to save a URL as a bookmark and display a snapshot image of the web page in use.

4. In the Geolocation App, add each of the updated Google static map images to a horizontal scrollable list.

▶ WHAT YOU LEARNED IN THIS CHAPTER

TOPIC	KEY CONCEPT
Determining support for the camera	Use `CameraUI.isSupported` to determine whether the web interface is supported on a mobile device.
Launching the camera app	Use `CameraUI.launch()` to launch the device's camera app.
Determining microphone availability	Use `Microphone.names` to retrieve a list of sound capture devices available.
Retrieving a microphone	Use `Microphone.getMicrophone()` to return a reference to a `Microphone` object for capturing audio.
Capturing audio from a microphone	Register the `SampleDataEvent.SAMPLE_DATA` event with a `Microphone` object and write an audio data stream to a `ByteArray` object using `writeFloat()`.
Audio stream data playback	Register the `SampleDataEvent.SAMPLE_DATA` event with a `Sound` object and call the `Sound.play()` method. Re-write an audio data stream to the `data` property on `SampleDataEvent` object using `writeFloat()`.
Determining support for web control	Use `StageWebView.isSupported` to determine whether the web control is supported on a mobile device.
Displaying dynamic HTML content	Use `StageWebView.loadString()` to load HTML.
Displaying web browser content	Use `StageWebView.loadURL()` to load a web page.
Navigating the browsing history	Use `StageWebView.isHistoryBackEnabled` and `StageWebView.isHistoryForwardEnabled` to determine whether historical navigation of the `StageWebView` instance is permitted. Call `historyForward()` to navigate forward and `historyBack()` to navigate back.
Determining support for the geolocation	Use `Geolocation.isSupported` to determine whether a device supports retrieving geolocation data.
Retrieving geolocation information	Register the `GeolocationEvent.UPDATE` event with a `Geolocation` object to receive updates on geolocation data.

INDEX

U

V

W

X

Y

Z